MW00624373

The Battle of Stonington

The Battle of Stonington (greatly enlarged) from an English commemorative water jug. Although the depiction is fanciful in many details, the general sense of the action, including the attempted landing on the east side of the village (at top), is accurate. The complete water jug is shown at the end of the text. (Author)

JAMES TERTIUS DE KAY

THE BATTLE OF STONINGTON

Torpedoes, Submarines,
and Rockets in the
War of 1812

Naval Institute Press
Annapolis, Maryland

This book has been brought to publication by the generous assistance of Marguerite and Gerry Lenfest.

First Naval Institute Press paperback edition published 2012.

ISBN 978-1-59114-202-7

© 1990
by the United States Naval Institute
Annapolis, Maryland

All rights reserved. No part of this book may be reproduced without written permission from the publisher.

The photograph on page 130 is Crown copyright: Public Record Office, London: ADM 1/4369.

Library of Congress Cataloging-in-Publication Data

De Kay, James Tertius.
    The Battle of Stonington : torpedoes, submarines, and rockets in the War of 1812 / James Tertius de Kay.
        p. cm.
    Includes bibliographical references and index.
    ISBN 0-87021-279-6
    1. Stonington (Conn.)—History—Bombardment, 1814. I. Title.
E356.S8D4 1990
973.5′2—dc20   90-6265
                            CIP

Printed in the United States of America on acid-free paper ∞

First printing

23 22 21 20 19 18 17   11 10 9 8 7 6 5

To

FRANK LYNCH
(1914–87)
Captain, United States Navy

He is the keel and rudder
of this book.

Contents

Acknowledgments

This book could never have been written without the painstaking research of the late Frank Lynch. Working over a number of years in both Britain and the United States, he searched through the densely packed captains' letter boxes at the University of Hull, the National Library of Scotland, the Public Record Office at Kew, and the Library of Congress; traced with patient scholarship the Byzantine trail of the Stewarts' quest for a pension; charted the vagaries of the Connecticut militia; and finally assembled on computer disc and microfilm his rich collection of naval correspondence concerning the War of 1812 in general and the Battle of Stonington in particular.

My own interest in the battle developed years after most of Frank's work was completed. My curiosity was piqued by the strange outcome of the battle, and later when I read Captain Hardy's singular letter of 10 August 1814 (see page 161), I was hooked. Torpedoes? I wondered. Mrs. Stewart? I poked around through local libraries for answers, and in the process discovered that Frank Lynch, a retired naval officer living in Stonington, was a leading authority on the battle and had written a comprehensive piece on it for the 150th anniversary of the event in 1964. Frank shared his research with me, and eventually we began considering the possibility of writing a book on the subject. And then in the fall of 1987 Frank Lynch died. Since then his widow, Emily, has been as generous with her time and help as Frank was and has allowed me continued access to the wealth of material Frank amassed.

I have had help from many other quarters as well. Anthony Bailey, the novelist, memoirist, *New Yorker* writer, yachtsman, and sometime neighbor, painstakingly went through an earlier draft to exorcise the mangled nautical terminology of a writer who barely knows the difference between a halyard and a trunnion. Mary Thacher, burrowing in the National Archives, came up with an invaluable collection of cartographical material, including Hardy's own chart of the eastern end of Long Island Sound and the only map of Stonington I have ever seen that includes the location of the fort. Victor Taliaferro Boatwright, who has a seemingly inexhaustible knowledge of the wooden navies of the world, provided guidance in many areas, particularly concerning the early history of submarines. Linda M. Maloney, the biographer of Isaac Hull, was helpful in a hundred ways—literally—most notably by providing a reasonable motive for Decatur's attempted kidnapping of Hardy. Rollie McKenna, another neighbor, went out of her way to help me locate rare photographs.

I would also like to thank various institutions for their valuable help: the staff of the G. W. Blunt White Library at the Mystic Seaport Museum, and particularly Bill Peterson, who established for me the authority of the Frederick Denison articles in the 1859 Mystic *Pioneer*; the Stonington Free Library and its chief librarian, Ann Gray; the Nautilus Memorial Submarine Force Library & Museum in Groton, Connecticut, and archivist Theresa M. Cass; the New-York Historical Society Library, which I discovered only by chance has one of the great naval research collections in the nation; the Old Lighthouse Museum in Stonington, and especially its curator Louise Pittaway; and the National Maritime Museum at Greenwich, London, and the helpful people administering its magnificent picture collection.

I owe a very special thanks to George Lord for providing me with information on his ancestor William Lord, as well as for his helpful introduction to the Beineke Library at Yale, where Hardy's letters to Stonington reside. Other special thanks go to Dan Jones, for helping locate Hardy at Block Island a month before I thought he got there, and to Peter M. Coy, for supplying proof in the form of a spy's letter.

Many people in Stonington have been helpful, and of these I would particularly want to single out Margaret Davol and the late Robert Newman, whose encouragement at different times was crucial to the completion of this little book.

There are no words to express my love and appreciation of my wife, Belinda, and daughter, Kate, for the innumerable times they cheered me out of a writer's block and general sullenness, and whose good spirits and intelligent criticism made this project so much fun.

Stonington
April 1990

A Note on the Text

All spelling and punctuation in quoted
extracts is faithful to the original sources.

The Battle of Stonington

1

9–12 August 1814

The British attack in brief—the curious outcome of the battle—the action seen as a part of the Battle of Long Island Sound

FOR four days in August 1814 the tiny seaport of Stonington, Connecticut, was attacked by a large, heavily armed British naval squadron, intent on destroying it. Day after day, the village was bombarded with explosive shells, rockets, incendiary missiles, and cannonballs. All in all, at least fifty tons of British ammunition were thrown into the village.

Stonington fought back against this massed armed might as best it could, but it was hopelessly outgunned. The British had over 160 cannon, while the village could muster only two 18-pounders and a brass 6-pounder. (To get an idea of the strength of the British squadron, its ordnance was ten times greater than the total of all of Andrew Jackson's artillery at the Battle of New Orleans.)

After the better part of a week of banging away at each other— the Royal Navy with its 160 guns and Stonington with its two 18s— the village remained largely intact, having suffered surprisingly little damage. Of its hundred or so wooden houses, the British managed to destroy only four and to damage another thirty or forty. The record showed only half a dozen American wounded (none seriously) and no

1

deaths. British deaths amounted to anywhere from two to twenty-one, depending on who did the counting.

Finally, on the fourth day, having utterly failed to achieve their goal, the British pulled up anchor and sailed away.

End of battle.

The news of this curious little action caused a sensation throughout the young United States. The country was just then entering the third year of the War of 1812, which was not going at all well, and the story of brave little Stonington was a refreshing break from the dreary reports arriving from other fronts. From border to border Americans acclaimed it as a stunning victory, a modern Thermopylae, in which a handful of gallant Yankees held off the might of the British navy.

How does one explain this lopsided victory? It certainly was a victory, no question about that. The enemy picked the fight, declared his intentions, committed his forces, and then, despite his vast superiority in men and arms and the total absence of any threat of counterattack, summarily called off the action without accomplishing what he had set out to do. By any definition the battle was an American victory, but such a strange one that no one has ever been able to provide a reasonable explanation for it in all the years since.

The year 1814 was still the era of sailing ships, of course, and it is easy to dismiss those old square-riggers with their clumsy muzzle-loading guns as charming but overrated artifacts of a simpler age. For all their grace and elegance, it is sometimes difficult to see them as serious or effective machines of war, and yet that is exactly what they were: *very* serious machines of war, designed and built by the best technicians of their day and tested and perfected under fierce conditions of combat. Even by today's standards they were weapon systems of considerable destructive power.

Some of them were huge. A single ship-of-the-line such as the *Ramillies*, which led the attack on Stonington, required fifty-four acres of oak forest for its construction—that is, about three thousand full-grown oaks—and was manned by a crew of over six hundred sailors. She was a 74-gun ship, which meant she usually carried twenty-eight 32-pounders—guns that fired iron balls of thirty-two pounds weight—as well as twenty-eight 18-pounders and eighteen 9-pounders. A single 32-pounder could smash through two feet of solid oak at half a mile's distance, and a broadside from such a ship, with all the guns on one side firing simultaneously, was powerful enough to knock down a building the size of Liberty Hall in Philadelphia.

It is tempting to shrug off the battle as an irrelevance, just a case of King George's men bumping into the furniture. After all, such inexplicable encounters happen all the time in combat and are the common currency of war. Yet questions remain.

For instance, what prompted the attack? It was totally unexpected and completely unprovoked. There was no sound military reason for it. From the outset, the attack was clearly defined as a punitive action designed to destroy civilian property. The British commander, Captain Sir Thomas Masterman Hardy, said afterward that he believed Stonington manufactured torpedoes, but he never produced a scintilla of evidence to back up his claim, which was in fact untrue.

Just as puzzling as the British attack was the American response to it. What made the Yankees so preposterously brave? What could have possessed the villagers to think they had the means to fight back against such odds? Why such foolhardy courage?

Most puzzling of all is the ineffective nature of the attack. Why was there so little damage to the village? Five powerful vessels participated in the action, manned by veteran crews and commanded by some of the best naval officers in the world, a total of roughly 1500 men against perhaps twenty civilians. How could the British possibly lose?

The day after Hardy withdrew his ships, the people of Stonington repaired to the Road Church a mile or so north of the village to give thanks and to share their joy and relief, convinced that they had been preserved by a miracle. Their belief in divine providence is understandable, but a later and more skeptical age may be forgiven for seeking a more rational explanation. What follows is an attempt to understand the small historical anomaly known as the Battle of Stonington, and to try to make sense of something that has not made much sense for almost two hundred years.

In rummaging around through the old naval records, ships' logs, and newspaper reports in search of answers, it became evident that the root causes of the battle were surprisingly complex and involved some totally unanticipated elements. Although the battle itself was very small and circumscribed, the principal actors, military and civilian, British and American, played out their parts in the run-up to the battle

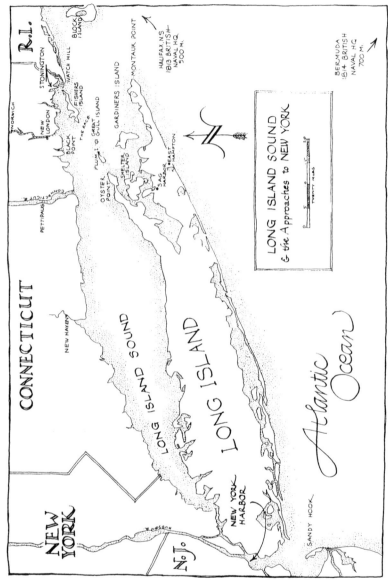

Map One: Approaches to New York

on a huge stage stretching the length of the Atlantic coast and from London to the Great Lakes. The time factor was equally expansive. Certain aspects of the battle cannot be understood without reference to events that took place up to forty years before the British attack.

Significantly, it is impossible to isolate the tiny Battle of Stonington from something that might be called the Battle of Long Island Sound. That remarkable and long forgotten aspect of the War of 1812 involved the world's first generalized application of underwater warfare. The seemingly anachronistic image of naval officers in cocked hats and knee breeches wrestling with the problems and opportunities of submarines and torpedoes a full hundred years before the First World War is in itself as curious a phenomenon as the little Battle of Stonington itself.

In the end, the battle turned out to be not so much a mystery as a story of divided loyalties, of new ideas versus traditional values, a story of honor and bravery and of people on both sides who wanted very much to do the right thing.

2

Causes of the War

Complex nature of the War of 1812—Britain's
war with Napoleon—impressment of American
seamen—the Canadian option—Congress declares
war—the blockade

ANY understanding of events during the War
of 1812 must begin with at least a rudimen-
tary grasp of the causes of the war. It was a very small war (few
Americans know much about it, and the British seem never to have
heard of it at all), but it was also a very complicated war, so complicated
that to this day it is unlikely that any two scholars will even agree how
it came about. Trying to define the actual causes of the war is one of
those angels-on-the-head-of-a-pin questions beloved of academics.
Suggested *casus belli* range from Napoleon's shifting interpretations of
his own Milan Decree to the British cabinet's insistence on something
called Orders in Council. There were in fact a good half dozen legitimate provocations, but it is probably safe to say that the basic impetus
towards war can be found in America's hurt sense of pride and self-
respect, or what diplomats refer to as the issue of national sovereignty.

At the end of the eighteenth century the newly minted United
States was one of the three leading trading nations in the Atlantic,
along with Britain and France. When the two European countries went
to war with each other, the neutral United States found itself inadvertently caught up in the action. If American ships traded with Britain,

6

they were attacked by the French. If they traded with France, the British attacked. As the smallest and weakest of the three powers, America, which had literally no army and almost no navy with which to defend itself, was in consequence battered about the head and shoulders by both rivals.

Over the course of years, as the European war dragged on, the American government made several attempts to solve the problem, all of them failures. American shipping interests continued to find plenty of reasons to be outraged by both Britain and France, but what finally tilted American public opinion conclusively against Britain was the matter of impressment.

In the years following the American Revolution a considerable number of British sailors, probably several thousand in all, took jobs on American vessels, attracted by the better pay and superior working conditions. The United States encouraged naturalization, and many of these men became American citizens. When Britain went to war with France, more thousands of British sailors found their way into American ships, and many doubtless sought the protection of American citizenship as well. The British navy, desperate to find crews to man its immense fleet, refused to recognize such naturalizations, claiming that a British subject born was a British subject until he died and, therefore, owed service to his king and country in times of war. Royal Navy captains, to flesh out their inadequate crews, took to stopping American merchant ships at sea and forcibly removing any seaman they suspected of being British born. American sea captains, brought to in the middle of the ocean and standing by in the shadow of loaded cannon, were powerless to protest. Inevitably, as Britain's need for manpower grew more acute, British officers became increasingly less particular in their selections and began the practice of impressing any likely sailor that fitted their needs, whether British or American. During the course of the Napoleonic wars the Royal Navy forcibly impressed about ten thousand native-born American citizens, and these illegally conscripted sailors made up anywhere from 2 to 4 percent of the total British crews. (Two of George Washington's nephews were impressed, and the British navy never bothered to release them, in spite of impassioned pleas from their own minister in America.)

Americans were enormously frustrated to see their countrymen impressed into British servitude while the government of the United States stood by, too weak to protect the interests of its own citizens.

Eventually, spurred by that frustration, more and more Americans began to examine and to seriously consider a seductively simple scheme specifically designed to put pressure on Britain: namely, to invade Canada.

Canada was a vast, virtually empty wilderness lying at America's doorstep, and Britain, busy with Napoleon on the other side of the ocean, would have a very difficult time trying to protect it from a determined American attack. What made the idea of a campaign to the north all the more attractive was the belief that the conquest of Canada would be almost effortless. Thomas Jefferson airily predicted that Canadians would rally to the Stars and Stripes the moment the American militia crossed the border.

The British were aware of this threat to their remaining North American colonies, and to discourage an invasion the government in London sent agents to mobilize the Indians living along the frontier in what is now Indiana, Michigan, and Ohio, and to encourage hostile actions against American settlers. As tales of the Indian massacres sponsored by the British spread along the frontier, the Americans came to look upon the Canadian invasion as simply a means of self-protection.

The tense diplomatic situation dragged on for years but might never have led to a declaration of war if Britain's war with Napoleon had not dragged on even longer, occupying the best minds of the British cabinet and distracting them from North American matters. Eventually, in June 1812, a sullen and divided Congress, stung by decades of cavalier treatment by Britain and believing it had in Canada a means of settling the score, decided it would take no more insults, no more embarrassing snubs to its sovereignty, and declared war on the world's greatest naval power.

London greeted the news from Washington with genuine regret. The British cabinet saw no particular advantage in war with the United States, and there were obviously serious drawbacks inherent in the situation. But the truth of the matter was that no one in London had much time to spare for the bumptious Yankees. Everyone's attention was concentrated on Napoleon. Wellington's army was busy fighting Bonaparte in Spain, so the principal role of answering the Americans fell to the Royal Navy, which since the great victory at Trafalgar in 1805 had ruled the seas unopposed. The Admiralty quickly instituted an enormous blockade that, it was hoped, might dampen Yankee war fever, and it is with this blockade that the Battle of Stonington begins.

3

Spring 1813

Hardy of the Ramillies—*Jeremiah Holmes runs
the blockade—the making of a gun captain—the
homeward dodge—Decatur leaves New York—a
"noble fellow" makes a promise—Decatur
trapped—a singular Act of Congress*

IN early March 1813 the man who would
eventually lead the attack on Stonington
stood over a table in his large, comfortable cabin aboard his flagship, the *Ramillies*, and methodically leafed through the Admiralty
charts spread out before him. Captain Sir Thomas Masterman Hardy,
Baronet, hero of Trafalgar and veteran of over thirty years service in
the Royal Navy, was taking the *Ramillies*, 74 guns, south from Halifax,
Nova Scotia, to rendezvous with the rest of his squadron.

He was a ruddy, muscular man in his mid-forties, thick necked
and bald. He stood a commanding six feet three inches tall, and a
lifetime at sea had given him the unmistakable poise and grace of a
natural sailor. Even as he studied the charts, his body moved uncon-
sciously in perfect harmony with the motion of the ship, reacting to
and anticipating even the slightest shift under his feet, precisely
matching the pitch and roll of the deck as the *Ramillies* cut through
the choppy seas off New England.

The charts were of varying size and projection, and he studied
them for a long time, analyzing the shoals and inlets, memorizing the
island groups and points of land, making note of likely tidal flows and

9

Captain Sir Thomas Masterman Hardy, Bart., as painted by Domenico Pelligrini in Portugal in 1809, two years after Hardy's first tour of duty in the Chesapeake and four years before his attack on Stonington. He is wearing his Trafalgar medal. (The National Maritime Museum, London)

potential hazards that he could only guess at in the complicated engravings.

The charts detailed the approaches to New York Harbor and were of utmost interest to Captain Hardy, for he had just received orders to establish a blockade of that city.

England had not sought this war with America and wanted to get it over with as quickly as possible. Toward that goal, the Admiralty in London had ordered a stranglehold placed on the ports and sea-lanes of the United States, to thwart America's tough but tiny navy and choke off the trade of the brash young nation that had the temerity to declare war on Britain. Central to the success of the blockade would be the closure of the port of New York. The city was quickly growing into America's principal commercial center. Just as important, it was the home base for Commodore Stephen Decatur, one of the most dangerous naval officers Britain had encountered in the last hundred years.

Decatur was one of the handful of brilliant young American naval officers who, in the early months of the war, had already handed the Royal Navy a stunning series of defeats. The previous October, commanding the *United States*, he had forced the surrender of the British frigate *Macedonian* in a dazzling display of seamanship and gunnery that remains one of the classic single-ship actions in the age of sail. The British suffered more than a hundred dead and wounded in the murderous confrontation, or almost a third of the entire ship's company. American casualties totaled eleven.

Now Decatur and the *United States*, along with the *Macedonian*, which after her complete refurbishing now flew American colors, were riding at anchor in New York, preparing to go to sea once more. They represented a serious threat to British interests in the western Atlantic, and the Admiralty had good reason to want to keep them locked up.

Hardy's job was to nail down the northern end of the blockade, which was to stretch south from New York to Georgia and then around into the Gulf of Mexico as far as the Mississippi delta and New Orleans. By any measurement, the blockade was an ambitious project, and it is indicative of the size and strength of Britain's navy that no one in the Admiralty entertained the least doubt of its success.

Captain Hardy knew a great deal about blockades. During almost twenty years of war with Napoleon, he had seen action from one end of the French coast to the other and had distinguished himself in some of England's greatest victories in the epic struggle that now seemed finally to be drawing to a close. (Waterloo was still two years in the future, but already news of Napoleon's spectacular defeat in Russia was filtering through to the west.)

Hardy was no ordinary, off-the-shelf naval officer. Circumstances had made him unique, for he was "Nelson's Hardy," the most trusted aide to the late Rear Admiral Horatio, Viscount Nelson. The reflected glory gained from his close association with the world's greatest and most glamorous naval commander made Hardy famous beyond his rank. He was probably the best known of all the twenty-five hundred officers then serving in the Royal Navy, at least to the general public.

Hardy had served with Nelson at each of his three greatest victories—the Nile, Copenhagen, and Trafalgar—and at the last had brought his mortally wounded leader the news of the overwhelming victory over the combined fleets of France and Spain. "Kiss me, Hardy," the dying Nelson pleaded; and his request, so freighted with drama and heartbreak and mystery, became a catchphrase that is still known to every schoolchild in Britain, although few can tell you anything of the man to whom it was addressed.

As Hardy continued to study the Admiralty charts with a practiced eye, the most obvious—and most significant—detail that occupied his attention was that the port of New York had two entirely separate entrances. One mouth of the harbor opened south, directly into the Atlantic, while the other opened to the east, into Long Island Sound.

The first of these gateways was protected by the long curving arc of Sandy Hook, New Jersey, and represented a fairly typical harbor mouth similar to those of Brest, Toulon, and other French ports with which Hardy was familiar. But the Long Island Sound exit was an entirely different matter. A ship leaving New York by the eastern route would not reach the Atlantic until it had traveled a hundred miles or so between the shorelines of Long Island and Connecticut. New York's complicated geography meant that to blockade the port effectively Hardy would have to split his squadron into two quite distinct units, which would be forced to operate as much as two hundred miles away from each other and would, for the most part, remain out of ready communication.

A casual analysis of the charts might suggest that the Long Island Sound exit would be the easier to blockade since it appeared to form a large trap, easy to close at either end. But such an optimistic perception would not have fooled Hardy. He could see that on either side of the sound the shoreline was broken into a myriad of coves and inlets, and that to the north the coast of Connecticut included two large seaports capable of handling ocean traffic, as well as a major river. All of these locations would be ideal hiding places for even the largest ships. Hardy could see that his ships would be able to handle the blockade of Sandy Hook in a routine manner, but maintaining control of Long Island Sound was going to require a large number of naval vessels and most of his time.

It is indicative of the excellent coordination and superior communications of the Royal Navy on the North American Station that within a fortnight Hardy was able to rendezvous with all the ships assigned to his command and to establish precisely that degree of control of the waters adjacent to New York that his orders called for.

As he had anticipated, he himself took up position off the eastern end of Long Island. On the first of May, with the *Ramillies* patrolling just beyond Block Island, and with the latest intelligence reports from New York in his pocket, he wrote to his brother Joseph back home in Dorset, "The *United States* and *Macedonian* Frigates . . . are both ready for sea and laying at New York; however, I would rather wish they would put to sea for the chance of our falling in with them."

Jeremiah Holmes, master of the coasting sloop *Hero* and the man who would one day lead the defenders of Stonington, left his home on the Mystic River in February 1813 and set sail for New York with his two partners to pick up a cargo for Charleston, South Carolina. The *Hero* was a sturdy coaster, just forty-seven feet in length, known for her good speed and sound construction. She had been built in 1800 by Eldredge Packer in a shipyard on the Groton side of the river, directly across from Jeremiah Holmes's house, and all three partners were familiar not only with the ships carpenters who had built her but also with the merchant seamen who had sailed her through the years. She was, they knew, a good, reliable vessel. By agreement, Holmes held a one-quarter share and served as captain.

The strict British blockade of the eastern seaboard south of New York made a long coastal trip an extremely dangerous undertaking, but one that was sure to be highly profitable for those who succeeded. Wartime shortages had raised the value of certain cargoes to the point where it was possible to make enormous profits as a blockade runner.

An enterprising captain could buy flour in Virginia for $4.50 a barrel and sell it in Boston for $11.87, for a 264 percent profit. Or he might buy rice in Charleston for $3.00 and sell it in Philadelphia for $12.00, a 400 percent profit.

When the three men got to New York, they learned the British had recently increased their blockade off the Chesapeake, and Holmes's partners grew nervous about the venture and began to argue in favor of a postponement. But the captain felt confident he could trust the *Hero*'s keel and the strength of her cordage to get him past the Royal Navy, and he prevailed over the others' doubts. Soon after, with his cargo safely stowed on board, he bade his partners farewell and headed the *Hero* out the Narrows.

Since so many of the people involved in the events leading up to the Battle of Stonington were ship's captains—both military and civil—it's worth taking note of just how very out-of-the-ordinary and generally superior such men were from the average run of humanity. No one became a ship's captain by chance, nor could inheritance or training alone guarantee success. The process began with the man, or more precisely, the boy. Early in life every skipper had made a conscious decision to go to sea, to deliberately subject himself to one of the most unpredictable, most ungovernable, and most dangerous lines of work in the world. The open ocean is always perilous, but it was particularly so in the age of sail when captains depended entirely upon winds and tides to move their vessels and had to contend with pirates and privateers and the vagaries of international politics as well as foul weather to wrest a living from their calling. That these men deliberately chose to turn their backs on the safety and familiarity of life on shore to go to sea tells us a lot about them.

They were men of tremendous spirit, men who actively sought challenge. They were by nature adventurous men, with strong egos, attracted to novelty and surprise. In many cases they were acquisitive men who accepted the risks of a life at sea for the potential wealth that might come their way. By and large they were men of singular native intelligence, with the kinds of minds that thrived on processing a number of data simultaneously—the wind, the tide, the character of the sea, the sailing qualities of the ship, the reliability of the crew, the value and nature of the cargo—and on juggling all the possible permutations of these factors. They were men whose lives and fortunes depended on the ability to make quick and complicated decisions under great duress—and their judgments had to be right because their lives often depended on the subtlety of their choices.

Whatever else they might have been, sailing ship captains were a breed apart.

For his first day or so at sea Holmes had little trouble avoiding the blockade. He fell in with a pilot boat, the American schooner *Ulysses*, which was cruising off the coast to warn returning American ships of the blockade. Having the *Ulysses* close at hand was a comfort. Her extra guns might well prove useful if they ran into trouble. Trouble in this case did not mean Royal Navy ships, which were far too powerful for the *Hero* to even attempt to fight. Trouble meant privateers, small, heavily armed British merchant ships, often no larger than the *Hero*, captained and manned by civilians. With the outbreak of hostilities, hundreds of them had swarmed across the Atlantic as auxiliaries to the Royal Navy to seek out and harass American shipping.

On the second night out of New York the *Hero* and *Ulysses* ran into a squadron of what appeared to be five British ships-of-the-line, but by skillful sailing Holmes and his escort were able to escape undetected.

The following evening, toward sunset, Holmes spotted a large English schooner, which immediately put on sail and gave chase. Luckily for Holmes, the *Ulysses*, which was still in the neighborhood, appeared on the horizon, moving in the opposite direction. The English ship, seeing that this other quarry was larger and in all probability more valuable, abandoned the chase of the *Hero* in favor of the larger prize. Holmes escaped. The *Ulysses* was sent to the bottom.

Holmes's penciled account of his harrowing trip to Charleston, still carefully preserved in the library of the Mystic Seaport Museum, gives a graphic picture of the enormous strength of the British blockading fleet off the American coast in early 1813. On each of the six days of his trip south he was forced at least once and sometimes several times to evade or escape the British patrol.

After a week the *Hero* finally ran over the bar into Charleston, to the astonishment of the people of that city. Holmes learned that just the day before a British brig and a larger ship had been prowling the area and had captured the schooner *Federal Jack*. The collector of the port complained that no vessel seemed fast enough nor any captain sly enough to evade the British presence on the coast; as a result bales of hemp were rotting on the quayside, and mountains of rice falling prey to weevils for lack of means to ship the produce to market. This last news was of particular interest to Holmes, for it meant he could in all likelihood strike an even better bargain than he had hoped for.

Jeremiah Holmes was taking a considerably greater risk than almost any other American captain running the blockade that spring. Most ships' officers captured by the British could expect to be exchanged as prisoners of war, but if Holmes ever fell into enemy hands, he had every reason to believe he would hang from a British yardarm, for Jeremiah Holmes of Stonington, Connecticut, had committed one of the most heinous crimes in the Royal Navy: desertion.

Almost ten years earlier, on 2 July 1804, young Holmes, already a veteran world sailor at the age of twenty-two, had arrived destitute on the island of St. Helena with nothing but the clothes on his back, the victim of French privateers.

St. Helena was a British possession, the south Atlantic head-quarters for the fleet that guarded the sea-lanes to India and the Orient. At the time of his arrival several Royal Navy warships were anchored in the harbor. Typically, they were short of crewmen, and their captains were on the lookout for any likely recruits. Within a day of his arrival on the island Jeremiah Holmes was unceremoniously pressed into service aboard the British ship-of-the-line *Trident*, 64 guns. Years later, in his handwritten memoirs, Holmes recalled the scene in detail. "But I'm an American!" Holmes protested to the lieutenant taking his name. "We'll soon make an Englishman of you," the lieutenant said mockingly. "No sir. You will never do that," Holmes said, mustering what dignity he could.

Within days the *Trident* set sail to the north, and Jeremiah Holmes began his three years of forced service in the navy of His Britannic Majesty King George III, suffering the brutalizing discipline, degradation, insult, and disease common to British vessels of the period, as well as experiencing the grinding despair brought on by official duplicity and the consequent loss of hope.

As soon as he could find means to do so, Holmes began sending desperate pleas across the world to anyone who might help extricate him from his impressment, but to no avail. The British transferred him to the *Saturn*, 74 guns, and sent him to the Mediterranean. He later recorded that in an engagement off Cabarena Point near Gibraltar he distinguished himself with his work with a cannon and was soon made captain of his own gun crew. Warships of the day rarely used both port and starboard guns simultaneously, so his crew was responsible for one gun on each side. It was a minor but important job and put him in command of a ten-man team. It took skill and discipline to organize the loading, aiming, priming, firing, and sponging out of a three-ton monster on wheels that was constantly threatening to break loose and go careering about the deck, lethal and unchecked. It was wickedly uncomfortable and backbreaking work that eventually deadened a man's eardrums (Holmes never recovered his full hearing) and forced him to crouch in a stooped posture at all times because the headroom on the gun deck was barely five feet. It was not without reason that the gun deck was known to British sailors as "the slaughterhouse."

It was in the Royal Navy that Jeremiah Holmes learned the arcane technology of cannon: that the best cartridges were made of felt, which always burned clean, leaving no smoldering residue in the chamber that might accidentally set off the next cartridge; that it was up to the gun captain to see that his second captain's lint stock was properly supplied with slow match, and that the slow match was alight; that the powder monkeys—mere boys, most of them—were careful with the cartridges and kept the gun well supplied; that his powder horn was ready to hand, and, of course, that the powder in it was dry.

Hitting a moving target with a cannonball fired from a moving ship took great skill and months of practice and Holmes had to learn the rules: elevate the side sights and point by the upper sights; use a crowbar on one side of the gun to move it, and a handspike on the other to hold it where you wanted it; and at all times keep this monster they all served, and for which they were all responsible, from knocking down or crushing your busy crew.

Every time his ship reached port Holmes would write off again to anyone who might help him escape his grim condition. The American minister in London, spurred by Holmes's direct entreaties and those of his relatives back in Connecticut, again and again sent requests for his release to the Admiralty, supported by affidavits of Holmes's nationality; but the Admiralty refused to let him go, citing pettifogging bureaucratic objections. Unstated but implicit in the correspondence was English petulance at being asked to do a favor for a one-time colony, particularly a favor involving a common seaman.

It was clear that legal action was fruitless and that the only recourse was escape. But how? Obviously he could not get off a ship at sea; and even on those rare occasions when the ship returned to home port, Holmes was never allowed on shore for the perfectly sensible reason that his officers knew he would run away. Twice he attempted to escape during tours in the Mediterranean, once near Gibraltar and again in Africa, only to return to his ship when he found his way insurmountably blocked. (Samuel Johnson wondered drily why England bothered to maintain prisons when it already had a navy.)

Finally, on a winter's day in Portsmouth harbor, after years of frustration, Holmes managed to escape to an American ship, and from there eventually reached home in March 1807. The experience left him with a deep hatred of the British navy. It also taught him how to fire a cannon both quickly and accurately, a skill that would come in handy years later during the attack on Stonington.

The *Hero* lay in Charleston Harbor a fortnight, and Jeremiah Holmes used the time to scrub and tallow her hull so that she might make a clean furrow on the return cruise. As the time approached for him to set sail, prospects for the journey north dimmed with the news that two other Mystic River schooners, the *Nimble* and *Revenue*, which sailed the day before Holmes's scheduled departure, were both captured off Cape Hatteras. Their crews, Holmes knew, would be shipped off to prison hulks in Bermuda.

This fresh evidence of British strength in the area undoubtedly concerned Holmes, but he had spent all his cash on his new cargo and could not afford to stay on shore any longer. Reluctantly, he set sail on schedule, and the *Hero*, loaded to the gunwales, started on what he described as her "homeward dodge." All went well for the first two days out; but on the third he came across an English frigate off the Virginia Capes that chased him from morning to night. As darkness fell she managed to come within two hundred yards of him, but under cover of night Holmes took in his small sails, hauled in toward land, and then tacked to the north to avoid his pursuer.

Holmes decided to try to improve his chances by sailing well out to sea, beyond the range of most British patrols. The maneuver proved successful, and for several days he experienced no further dangers until he judged it was time to head west again, toward the coast. His first landfall was the island known as No Man's Land, to the south of

Martha's Vineyard, which meant he had slightly overshot his mark and
sailed too far north. At daylight he discovered a brig on his weather
quarter busy making sail and heading in his direction. Holmes, with
good reason, assumed she was a British privateer and took evasive
action. He spread all his canvas and squared away before the wind,
which was now from the north. The brig followed close behind. For
about two hours they remained in sight of each other, but with the
Hero too far ahead to be taken as prize. Then, in a very unwelcome
surprise, two British frigates appeared on his bow, and Jeremiah
Holmes suddenly found himself with less sea room than he might have
desired.

As one of the frigates joined the brig in chase, he jibed and stood
to the east. What happened next proved Holmes still had luck on his
side. The brig, while continuing her chase of the *Hero*, began to move
away from the frigate, and Holmes could guess the reason. She was,
as he had thought, an English privateer—the *Sir John Sherbrooke* of
Liverpool, Nova Scotia—and she did not wish to come within reach
of the frigate, which could impress a portion of her crew. The chase
became a three-way hunt, with the privateer tracking the *Hero* and
the frigate running after both of them. The divided nature of the chase
could only benefit Holmes. The privateer hauled her wind to the
north, and the *Hero* headed toward the Vineyard.

The frigate eventually gave up the chase. The brig continued,
but before she could make any headway the wind died down and left
both vessels becalmed. Determined not to lose his prize, the captain
of the *Sherbrooke* ordered her boat lowered, and a small crew armed
with muskets attempted to row over to the *Hero*. The man in the bow
of the boat fired a shot that passed through the *Hero*'s sails.

One of Holmes's passengers, a crack shot from Vermont named
Spencer, loaded his rifle—a far more accurate weapon than a musket—
and proposed killing the musketeer in the boat, but Holmes prevailed
on him not to. He readied the *Hero* for a defense and told his passengers, "Now, gentlemen, you have got to fight or go to Halifax."

Fortunately for the Americans the wind picked up again before
any fighting could start, and the *Hero* began to move off and out of
range and soon left the brig and her boat behind. Holmes then ran
his sloop between a reef and No Man's Land and stood to the north.
The brig dared not follow but remained outside Rhode Island Sound
and was again becalmed. Holmes, safely on the other side of the reef,

saw the privateer run up an American flag on her fore-topgallant mast-head as a signal that she wanted a pilot.

One of the greatest difficulties that bedeviled British captains throughout the war with America was the problem of operating along a coast that had an almost endless number of reefs, islets, and dangerous shoals. At almost every point on the continental shelf a ship would need an experienced pilot, which of course the British did not have. To solve the problem, they paid exorbitantly high fees, as much as a hundred dollars a day, to obtain the services of local pilots. A British ship at anchor in enclosed waters, displaying an American flag, was usually enough of a signal to attract the attention of a local pilot whose greed exceeded his patriotism. If he made his way out to the British after dark, he could often protect his reputation while he secured a fat profit.

Holmes's reaction to the signal flag tells us a lot about the boyish, adventuresome character of the man and about the times in which he lived. He actually discussed with his mate the possibility of waiting until dark and then running back down to the privateer and offering the mate as a pilot. The mate could then earn an inflated fee from the privateer while surreptitiously steering the brig into Newport, where the American authorities would of course take her as a prize. Eventually they discarded the plan as too risky.

Later, as they neared land they fell in with the smack *Fair Haven* of Edgartown. Holmes told her captain of the British brig, and it was he who ran down and furnished her with a pilot.

With a change in wind Holmes now put his head in for Point Judith and by four o'clock in the morning was off Watch Hill. When dawn broke he was surprised and not a little distressed to discover the very same privateer, the *Sherbrooke*, not a mile distant. Holmes immediately put on all sail before the brig could give chase, taking his sloop through the reef safely into Noank and up the Mystic River, home at last.

Jeremiah Holmes was no coward, but he was a prudent man, and the presence of so many enemy vessels along the coast caused him concern. The large profits a blockade runner could make greatly attracted him, but with the terrible price on his head should he be captured, he had every reason to wonder whether the game was worth the candle. He determined to sell his share in the *Hero*—either to his partners or to another party—and find some other means of occupying his time.

Captain Stephen Decatur, U.S. Navy, with his boundless energy, his nervous high style, and his dark, Byronic good looks, was one of those larger-than-life characters who seemed to flourish in the early nineteenth century. He was audacious to the point of folly, impatient, and incredibly brave, all of which helped him cut a glorious figure that the public adored. The fact that at least ten American towns and cities still bear his name attests to his popularity with his compatriots.

Decatur first gained fame in 1804, when he and his crew stole into Tripoli Harbor under cover of darkness and burned the frigate *Philadelphia*, which had been captured by Barbary pirates. When Lord Nelson heard the story he is said to have roared with appreciative laughter and proclaimed the feat to be "the most bold and daring of the age." Doubtless Nelson's flag captain, Thomas Masterman Hardy, would have shared his admiral's opinion of the dashing young American's exploit.

Now, nine years later, the hero of Tripoli was preparing to escape from New York, and to do so he would have to evade Nelson's flag captain. The date was 23 May, and Commodore Stephen Decatur, thirty-five years old and impatient as ever, stood on the quarterdeck of the frigate *United States* and studied his officers as they supervised the tricky business of taking on gunpowder from the naval arsenal and carefully stowing it in the ship's magazine well below the waterline.

Gunpowder was frightening stuff, particularly in the amounts needed by a fighting ship. Any accidental spark—from something as simple as a shoe nail striking a steel plate—could instantly transform the entire *United States* into a gigantic exploding fireball, atomizing everything within a cable's length. The ship's armorer and the powder monkeys who worked for him gingerly shifted and stacked the small casks and prepackaged cartridges of static-free paper and felt. For good reason, gunpowder was the last of the supplies taken on board a warship before she set out on a cruise, just as arsenals were located as far as possible from the rest of the navy yard facilities.

Decatur's restless nature and single-minded pursuit of glory made him ache to get to sea. He knew the *President* and *Congress*, two of America's eight precious frigates, had already slipped past the Royal

Navy guarding Boston on 30 April. They were now safely on the open ocean, menacing British merchant shipping, disrupting the sea-lanes, and forcing the Admiralty to withdraw ships from the American coast to protect merchantmen.

Only a week earlier, on 17 May, Secretary of the Navy William Jones had written suggesting that if he managed to make it past the blockade there might well be easy pickings in the West Indies. Decatur could well imagine: hundreds of merchant vessels, heavy laden with cargoes from the plantations and homeward bound to England, ripe for the plundering. If there was glory to be got at sea, there were riches, too.

Navies of the era encouraged the zeal and fighting spirit of their crews by practicing a peculiar form of free enterprise known as the prize system. When a warship captured an enemy vessel, the entire crew of the victorious ship shared in the value of the capture. The lion's share went to the officers, by a formula that established a precise division of spoils according to rank. Many a lucky captain had grown rich in the service of his country. Decatur was one of them.

When Decatur captured the British frigate *Macedonian*, his personal share of the prize money—three-twentieths of the total—came to about $30,000, which in those days was a very substantial sum. To get an understanding of the value of the dollar at the time: in 1813 the total cost of a four-year education at Harvard, including food and lodgings, was about $1200. A certain Abijah Weld, the pastor of the Congregational church in Attleborough, Massachusetts, maintained a hospitable home, gave charity to the poor, and brought up eleven children on his salary of $240 a year. An educated guess might put the present-day value of Decatur's personal share of the prize money at about $300,000—and he earned that very substantial fee in a single naval action that lasted less than ninety minutes!

On the strength of that victory Decatur was promoted to a command that included three warships. Although his rank was captain—the highest rank in the American navy at the time—his command over more than a single vessel carried with it the title of commodore. (In this respect he exactly paralleled Captain Hardy, who as commander of the blockading squadron was also a commodore.)

Decatur's flagship was the *United States*, 44 guns. She was old and slow, but she was very special to Decatur. She was the ship he had first served in as a midshipman at age nineteen, and he knew her intimately, from keel to main top royal, even to the nicknames of her guns: Glory, Lion, Sally Mathews, Brother Jonathan, Torment, Jumping Billy, Bruiser, Bulldog, Happy Jack, and Long Nose Nancy. There was even one gun that honored a British hero: Nelson. These were the guns he'd grown up with, and the guns that had forced the *Macedonian* to surrender.

Besides the *United States*, the other ships under his command were the prize *Macedonian*, 38 guns, and heavy sloop *Hornet*, 18.

By 24 May Decatur had reconnoitered the Sandy Hook exit from New York and found it crowded with enemy vessels, including two 74-gun ships-of-the-line, each one half again as large as anything in the U.S. Navy. Attempting escape by the southern route would have been foolhardy. He decided to turn east and try a dash up the sound to Montauk. He ordered his commodore's broad pennant hoisted, and he and his little squadron moved up the East River. They successfully passed through the treacherous Hell Gate, where the tides of the sound meet and battle those of the harbor, and moved steadily past Hunter's Point and into the sound itself.

As the land fell away on either side, with the green farms of Long Island to starboard and the forests of Connecticut to port, the waters of the sound opened up before him with no British ships in sight. The only hint of trouble lay in an angry squall making up to the southeast.

By the time the sun went down behind the ships the squall had evolved into a full-scale storm, with the dull growl of thunder in the distance punctuating the occasional flicker of lightning. Even in the enclosed waters of Long Island Sound the sea grew uncomfortably choppy. As the sky darkened and the air thickened the three ships, with the *United States* in the van, experienced difficulty maintaining visual contact. Decatur signaled with hooded lanterns to the other ships to draw within a half cable's length to each other, that is, about a hundred yards' distance.

Suddenly, with a deafening peal of thunder, an enormous bolt of lightning crashed into the main royal mast of the *United States* and with an almost whimsical precision tore away Decatur's commodore's pennant, which dropped to the deck, a singed and tattered ill omen. Not content with this bit of mischief, the lightning bolt danced crazily down a conductor and jumped to a gun through a main-deck port, slithered down the wardroom hatch, ricocheted around the magazine scuttle, passed through the locked door of the surgeon's cabin, doused his candle, and tore his bed to pieces—with no harm to the surgeon lying therein. The charge finally burrowed through fifteen feet of solid oak planking and vanished into the sea, carrying away a patch of copper from the hull and twenty studding nails.

Aboard the *Macedonian*, which was following close behind, the officer of the deck could think of only one thing: gunpowder. Desperately he ordered all aback, to put more room between his ship and the *United States*, should the lightning—or some fire started by it—reach the magazine. The great prize creaked and groaned with the effort, but as the minutes passed and the *United States* failed to explode, calm returned to the little squadron. The ships reestablished their positions in the dark and continued on their eastern passage.

Decatur was not a particularly superstitious man, but he knew that his crew was likely to be so, and the obvious symbolism of a bolt from the blue striking down his personal talisman would not have been lost on them. A more circumspect commander might have found an excuse to heave to on a temporary basis and use the time to placate his crew. But practicing caution was simply not in Decatur's character. He knew his country needed his ships at sea. Besides, there were glory to be won and prizes to be taken.

As the winds abated he ordered more canvas set on the *United States* and signaled to the *Macedonian* and *Hornet* to do the same.

While Decatur was caught up with his troubles at the western end of Long Island Sound, Captain Hardy was moving to establish British control of the eastern end. Hardy was quickly learning that the Yankee mariners living along the sound were an independent lot, with a thick streak of larceny in them, and they promised to remain a permanent nuisance unless dealt with firmly. On his orders his officers and men were fanning out in long boats and pinnaces to burn fishing boats and take coastal merchant vessels whenever they could catch them.

What made the Yankee sailors such a trial was their determination to profit from the almost unlimited opportunities for making money that the war had created. The potential rewards were so great that they were worth almost any risk. As a result, despite the overwhelming superiority of the British naval presence, Long Island Sound—at least the nooks and crannies around its edges—was alive with Yankee shipping. For the most part the skippers of Long Island and Connecticut kept their sloops and brigs as close to shore as possible, particularly during daylight hours, and were ready at a moment's notice to make a dash for cover if enemy patrols appeared. As Jeremiah Holmes's trip to Charleston demonstrated, the coastal trade was a gold mine for anyone brave enough—and lucky enough—to evade the British blockade.

Beyond the coasters operated the privateers, captained and crewed by the most adventurous of the sea-going entrepreneurs. These swift and heavily armed marauders spent their time far out at sea, harassing English merchantmen in the Atlantic, and used Long Island Sound only as a base. Every privateering vessel was articled with an official letter of marque backed by the U.S. government, which guaranteed the safety of the crews. If captured by the British, they had to be treated as prisoners of war rather than as licensed pirates, which was a closer description of their actual character.

From Hardy's point of view, running contraband and privateering on the high seas were not serious problems. In time the Royal Navy would undoubtedly find the means of discouraging such practices. What was bothersome was that certain of these local sailors were not content to limit their activities to smuggling and preying on British merchantmen. Some were actually beginning to practice a form of guerilla warfare directly against the blockading fleet.

In April 1813 a Yankee vessel from the Mystic River (in fact, she was the same *Hero* Jeremiah Holmes had skippered to Charleston) had deliberately hunted down and captured a British brig captained by one of Hardy's own lieutenants, taking the brig as prize and holding the crew for ransom.

Fortunately for all concerned, none of the British crew had been killed or wounded. Even so, the British were not going to tolerate this sort of horseplay on the part of civilians. Hardy fired off a letter to the governor of Connecticut, threatening to destroy nearby New London unless the lieutenant and his men were returned forthwith. There was a subsequent exchange of letters between Hardy and the governor's office, and in due course, at the end of May, a peaceful exchange of prisoners was arranged in the waters off New London. The report of the event in *Niles' Weekly Register*, a news magazine of the day, is particularly interesting in view of Hardy's subsequent attack on Stonington, still a year in the future.

According to *Niles' Register*, the prisoners were returned to the *Ramillies* on board a barge flying a flag of truce, accompanied by the inspector of customs in New London, who was present in his capacity as the most senior federal official in the city. Hardy greeted the inspector cordially and, after showing him around the ship with the utmost courtesy and wining and dining him, took the opportunity to address several messages to the American public through him. The captain said he was aware that the newspapers were just then carrying horrifying reports of the terror raids of British Admiral Cockburn, who had recently leveled the defenseless village of Havre de Grace, Maryland, and who was promising to deal out the same treatment to other Chesapeake ports. Hardy stated clearly that he personally deplored Cockburn's attacks against civilians. Upon learning from the inspector that some New London families were planning to move away out of fear of similar attacks upon their own coast, Hardy "begged him to assure the ladies that they may rely on his honor, that not a shot should be fired at any dwelling (at least while he had the command) unless he should receive very positive orders for that purpose, which he had not the most distant idea would be received."

It being too late to return to New London that evening, the customs inspector spent the night in the *Ramillies*. The following morning, when bidding his guest farewell, Hardy said he hoped soon to have the pleasure of making New London a visit, not as an enemy but as a friend. The New London press snapped up and printed all these comments, which newspapers around the country quickly copied. At the end of the article in *Niles' Register*, the editor, Hezekiah Niles, a man known for his acerbic and mordant dislike of the British, felt constrained to admit grudgingly, "On the whole, Hardy must be a noble fellow."

With the memory of the freak lightning bolt behind him, Decatur was inching his little squadron cautiously up Long Island Sound. The ships had difficulty escaping attention. Hiding three large warships was virtually impossible: while he might have preferred to limit his movements to the hours of darkness to best evade the notice of Hardy's lookouts, he was dependent upon the winds and tides, so a good deal of movement in daylight was simply unavoidable.

Decatur was acutely aware that the masts of his ships were visible from as far away as thirteen miles. This meant that as his vessels moved eastward they continued to form the center of a circle of visibility twenty-six miles across, and anyone within that circle could see them. Since the sound was only about fifteen miles wide, his squadron was always in sight of the people on shore. This fact did not overly concern him, since those on shore were fellow Americans, but he was very worried about the Royal Navy. A British sailor standing watch on the foretop of a 74 in Gardiner's Bay could pick out his squadron as it passed the mouth of the Connecticut River. For the most part Hardy had kept his ships out of the sound proper, but Decatur had every reason to believe that they would soon begin to enter it, particularly since they must have learned by now of the American ships' departure from New York.

By Monday, 31 May, a day or two after Hardy had entertained the customs inspector, Decatur managed to reach the eastern limit of the sound, apparently without attracting the attention of the British. He now lay at anchor on the Connecticut side of Fishers Island, awaiting only a fair wind and a favorable tide to move through the Race on his final dash to Montauk Point and the open Atlantic.

The captain of a passing Swedish merchantman heading for New Haven made note of the American ships that morning. A bit later, as he continued on his way rounding the end of Fishers, he saw on the other side of the island, not more than five miles from Decatur, another ship at anchor. It was Hardy in the *Ramillies*.

Was Decatur aware that the *Ramillies* was so close at hand? For that matter, was Hardy aware of the Americans? Nothing in the records indicates that either commodore had knowledge of the other; but large warships are difficult to hide, and since both men were experienced officers and outstanding captains, the likelihood is that at least one of them knew of the other's proximity, and probably both knew.

Assuming they knew of each other's presence, neither Decatur nor Hardy would have been anxious to attack the other. In theory, the Americans held a slight advantage in terms of weight of metal—that is, the weight of all the cannonballs Decatur could fire from all his ships was greater than the weight of all the cannonballs the *Ramillies* could fire. This was a rough but accurate way of measuring fighting potential, and given this advantage, slight as it might be, a fiery sea dog like Decatur might reasonably jump at the chance to attack, particularly with the promise of such a glorious prize as a 74. But Decatur was mindful that the *Ramillies* had many allies in the neighborhood and that they might appear at any moment and make a shambles of his assault. In any case, Decatur's job was not to destroy a blockading ship—even a ship-of-the-line. Britain had ninety-eight more 74s in commission and could easily replace a lost one. Decatur's job, as he well knew, was simply to slip through the blockade and get to sea. From there he could keep ten times as many British warships busy hunting for him than he could ever take in prize.

Hardy, on the other hand, would not feel under any pressure either to attack Decatur or to run away, if he judged the weight-of-metal ratio too far out of his favor. He was already in a perfect position to keep an eye on the Americans while he sent for the reinforcements that would guarantee victory. Besides, Hardy had other reasons not to go in after Decatur. The waters north of Fishers Island were full of shallows, and the *Ramillies*, with a draft of eighteen feet or more, could easily run aground. If Hardy did have to fight Decatur he would want to do so on the deep-water side of the island.

In any case, Decatur could not afford to wait. Hardy had only to send for more ships, and Decatur would find his little squadron hopelessly outnumbered. Early in the morning of 1 June the *United States*, *Macedonian*, and *Hornet* weighed anchor and, with the *United States* in the lead, rounded Fishers Island. Setting full sail before a following wind, the three ships stood boldly out to engage the *Ramillies*. Almost certainly Decatur meant this action only as a feint and was primarily interested in simply getting past the *Ramillies* and making the ten-mile run to freedom and the open sea.

The squadron drew close to the lone ship-of-the-line. The crews stood at their battle stations, their guns double-shotted with grape for a first broadside that would, Decatur hoped, tear away the Britisher's rigging and play havoc with her spars. With luck, the Americans might immobilize the *Ramillies* as they had the *Macedonian* the previous October, when she still flew the Union Jack.

They were almost within gunshot when Decatur, who had been searching the horizon, caught sight of a three-masted ship, hull down and approaching from Montauk. She quickly revealed herself as the *Valiant*, 74. With her were two frigates, the *Acasta*, 48, and *Orpheus*, 38. All three ships held a course that promised to cut off the Americans and force a hopeless fight.

Decatur had no choice. Hurriedly he ordered his squadron to tack. The *United States*, which had led the column, now had the honor of covering the retreat. Fire was opened and returned, but no real damage was done to any of the ships. Every captain on the scene knew where the Americans had to go. Their only chance was to make for New London, to anchor under the lee of Fort Griswold and Fort Trumbull, which guarded the mouth of the Thames River, and eventually to move up the river to the port itself, directly under the guns of the forts. Decatur's ships, ignominiously chased by the swift *Acasta*, barely made the sanctuary. Hardy's squadron stopped at Gull Island, and the British watched two of the three American ships temporarily ground themselves on the shoals of the Thames before finally reaching safety.

A few days later Decatur moved his ships up beyond the mouth of the Thames to a safer anchorage above the city. "Here we are," he wrote disconsolately to a friend, "John Bull and us, all of a lump."

Thus was established the cat's cradle of forces and counterforces that was to govern military action in Long Island Sound for the remainder of the War of 1812, and incidentally to help bring about the Battle of Stonington: Stephen Decatur, America's most dashing naval commander, impotent and furious, held prisoner up the Thames River, but always threatening to break out, while Thomas Masterman Hardy, "Nelson's Hardy," sat staunchly guarding him. The irresistible force facing the immovable object. It was not a situation that lent itself to stasis.

As it turned out, Congress had already passed an act in March 1813 that virtually guaranteed that the forces ranged against each other at the eastern end of Long Island Sound would remain in a state of instability:

AN ACT TO ENCOURAGE THE DESTRUCTION OF THE
ARMED VESSELS OF WAR OF THE ENEMY

Be it enacted by the Senate and House of Representatives of the United States of America in Congress assembled—That during the present war with Great Britain it shall be lawful for any person or persons to burn, sink or destroy any British armed vessels of war except vessels coming as cartels or flags of truce; and for that purpose to use torpedoes, submarine instruments, or any other destructive machines whatever. And a bounty of one half the value of the armed vessels so burnt, sunk or destroyed, and also one-half of the value of her guns, cargo, tackle and apparel shall be paid out of the treasury of the United States to such person or persons who shall effect the same otherwise than by the armed or commissioned vessels of the United States.

In short, Congress was encouraging a whole new category of warfare, one that allowed anyone with a rowboat and an explosive device to become a one-man guerrilla force. This singular piece of legislation would open the door for a remarkable series of mischief makers, who in turn would make the year to come a memorable one for Thomas Masterman Hardy.

4

Summer 1813

The djinni in the bottle—the Eagle *incident—
Thomas Masterman Hardy—a kidnapping
attempt—a spy network—building a "Hornet's
Nest"—torpedo warfare*

THE sudden and unexpected appearance of
Stephen Decatur's squadron in the harbor
threw New London into a panic. Throughout the first days of June
the city of five thousand souls buzzed with rumors. It was obvious to
everyone that Decatur was hopelessly caught, and that Hardy not only
had the upper hand, but had such total control of the situation that
he could take any action he chose at whatever time he chose to take
it. It was commonly accepted that he would sail in on the next tide
and burn their little city to the ground in his eagerness to get at
Decatur, and the newspaper reported, "A desperate engagement may
be hourly looked for." In preparation for the expected attack the banks
prudently removed their gold and silver holdings upriver to Norwich
for safe keeping. Those citizens fortunate enough to find a place of
shelter outside the city made arrangements to leave.

Decatur shared the conviction that the British would momentarily
run up the Thames and blast the three American ships into kindling
or force their surrender. Certainly he would have taken that course of
action were the situation reversed. In anticipation of the attack he
bent every effort to prepare a defense.

31

In a quick survey he discovered that both of the forts guarding the river's mouth were virtually derelict and almost useless as they stood. Strengthening them before the British learned how weak they were was imperative. He landed some of his own guns from the *United States* and laboriously manhandled them up the hills to the forts. A few days later, detecting a sullen insolence and lack of discipline on the part of the militia assigned to the forts, he decided he could not trust New London's homegrown soldiers and assigned his own men to permanent duty at the forts.

He moved his ships farther up the river, to a place above the city called Allyn's Hill, where the British 74s could not follow, and ordered his men to throw up earthworks in preparation for a desperate defense.

On the heels of his suspicions of disloyalty among the militia, Decatur made another disagreeable discovery: far from hailing him as a hero, most of the citizens of New London bitterly resented his presence. They saw him as a Jonah bringing fresh miseries to their city. Only a fortnight earlier Hardy had comforted them with protestations of friendship and reassuring promises not to attack; but with Decatur's squadron now lying upriver, New Londoners could no longer hold Hardy to those promises, and the old fears were rekindled. Everyone was intensely aware that the sole cause for the dramatic and unwelcome reversal of the city's fortunes was Stephen Decatur.

The situation held a special irony for the commodore. Only six months earlier New London had been the scene of one of his greatest triumphs. In December 1812 he had made his landfall at New London after his victory over the *Macedonian*. From here the glorious news went out to the nation of the first British prize frigate brought home in triumph, and here Decatur and his men were first feted as heroes.

If Decatur had been a sensible man, a realist, he would have seen that for him—or at least for his ships—the war was over. But accepting the inevitable was not in his nature. He was a warrior, a fighting leader who would go to any lengths to free himself from this unacceptable impasse. If there was a way out, Decatur would find it.

As it turned out, Commodore Hardy had no intention of storming the forts and going in after the Americans. Why should he? He had already accomplished everything that his orders had asked of him, and he was content to let matters rest as they were. In one brief action he had managed to trap America's most mischievous djinni inside the

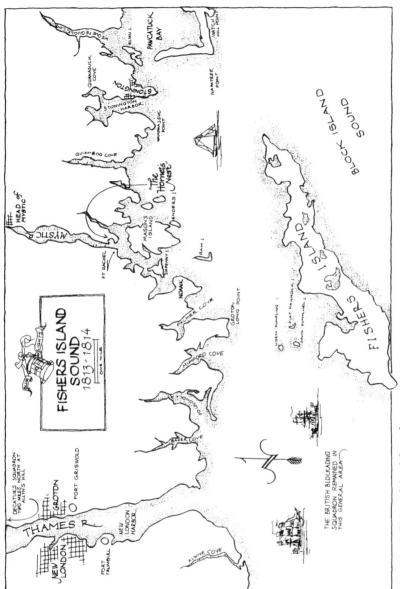

Map Two: Fishers Island Sound

bottle of New London, along with more than one quarter of the entire U.S. Navy to boot. Furthermore, he had managed it without the loss of a single life on either side. While it is unlikely that Hardy had ever heard of *The Art of War* by Sun-tzu (c. 350 B.C.), he would have heartily concurred with that book's basic tenet, which championed the desirability of achieving military objectives without actually fighting.

In the meantime other matters occupied Hardy's attention. As more ships continued to join his squadron, Hardy busied himself with the deployment of the new arrivals, including the *Statira*, 38, and *Endymion*, 50. Long Island Sound was a particularly complicated area to patrol, and employing each vessel in his command to maximum effect was important.

At this stage, neither the British nor the Americans fully perceived that Decatur's entrapment had subtly changed the nature of Hardy's blockade. While he could still assign the bulk of his squadron to patrol, a considerable number of Royal Navy vessels would now perforce be obliged to stay near the mouth of the Thames to keep their dangerous prisoner in his place. This meant that large British ships, including ships-of-the-line, would remain at anchor within sight of shore and, therefore, within reach of civilian mariners along the coast. These were precisely the circumstances anticipated by those in Congress who had drafted the Torpedo Act.

On 15 June 1813 an enterprising businessman in New York named John Scudder, Jr. put the finishing touches to a complicated machine of destruction that would within the next ten days put an entirely new twist on the nature of the war in Long Island Sound and usher in a form of naval combat a full century before its time.

Scudder and his six partners had pooled their cash and resources in a project designed to make them a lot of money while at the same time furthering the American cause. The device by which they meant to effect this goal was a schooner they had recently purchased and totally refurbished, called the *Eagle*.

Deep below the deck of the *Eagle* Scudder and his men planted a large cask filled with ten forty-pound kegs of gunpowder, with a quantity of sulphur mixed into it. They surrounded the cask with huge stones that in the event of an explosion would be hurled outward under tremendous force and, it was hoped, inflict great damage and injury. For good measure they placed large containers of turpentine on top of this immense bomb, which was "sufficient," in Scudder's testimony, "to destroy any vessel that ever floated on the water."

To the top of this lethal contraption Scudder fixed two firing mechanisms—actually, they were flintlocks—cocked to strike the sparks that would ignite the gunpowder. Cords of twine led from the flintlocks to two innocent-looking barrels of flour on deck, and the cords were attached in such a way that moving the barrels would set off the flintlocks and ignite the enormous booby trap down below. A prodigious explosion would result.

The entire *Eagle* from stem to stern was in fact a single self-propelled floating bomb, and a very expensive one at that; but as far as Scudder and his partners were concerned, she was an excellent investment. They had rigged her for the sole purpose of sinking the *Ramillies*, and if the bomb proved successful, the investors stood to receive $150,000 in prize money from the U.S. government, under the terms approved the previous March by act of Congress.

The evening of 15 June the *Eagle*, under the command of a Captain Riker, set off on the same route Decatur's squadron had followed three weeks earlier. Issuing out of New York Harbor by way of Throg's Neck, the *Eagle* began her long journey down the length of the sound. As with Decatur's, her passage was covert and slow, and she took a total of ten days to transit to the mouth of the Thames where she arrived at about eleven o'clock on the morning of 25 June.

As planned, Captain Riker deliberately guided the *Eagle* to within tempting distance of the enemy so that, again as planned, the English lookouts spotted her. Within minutes a barge crewed by an officer and twenty sailors set out from the *Ramillies* to capture the schooner.

If the captain of the *Eagle* had been piloting a legitimate merchant vessel with a real cargo and found himself chased by the British, he would almost certainly have taken the standard measures used to avoid capture. First, he would have turned his ship toward shore and run her aground on the shoals. He and his crew would have jumped off and made their way to land; from there, safely hidden away behind the trees, they would have attempted to fend off the British with musket fire until the local militia arrived to help. Such was the established method of protecting a coasting vessel and her cargo.

But the captain and crew of the *Eagle* behaved differently. Instead of grounding the *Eagle*, they deliberately kept her in deep water and anchored her near Millstone Point, and from there they "escaped" in a small boat. Once on shore, they waited until the British had boarded the *Eagle* before beginning a heavy musket fire so intense and accurate that the British had to cut the cable holding the anchor to move out of range quickly. The unsuspecting British set sail back to their ship, just as Scudder and his partners had anticipated.

For all the British could see, the *Eagle* gave every evidence of being a valuable prize heavily laden with marine stores and provisions—Scudder and his people had purposely covered the deck with freshly minted barrels and coils of new line—but because the *Eagle* now had no anchor, there was no way to secure her in her own right and make an inspection of the cargo. As Scudder and his partners had planned, the British were forced to tie her to another vessel. The obvious one was the flagship, and the sailors worked for two hours to get her alongside the *Ramillies* so that she might be off-loaded.

As luck would have it, the wind died away and the tide turned against the British sailors before they could secure the *Eagle*. Captain Hardy finally ordered her crew to move the *Eagle* away from the *Ramillies* and to tie her to a sloop captured several days earlier, which was now anchored about three quarters of a mile away. Perhaps the order was just luck, or maybe some sixth sense warned Hardy that the Americans' evasive action had been suspicious. Whatever the reason, his decision undoubtedly saved his flagship.

At half past two that afternoon someone on board the *Eagle* hoisted one of the flour barrels, triggering the flintlocks, and the terrible engine of death erupted. The American Captain Riker, still watching closely from Millstone Point, reported later, "The body of fire appeared to rise upwards of 900 feet into the air, with a black streak on the spout side, and then burst like a rocket." The explosion was so great that a shower of pitch and tar fell on the deck of the *Ramillies*, almost a mile away. A Royal Navy lieutenant and nine seamen simply disappeared in the explosion, along with the *Eagle* and the schooner to which she was moored.

The effect of the *Eagle* incident on Captain Hardy is difficult to overstate. The enormity of the attack—the deceit, the trickery, the underhanded manner of the operation—the fact that the *Ramillies* owed its survival to good luck alone—these facts must have deeply shaken Hardy. He was a traditional Englishman to his fingertips, and "this new mode of warfare," as he characterized it, was antithetical to everything in which he believed.

For two centuries and more the warring nations in Europe had evolved a system that attempted—often successfully— to make a clear distinction between civilians and fighting men and to limit war to the combatants. Suddenly, one ghastly explosion on board the *Eagle* signaled the distressing fact that civilians operating on their own and with no control from the military could now endanger a machine of war even as large as a ship-of-the-line. The idea of "civilized war" was thrown into a cocked hat. To someone of Hardy's stripe, the *Eagle* incident must have seemed like the opening of the gates of Chaos itself.

Whatever his philosophical reaction, his practical response was both cool and quick. He immediately ordered a boat sent under a flag of truce into New London to ascertain whether the U.S. government had sanctioned the explosion of the *Eagle*, declaring that if it had "he would destroy everything American that floats." The local citizens quickly demonstrated that the fitting out of the *Eagle* was a wholly private undertaking and had nothing to do with either New London or the federal government. Of course, no one could gainsay that if the government had not "sanctioned" the explosion, it had clearly encouraged the incident with an Act of Congress, and the U.S. Treasury had just as clearly been ready and eager to pay off the members of the syndicate if they had been successful. Most worrisome to Hardy was the likelihood that someone would repeat the attempt if he did not immediately check the impulse. He ordered a new and more rigorous patrol calculated to neutralize the whole eastern end of Long Island Sound.

It was the beginning of a long, troublesome summer for Captain Hardy, a summer that would test his mettle—not to mention his character and cunning—to the limit.

"Hardy has not beauty, but he is very superior," wrote Sir Edward Codrington, one of his fellow captains at Trafalgar. Everyone who knew Hardy seems to have recognized there was something special about him. Sir William Parker called this quality "the very soul of truth," and a twentieth-century writer, Ludovic Kennedy, characterized Hardy's superiority as "a kind of natural and spontaneous authority, arising from a moral standard of the highest order."

Thomas Masterman Hardy holds the odd distinction of appearing as a character in two minor classics of English fiction—C. S. Forester's

Flying Colours, in which he rescues the redoubtable Horatio Horn-blower, and *The Trumpet Major*, written by his namesake and distant relative, Thomas Hardy. (After visiting the novelist Hardy in 1902, Lady Cynthia Asquith reported, "The only thing he seems to take the least pride in is his descent from the Trafalgar Hardy.")

Hardy was born in 1769 in Dorset, England, the sixth of nine children in a family of respectable and suitably ancient lineage. When he was nine his family moved into the ancestral holdings in the village of Portesham, near Weymouth. The building is still there today, a little doll's house of a manor, plain and stoutly made. Its size and character tell us something of the Hardys and their position in Dorset society. They were not wealthy, but they were people who counted—yeomen for the most part—small squires, local professionals, village industrialists, and the like. In short, the backbone of England.

Young Tom was sent off to grammar school twenty miles away in Somerset. There he remained for three years—it was virtually his only formal education—before he was apprenticed at the age of twelve to Captain Francis Roberts, a family friend, and shipped out as captain's servant on His Majesty's Brig *Helena*. Five months later he wrote a letter to his older brother, telling of his adventures convoying ships to Ostend. The letter still exists and is endorsed in Captain Roberts's hand, "Thomas is a very good boy, and I think will make a complete seaman one day or another."

Although he returned home briefly and even received a little additional schooling, young Tom never left the sea for long, and on 5 February 1790, just short of his twenty-first birthday, he joined the *Hebe* as a midshipman. Her captain was Sir Alexander Hood, a Dorset man and a neighbor. In 1793, after the outbreak of war between Britain and revolutionary France, Hardy was ordered to Genoa to join the Royal Navy squadron commanded by an extraordinary young leader already recognized as a naval genius, Horatio Nelson.

Nelson had a reputation as a high-strung officer who was difficult to deal with. His superior, Admiral Jervis, later Earl St. Vincent, described him as "devoured by vanity, weakness and folly." But the young Hardy, according to his biographer John Gore, "already knew how to direct vain men without their realizing it and to compose the moods of the heady and the irritable." The combination of Hardy and Nelson was to be a perfect match of personalities.

At Gibraltar in the autumn of 1796 Lieutenant Hardy was serving in Nelson's flagship, the large frigate *Minerve*. Off Cartagena they captured the Spanish frigate *Sabina*. Hardy was dispatched to take command of the prize; but before the little British squadron could get underway again, a large Spanish squadron, including ships-of-the-line, appeared over the horizon and bore down on them.

From his position on the quarterdeck of the captured *Sabina*, Hardy could observe the action. Nelson, in the *Minerve*, was in imminent danger. Small and fast Spanish sloops were closing in on her. While they were no match for *Minerve*'s firepower, they could detain the frigate long enough for the ships-of-the-line to reach the scene, at which point *Minerve*—and Nelson—would be forced to surrender.

Hardy's initiative and quick judgment alone saved the *Minerve* and laid Nelson under a debt of gratitude. Hardy realized that since the *Sabina* was still flying Spanish colors, the attacking squadron assumed she was one of theirs. He quickly shortened sail and simultaneously ran up the British ensign above the Spanish flag. The leading Spanish ship, catching sight of this closer and more vulnerable target, broke off her pursuit of the *Minerve* to attack, and soon to recapture, the *Sabina*. In the confusion, Nelson escaped.

Hardy and his prize crew were taken into Cartagena and spent Christmas as prisoners of war, but the event proved anything but a misfortune for Hardy. Nelson's dispatch was fervent in its praise of the lieutenant's courage and initiative, and an immediate exchange of prisoners was arranged. Hardy was on board the *Minerve* again in six weeks, his reputation enhanced, and with the legendary Nelson as his friend and patron.

The incident says a lot about Hardy. It shows he could grasp a subtle and complicated problem quickly and could intuitively take the right action. He sacrificed the *Sabina* and himself to save Nelson as quickly and as casually as a chess player would sacrifice a pawn to save a rook.

In May 1797 Hardy was given command of the cutting-out party sent to capture the French brig *Mutine*. The records show that he carried off the affair with such skill and swiftness that he was able to hoist British colors on board the Frenchman with only fifteen casualties and no loss of life, even though the attack was made in broad daylight. Admiral Jervis was so delighted he promoted Hardy and gave him the

Mutine as his first command. Nelson was pleased. "He has got it by his own bat," he wrote, "and I hope will prosper." An impressive number of Hardy's victories throughout his career are notable for their lack of bloodshed.

One last incident from that memorable Mediterranean cruise deserves mention. Upon taking over as captain of Nelson's flagship *Vanguard*, Hardy quickly discovered that the general standard of seamanship aboard her was much below what he wanted. When he gave an order to take in a reef in the main topsail and found half the crew ignorant of the duty, he took off his cocked hat and buckles, ran aloft, and lay out on the yard himself. This example made a great impression on the entire ship's company but particularly on Nelson, who for all his brilliance and zeal was no great shakes as a seaman.

After the Battle of the Nile Hardy was inseparable from Nelson and became, in fact, "Nelson's Hardy," as he remains known to this day. Between the two men an intense personal admiration grew up. Each respected the other for those qualities—the flashing brilliance of the one, the calm imperturbability of the other—that the other lacked. When Nelson was given HMS *Victory* there was never any doubt who his flag captain would be.

The bond between the two men was to develop and strengthen right up to the hour of Nelson's death at Trafalgar. Even there, it was Hardy who brought Nelson the news of the great victory and who carried out Nelson's last wish, cutting a lock of hair from his fallen commander and later delivering it to the admiral's great love, Lady Hamilton, a woman whom Hardy despised.

After Trafalgar a grateful Parliament voted £300,000 to the victors, of which Hardy's share was £2,389 7s 6d, which, along with prize money of nearly £1,000, translates to nearly a half million dollars in present American currency. Prize money made Hardy a wealthy man. At one point he was able to settle £20,000 on his wife—perhaps $4,500,000 in today's terms.

After a decade of fighting the French, Hardy's first direct experience with Americans came in 1807, two years after Trafalgar. That summer the uneasy peace maintained between Britain and the United States came close to breaking out into war when the British frigate *Leopard*, in a dispute over impressed seamen, made an unprovoked attack on the American frigate *Chesapeake*. The American public rose up in fury at the outrage. "For the first time in their history," Henry

Adams was to write, "the people of the United States learned, in June, 1807, the feeling of a true national emotion." Demands for revenge echoed from every corner of the nation. The fact that America was very weak and Britain very strong was immaterial. It was a matter of national honor. President Jefferson ordered all armed vessels of Great Britain to leave American ports. The militia was mustered from Massachusetts to Georgia. Mobs in New York and Boston roamed the streets in search of British targets.

Nowhere was the cry for revenge louder than along the shores of the Chesapeake Bay. On the day of the incident the mobs in Norfolk ran riot upon seeing their dead and wounded comrades carried from the stricken frigate. A few days later, when a British officer landed in Virginia with dispatches for the consul in Norfolk, the militia had to be called out to guard him from a lynch mob that instantly surrounded him.

The British ambassador, David Erskine, barely escaped the angry crowds in New York and appealed to London for an official apology from King George. While the royal apology was never offered, the nervous Tory cabinet recognized that the *Chesapeake* outrage was not only illegal and totally unproductive from Great Britain's point of view, but that it also needlessly upset the United States and might lead to war. Britain's resources were fully committed to the war against Napoleon, and for all the empire's military power the British could not afford to defend their western hemisphere possessions against even a tiny American force.

At this emotionally charged moment Captain Thomas Masterman Hardy of the *Triumph*, 74, was in Halifax, Nova Scotia, preparing to marry the daughter of his commanding officer; but before the ceremony could be performed his prospective father-in-law summarily ordered him to take over command of the Royal Navy squadron off Virginia. Hardy's handling of this very delicate situation is instructive. Immediately upon taking command, he ordered the offending *Leopard* to Bermuda, where her presence could no longer excite local anger by reminding Americans of the *Chesapeake* outrage. Just as decisively, he retired the rest of the squadron to an innocuous position beyond the capes, which led to an immediate relaxation of tension on shore. In Maryland and Virginia the militia was disbanded and the men sent home.

With the immediate danger under control, Hardy returned to Halifax to marry Louisa Berkeley (she was nineteen years old that autumn, and he was thirty-nine), and when he returned to the Chesapeake before Christmas, he made sure the local press learned that he was bringing Louisa with him. The Norfolk *Ledger* reassured its readers that as "the captain carries his newly married lady with him, it does not appear that he expects to have much fighting to do." The cheerful tone of the newspaper report is a far cry from the emotional outrage of June and July and says a lot about Hardy's skill at handling a crisis that was far more political than military. As he was to demonstrate repeatedly in the War of 1812, he had a highly attuned sense of the very modern concept of public relations.

The young Louisa Hardy never forgot the miseries of her first months of marriage, or the dreary loneliness of the Chesapeake. Many years later she remembered, "We spent from December 1807 to April 1808 in that gloomy, desolate Bay, not allowed to land, as the Americans were in such an exasperated state that they might have been very disagreeable." She used to tell her grandchildren that Captain Hardy insisted upon keeping the *Triumph* ready for action, so she was never even allowed to have a fire in her cabin.

During that long, quiet winter of his honeymoon Hardy had ample time to ruminate on the crisis in Anglo-American relations, and to draw whatever lessons from it he might. From the vantage of his quarterdeck he could survey the countryside with his spyglass (bequeathed to him by Nelson). Hardy could see that the shores of the Chesapeake were similar to the shores of Dorset, and that the Chesapeake farmers who tilled the fields were virtually interchangeable with those in Portesham. Over that winter of 1807–8 Captain Hardy came to know this foreign land where people spoke English and behaved in very much an English way, and yet insisted they were somehow different and seemed ready to go to war to prove it. The thought might have struck him that these tough, proud people, with their obsessive penchant for personal freedom and their angry determination not to truckle, were not such different people from his own.

Did Decatur have a hand in the *Eagle's* explosion? The question must have occurred to Hardy almost immediately after the event. Certainly Decatur stood to gain from such an attack, and the timing—barely three weeks after he was forced up the Thames—was suspicious. The circumstances, however, proved conclusively that Decatur was totally innocent of the scheme. Had he known of it beforehand, he most

Commodore Stephen Decatur, from a portrait by Gilbert
Stuart. Although Decatur played no direct role in the attack
on Stonington, the presence of his squadron at New London
focused British naval activity on the eastern end of Long
Island Sound and led (with Decatur's enthusiastic support) to
extensive antiblockade mischief on the part of resident
civilians. (U.S. Naval Institute)

certainly would have been preparing his ships for a quick escape during
the confusion. Instead, he spent the morning of the explosion moving
his squadron farther up the Thames channel toward Norwich.

But the fact that Decatur was not aware of Mr. Scudder's project
did not imply that he was in any way averse to it. He was a pragmatist.
He understood that the basic principle of war is to win. From Decatur's

point of view, if a secretly prepared infernal machine deliberately disguised and tricked out to appeal to the enemy's sense of material greed could help America fight a totally out-of-balance war with Britain, then so much the better. Besides, the scheme had a basic simplicity that would have appealed to his practical American nature.

Decatur was known within the navy for his keen interest in new weapons and new ways of fighting battles. Throughout his career he had used his influence—and sometimes his own prize money—to encourage all sorts of experimental and therefore "immoral" weapons. But perhaps the most novel means of waging war dreamed up by Decatur that summer of 1813 required nothing new in the way of naval hardware—just a long boat and a few men, some courage, and a lot of luck. With these, Decatur planned nothing less than the abduction of Captain Hardy. The commodore never openly admitted to the kidnapping scheme and later tried to dismiss the whole affair as simply an incidence of youthful high spirits on the part of his men; but the British always suspected a darker motive, and they were almost assuredly right. Pieced together from letters and news reports, the story strongly supports the British contention.

Not long after the *Eagle*'s explosion Captain Hardy moved his flagship from its original position near the mouth of the Thames to a location across the sound called Gardiner's Bay, an area about eight miles in diameter sheltered between the forks of Long Island and Gardiner's Island. Doubtless one advantage to such an anchorage lay in its proximity to the open ocean, and another in its remoteness from any local mariners with a penchant for explosive devices. In mid-July Decatur learned that the British might have found still a third advantage to the place. A certain Joshua Penny, a local pilot-cum-spy from Long Island, informed the commodore that when the *Ramillies* lay at anchor in Gardiner's Bay, Captain Hardy and his officers were in the habit of going on shore on Gardiner's Island and joining its owner, Mr. John Lyon Gardiner, for their meals. (Mr. Gardiner was already well known for his open collaboration with the British, and some patriots were quick to brand him a traitor. In truth, he was hardly in a position to defy the Royal Navy single-handedly and had little option but to cooperate with the enemy.)

The intelligence intrigued Decatur. To his mind it suggested a brand new opportunity for improving his almost hopeless situation. Hardy on board the *Ramillies*, surrounded by seventy-four guns and six hundred sailors, was untouchable, but Hardy on shore, and on an unfortified island at that, was an entirely different matter. Hardy sitting at Mr. Gardiner's table, with only a few crewmen to protect him, was too tempting a target to overlook. Decatur immediately set about devising a plan to kidnap the British commodore, or failing that, to capture at least a few of his officers.

So it was that in late July 1813 four small boats from the American squadron sallied forth at night from New London. Guided by Joshua Penny, they made their way across the mouth of the sound under cover of darkness. To protect Penny from being charged as a spy in case of possible capture (spying carried the death penalty), Decatur had secretly enrolled him into the *United States* as a seaman, although his duties lay purely in the area of espionage and dirty tricks. On reaching Gardiner's Island, the lead boat, captained by Midshipman Abraham S. Ten Eyck of the *Macedonian*, pulled up onto the beach while the three others turned and sailed back to New London. Among Ten Eyck's crew were the pilot Penny, who was familiar with the layout of the island, and a hand-picked selection of volunteer seamen, emboldened by the prospects of prize money.

After carefully hiding their boat near the shore, the men sequestered themselves on the western side of the island where they could observe the traffic in the bay. When the sun eventually rose they saw, as expected, the huge bulk of the *Ramillies* lying at anchor. What they perhaps did not expect to see was the frigate *Orpheus*, 38, nearby.

The day dragged on, and despite determined scrutiny they could detect little activity aboard the *Ramillies* and definitely no sign of a boat coming their way. Finally, with the sun well past the zenith, the men saw a pinnace set out from the *Orpheus*. Ten Eyck watched the boat pull for shore and made his decision. Clearly, a boat from the *Orpheus* would not be carrying Captain Hardy, but the fact that she was a pinnace suggested she had officers on board. He decided to settle for a bird in the hand—they would capture whomever might come on shore and make the best deal possible. From their hiding place behind the dunes the kidnappers watched the boat beach herself and eight men climb onto the sand. Then on a signal from one of them, the boat's oarsmen pushed her back into the sea and returned to the *Orpheus*. The Americans saw two men in officers' coats and a young boy detach themselves from the others and walk off in the direction of Mr. Gardiner's manor house. When they had passed from sight, Ten Eyck and his men quickly surprised and took captive the five men left on the beach.

These men turned out to be a midshipman and four ordinary seamen. Ten Eyck judged them not worth the trouble of capturing, so like a disappointed angler throwing back an undersized catch, he determined to parole all five. He quickly wrote out, and they quickly signed, the following document:

> We the undersigned acknowledge that we have been captured by a Party of Men belonging to the United States ship Macedonian and pledge our honour not to take arms against the United States until regularly exchanged.
>
>   Richard Chesterton, Mid. HMS Orpheus
>   John Thornelius
>   James Hickey
>   Thomas Jacques
>   Robert Lloyd

With this piece of paper in his pocket, and a caution to his recent captives to remain quiet and not attract attention or otherwise impede his plans, Ten Eyck felt secure enough to turn his attentions elsewhere. To modern eyes, such a mannered and legalistic device as a parole seems totally incomprehensible, yet they were commonly used throughout the War of 1812, and the fact that they were so widely employed and generally so scrupulously observed by both sides is perhaps indicative of a certain level of trust the warring parties held for each other.

Leaving most of his men with the paroled British, and accompanied only by Penny and one other hand, the midshipman hurried to Gardiner's house where, with sabres drawn, the Americans broke in and seized the other members of the *Orpheus*'s party, who turned out to be a lieutenant, a master's mate, and a servant boy. Despite the protests of Mr. Gardiner, Ten Eyck duly returned these men to the beach. The two captured officers—for the master's mate as well as the lieutenant was considered an officer—were but a poor substitute for Captain Hardy, but they would make valuable hostages just the same. Ten Eyck ordered his men to uncover the escape boat and prepare for departure.

At this point something happened. We don't know precisely what, but for some reason it suddenly became abundantly clear that fate had turned against the Americans. Their glorious adventure began to fall apart. Perhaps there had been a signal from Gardiner's house, or maybe the Yankee sailors spotted a boat being lowered from the *Ramillies*. Whatever the reason, the Americans hurriedly decided to abandon the whole project and to run for their freedom and their lives. As a practical matter, however, they could not even try to escape without first getting their remaining prisoners to cooperate, so once again Ten Eyck scratched out a parole, and once again passed it over to his hostages to sign, which they did:

PAROLE

We consider ourselves as prisoners of war and pledge our honours that we will not act against the United States during the war or till regularly exchanged.
Gardiner's Island, July 27, 1813

    T. W. Dance, Lieutenant HMS Orpheus
    W. Hope, Masters Mate, HMS Orpheus
    John Williams, boy on HMS Orpheus

Then, after this second document was in the hands of the ever-resourceful Midshipman Ten Eyck, disaster struck. Apparently the British crewmen, despite being disarmed and legally bound not to hinder the Americans, seized the Yankees' escape boat from under the noses of their erstwhile captors and started pulling toward the *Orpheus* with all their strength, leaving the Americans alone and trapped on the beach. In spite of this alarming and embarrassing setback, Decatur's men managed to get off the island before they could be taken by the British—undoubtedly by commandeering one of Mr. Gardiner's boats—and in due course made their way to Long Island, where the following night they were picked up by one of Decatur's boats and returned to New London.

Upon hearing the story from Ten Eyck and Penny, Decatur was livid. He was not so much angered by the failure of the mission, which at best had to be seen as a high-risk venture, as he was outraged by the duplicity of the parolees in stealing the escape boat. He dictated an angry letter to Hardy, demanding the return of the boat, and sent it off, along with copies of the paroles, under a flag of truce.

Decatur, who could toss off an orotund phrase when he so desired, made no secret of his abhorrence of the British action:

Whether this be viewed in the light of a mere seizure of the property of the United States or as tending to deprive the officer and his men of the means of leaving the Island, and thus rendering their capture almost inevitable, I presume, Sir, you will consider it an act of hostility and a violation of their parole. This entitles me to demand the Prisoners and by the common obligations of a Parole they are bound to surrender themselves; but . . . I am willing to waive this right. The taking of the boat, however, under these circumstances, was an act of hostility so unjustifiable that you cannot consider it as divesting us of our property in her and I trust [you] will order her to be restored. . . .

> I have the honour to be, Sir, with the highest
> consideration and respect your most obedient
> Servant
> Stephen Decatur, Captain
> Commodore U.S. Vessels at New London

Hardy's reply claimed that the men responsible for running off with the American boat had been two unidentified British sailors not signatory to a parole; and he, therefore, had no obligation to return the boat. The answer was feeble, and probably not entirely accurate, but Hardy might feel free to bend the truth a little, given Decatur's distinctly unsporting attempt to spirit him away.

Hardy closed his reply to Decatur by offering to return the boat as a gift, which offer the American stonily refused.

At first blush, Decatur's attempt to kidnap Hardy may strike some readers as a harebrained scheme. After all, the Admiralty had more senior officers than it knew what to do with and could easily have replaced Hardy if the Americans had managed to abduct him. But that analysis overlooks an important consideration: Hardy, because of his position as Nelson's flag captain, was unique. The loss of such a famous and distinguished officer would have had the same psychological impact on the British public as the loss of a large ship. If the Americans could have managed the kidnapping discretely, and sent an envoy to treat secretly with the British, the Admiralty just possibly might have offered Decatur his freedom in exchange for the return of the hero of Trafalgar.

Hardy recognized that it was vital to keep close tabs on the temper of the large, volatile population that surrounded his ships on all sides if he were to maintain the calm he so assiduously sought in the Long Island Sound area. Toward that end he spent a good part of the summer creating an intelligence network to help him keep track of the shifting moods of the public, and not incidentally to give him early warning of any further mischief coming his way.

One of his first steps in this direction was to enlist the help of the official British consul in New London, a man named James Stewart. Stewart was an Anglo-Irishman with an American wife, and he was allowed to remain at liberty in the city in spite of the war because he served as his country's agent for the transfer and return of prisoners of war. Because the British were constantly capturing fishermen and privateers, Stewart's work quite legitimately brought him into almost daily communication with Hardy, and this contact made him an ideal spy master.

The American army and militia commanders in New London were fully aware of Stewart's obvious value to Hardy and took steps to curb his access to the blockading fleet. In July, at the behest of the military, the consul was ordered to leave the coast and to relocate his office somewhere well into the interior. This order was a blow to Hardy, who needed a permanent set of eyes and ears in New London, but he soon came up with a solution to the problem. Rather than allow the Americans to move Stewart inland, he arranged for the consul to resign his position and come on board the *Valiant*, ostensibly to take the next packet to Bermuda or Halifax and there to seek reassignment elsewhere within Britain's foreign service. We shall hear from Stewart again. Significantly, he left his family behind him, and his American wife, Elizabeth, would remain in New London to serve as Captain Hardy's new native-grown spy master. We shall hear from her again as well.

As part of his information-gathering effort, Hardy also required a quick and expeditious manner of obtaining the American newspapers. Years before, during his tour of duty in the Chesapeake in 1807, Hardy had discovered the unique role newspapers played in America. The United States was a big new country committed to a national experiment in democracy, and its citizens depended heavily upon their newspapers to help them keep track of events. The government in Washington believed newspapers were so important that it established special cheap postal rates to encourage their distribution. But what made newspapers particularly valuable to Hardy was the fact that the American press was free to publish virtually anything it wanted to— it was by far the freest press in the world, even then—and it was, therefore, a valuable source of political and even military intelligence.

He arranged to get the local papers from New London fishermen, who were happy to deliver them along with fresh seafood for the wardroom mess. To obtain the newspapers from New York and beyond, Hardy contracted with Captain John Howard of the New London packet ship *Juno* for regular deliveries. Although Captain Howard was never proven to be in the pay of the British, the press of the day publicly remarked that while Hardy had made operating on the sound extremely difficult for any ship or boat, the *Juno*, sailing to and from New York in broad daylight, never missed a trip throughout the entire length of the war.

Hardy's most immediate concern, of course, was to obtain up-to-the minute intelligence on New London, and particularly on Decatur's squadron. Hardy was encouraged to learn of New London's disaffection with Decatur, and of how fear and anxiety had arisen again in the city as a result of Decatur's sudden appearance in its midst. In the short run, Hardy knew, the public antipathy toward Decatur could only serve the British cause, but the British captain was wise enough to recognize that, given enough time, the anxious population of New London was bound to wake up to the obvious fact that it was not Decatur who threatened their city, but Hardy himself who was the true cause of their misery. When the people came to understand the situation, Decatur was bound to find ways to capitalize on the change in mood, stirring up waves of mischief and patriotic fervor that would end up making Hardy's job much more difficult.

It was therefore important to Hardy to take advantage of the present pro-British sentiment so that New Londoners might continue to look upon him as "a noble fellow." What he needed was a fresh public gesture of some sort, calculated to demonstrate the benign nature of the British blockaders. An opportunity for just such a gesture arose when a letter addressed to Hardy arrived from the mainland under a flag of truce, concerning a seaman on board his flagship named John Carpenter.

John Carpenter was an American seaman impressed into the crew of the *Ramillies* five years earlier (long before Hardy took command) and held on board ever since. There was nothing unique about him, of course. A ship the size of the *Ramillies* was likely to have twenty-five or more illegally pressed Yankees on board. What made John Carpenter singular was that his father lived in Norwich, twelve miles up the Thames from New London. Somehow the son had found a way to get word to him of his presence in the flagship, and the father wrote to Hardy begging for his son's return. Hardy seized the opportunity to shine in the eyes of the local population and arranged for the father to come on board the *Ramillies*. After the elder Mr. Carpenter presented the proper testimonials and proofs of his son's nationality, an affecting scene took place when father and son were brought together on deck. Commodore Hardy ordered the sailor discharged and paid off, expressed his sympathy, and escorted them to the rail for their return to shore.

As expected, the news of John Carpenter's release from five years of servitude became the talk of New London and was seen as fresh proof of the decency and humanity of Thomas Masterman Hardy. Once more the people of New London were on his side. What Decatur may have thought of Hardy's gesture is not recorded. Perhaps he wondered why the people should so lavishly praise Hardy for the simple act of not committing a crime.

It is instructive to note that later petitioners with the same complaint were not to prove so fortunate. When a bottle washed ashore with a message from a John Banks of Hampton, Virginia, claiming that he too had been impressed five or six years earlier and was now serving in the *Ramillies*, Hardy made no move to right that particular wrong. But John Banks was not a local boy, and more importantly, by then the situation in Long Island Sound had changed radically, and Hardy was no longer interested in appeasing the Americans.

Hardy was determined to leave nothing afloat on Long Island Sound that could possibly prove dangerous to his ships. Since the *Eagle* had show that even the smallest vessel was capable of carrying enough gunpowder to destroy a 74, every vessel, down to the most innocent-seeming dory, had to go. Throughout the rest of the summer of 1813 the sound was alive with petty warfare.

As a step toward containing the danger, Hardy's forces soon established control over all the islands in the area, to deny roaming teams of Yankee "banditti" any convenient hideouts. Gardiner's Island was already in British hands for all intents and purposes. Now Shelter Island and Great Hog Neck Island to its south became sporting centers for parties of British officers who enjoyed hunting the abundant wildfowl of the area. Naval parties visited the scattering of islands that led across toward the New England shore—Plum Island, the Gulls,

Fishers, and Block Island—at regular intervals to make sure they did not become strongholds for American resistance.

Hardy's 74s and frigates were well suited to the job of subduing the islands and the more accessible points of land, but their clumsy bulk and deep drafts made them useless in securing the bays and creeks and rivers and coves that shaped the shoreline, each one large enough to hold at least a privateer or two and sometimes a whole fleet.

For Hardy to bring his power to bear on these sanctuaries, he relied on the small craft carried on the decks of all his larger vessels. These barges, long boats, cutters, and pinnaces came in a variety of shapes and sizes and could penetrate into even the shallowest bay if it was not guarded.

Inconveniently for the British, these small craft were often insufficient to deal with the people who lived along the coast. These Americans were seagoing folk, thoroughly familiar with guns and eager to use them in their own defense. They lived in at least a dozen locations along the Connecticut shore, independent and proud. One seaport that was particularly well protected and difficult to get at was the little community of mariners and shipbuilders living along the Mystic River, hidden behind the mass of Mason's Island.

Then as now the Mystic River formed the border between the towns of Groton and Stonington, and in consequence those living on the west bank were in a different town from those on the east bank. Today the area on both banks is known as the village of Mystic, but in 1813 the area had no generic name, and the people who lived there defined themselves by which township they happened to live in. Jeremiah Holmes, living on the east bank, always described himself as a Stonington man.

In the early months of 1813 Holmes had just managed to outrun the blockade, and upon his return to the Mystic River he had reluctantly decided to retire from the sea, at least temporarily, in the face of the overwhelming British presence. He was joined by several of his neighbors, master mariners all. Each one had settled uncomfortably into a sedentary life totally unsuitable for such vigorous men, and some had grown restless and gone back to sea. Holmes, still under sentence of death as a British deserter, stayed on shore, but increasingly he found himself totally at a loss as to what to do with himself.

One day in late June, when Hardy's campaign to eradicate small craft was at its height, Jeremiah Holmes was standing on a hill near his house when he witnessed a scene taking place beyond Mason's Island at the mouth of the Mystic River. A sloop, which Holmes recognized as the *Victory*, owned and captained by one of his neighbors, had run aground near Ram Point. She was heavily laden with cargo, and her crew had no hope of freeing her before the next tide. Of itself, this did not necessarily pose a serious problem for the sloop's captain, but Captain Holmes, from his vantage point on the hill, could see an approaching peril not visible to his friends on board the grounded *Victory*. The British anchored off Fishers Island had obviously spotted the *Victory*, and two enemy barges were now rounding the end of Fishers and bearing down on the marooned vessel, clearly intent on taking it as prize. Holmes immediately gave the alarm and collected a band of volunteers to save the *Victory*. With Holmes in the lead, they commandeered a smack called the *Charleston*, hastily armed her with a British 4-pounder and some small arms captured in an earlier foray, and set off to the rescue. They arrived just before the enemy, and in a long and sporadic battle the Americans were able to face down the British barges, forcing the enemy to return empty-handed to their mother ship. With a good deal of self-congratulation, the band held an impromptu party until the tide returned and floated off the *Victory*.

This small action, inconsequential in itself, served to alert Jeremiah Holmes and his neighbors to the haphazard nature of their defenses, and especially to the vulnerability of their shipping and boat yards, both prime targets for Hardy's depredations. All agreed they vitally needed to find some means to safeguard their property.

Under Holmes's leadership, the local people instituted a round-the-clock watch against British incursions. To protect themselves against raids, they built a fort on the Groton side of the river, fitting it out with the same 4-pounder they had used against Hardy's barges. From its commanding position, the gun could readily sink boats far out in the channel and could annoy an enemy at even greater distances. They dubbed the battery Fort Rachel, in honor of the widow who lived in a cottage below it.

To complement Fort Rachel, Holmes and his people threw up a redoubt on the Stonington side at Pistol Point, arming it with a 9-pounder left over from the Revolution and eventually two brass 6-pounders. Jeremiah Holmes himself, a man of considerable experience with cannon, took personal charge of the Pistol Point battery.

Thus was created the tough, troublesome little bastion of Yankee intransigence that the British officers quickly dubbed "The Hornet's Nest," just one of many such communities populated by experienced sailors, and each one capable of delivering some new and unnerving surprise, similar to the *Eagle*, to Captain Hardy's blockading fleet.

Just two weeks after the *Eagle*'s explosion a shadowy figure, known to the world only as "a gentleman from Norwich," introduced another new element into the War of 1812: submarines. On 10 July 1813 the New York *Herald* broke the story of a mysterious and unnamed gentleman from Norwich, Connecticut, who, having invented a "diving boat" that was propelled by paddles, managed on three separate occasions to submerge his craft off the New London coast and maneuver it under the bottom of the *Ramillies*, with the intent of blowing a hole in the bottom of said vessel.

After remaining underwater for a considerable length of time on his first attempt, he ran short of air and had to surface only a few feet from the target ship, where a sentinel immediately spotted him and gave the alarm. According to the newspaper story, the gentleman from Norwich hastily submerged again to avoid the musket fire directed at him. Simultaneously, the *Ramillies* cut her cables and got under way with all possible dispatch.

On a subsequent night the same gentleman tried to get underneath the *Ramillies* again, once more without success. But on his third attempt he came up directly under his target and fastened himself and his boat to her keel, where he remained for half an hour, eventually succeeding in drilling a hole through her copper sheathing. He then tried to attach a watertight bomb to the drill lodged solidly in her bottom. The apparatus was what we would today call a time bomb, with a clockwork device as a detonator. Unfortunately for the gentleman from Norwich, the auger broke, and he was left with nothing to attach the bomb to. He had to abandon the project, and for reasons not stated in the article he made no further attempts against the *Ramillies* or any other ship.

Who was the gentleman from Norwich? Local legends suggest that he was a Mr. Halsey, who died during an unspecified attack on a blockading ship. Another theory connects the gentleman from Norwich with David Bushnell, a native of nearby Saybrook, Connecticut, who had in fact designed and built a working submarine during the

The submarine *Turtle*, designed by David Bushnell of Saybrook, Connecticut, during the Revolution to attack the British fleet in New York. It is likely that an identical craft, or one very similar to it, was obtained from Bushnell in 1813 and employed by "a gentleman from Norwich" in an unsuccessful attack on the *Ramillies* off New London. (U.S. Naval Institute)

Revolution. That submersible, name the *Turtle*, was actually used in New York Harbor in 1776 in an attempt to sink Admiral Howe's flagship. The *Turtle* failed under circumstances similar to those given in the account concerning the gentleman from Norwich. Bushnell was still alive and active during the summer of 1813, and some have suggested that an updated version of the *Turtle* was the vessel used against the *Ramillies*.

Whatever the facts in the case, the story of a "Bushnell II" submarine, coming so close on the heels of the *Eagle* incident, clearly signaled that the United States in general, and a group of its citizens living principally along the boundaries of Long Island Sound in particular, was moving toward a radically new understanding of the nature of naval warfare. Certainly Hardy must have arrived at that conclusion. He gave orders that his ships were not to remain anchored in a single place for any longer than was absolutely necessary, and he caused the bottom of the *Ramillies* to be swept by a cable every two hours night and day.

While the new mode of naval warfare seemed to be centered on Long Island Sound, news from the Chesapeake that summer showed that Americans were pursuing further experimentation there as well. In July the U.S. Navy provided a civilian named Elijah Mix with a small boat, six volunteers, and the necessary gunpowder for an attack on British blockaders in Lynnhaven Bay. It turned out later that both the navy and Mr. Mix were working clandestinely with the inventor Robert Fulton, whose successful steamboats on the Hudson and elsewhere were already changing the nature of shipping. Fulton's contributions to Mr. Mix's operations were the waterproof copper-clad casings designed to hold the gunpowder, as well as the self-contained firing mechanisms designed to set them off. The whole instrument was something Fulton called a "torpedo," a name coined originally by Bushnell and derived from the torpedo fish, a slow-moving skate that produces a painful electrical charge when touched.

Fulton's torpedoes were similar to what we would today call sea mines. They were not self-propelled, like the modern torpedo, but they could be made to explode against the hull of any enemy ship in a variety of ways.

In the Lynnhaven incident, Mix used floating torpedoes and rafted them toward his target, the *Plantagenet*, 74, on the appropriate tide. A pressure-sensitive fuse was designed to trigger the bomb when it touched the hull. Unfortunately for the torpedoist, he misjudged the tide, and his first attempt proved a failure. The British were able to fish the torpedo out of the water and examine it closely before detonating it harmlessly. A few days later Mix tried again, and this time his second torpedo exploded near the bow of the *Plantagenet*. It failed to inflict any damage on the ship-of-the-line, but the Norfolk *Herald* gave the description of the attack, which took place in the pitch dark, in rhapsodic detail:

The scene was awfully sublime! It was like the concussion of an earthquake, attended with a sound louder and more terrific than the heaviest peal of thunder. A pyramid of water 50 feet in circumference was thrown up 30 or 40 feet, its appearance was a vivid red tinged at the sides with a beautiful purple. On ascending to its greatest heighth [*sic*], it burst at the top with a tremendous explosion and fell in torrents on the deck of the ship, which rolled into the yawning chasm below and nearly upset:—Impervious darkness again prevailed.

Captain Hardy could take little comfort from the failures of all three "torpedo" attacks on British ships. There was bound to come a time when those "damned Yankee barnacles," as he called them, could be made effective, and before then he wanted the people using them to know that British sailors would not suffer the consequences alone.

Hardy directed letters to the governor of Connecticut and other officials, warning that the *Ramillies* would hereinafter carry on board fifty to a hundred American prisoners of war "who," he warned, "in the event of the efforts to destroy the ship by torpedoes or other infernal instruments being successful, would share the fate of himself and his crew."

The threat to American lives sparked a number of public meetings in which concerned citizens spoke out against torpedoes as uncivilized and sinister. Not everyone agreed. The Philadelphia *Aurora* compared the new form of warfare to the equally novel Congreve rockets, a British development that had been responsible for burning Copenhagen to the ground in 1807. Reliable reports indicated that the British had already shipped over a million Congreve rockets across the Atlantic for use against America. As the *Aurora* put it,

> We would respectfully solicit the pious men to explain to us the difference between waging war with sub-marine machines, and with aerial destructive weapons—fighting under water or fighting in the air? The British . . . send us Congreve rockets to burn our towns and habitations—we, in return, dispatch some of our Torpedoes—to rub the copper off their bottoms.

A man named James Weldon—or perhaps it was Thomas Welling; there seems to be an understandable confusion about his actual name—was of like mind to the *Aurora*. Early in the summer 1813 he approached Robert Fulton in New York. Having obtained a partnership agreement with him similar to the one Elijah Mix struck with the inventor (under the terms of which Fulton would provide the torpedoes and take a third of any prize money they brought in), he made his way to New London to discuss matters with Commodore Decatur. No record of that conversation has ever come to light, but the nature of the meeting is easy enough to guess. What makes it particularly noteworthy, other than that it is the first incident that clearly ties Decatur to the emergence of torpedo warfare in Long Island Sound, is its unexpected aftermath.

When Weldon—or Welling—had completed his business with Decatur, he rendezvoused on the banks of the Thames with the Long Island pilot Joshua Penny (whom we have already met in connection with the attempted kidnapping of Captain Hardy). The two men ate dinner, and then after sunset they set out for Long Island in a small skiff, rowing with muffled oars past the watchful eyes and straining ears of the British squadron outside the Thames. Once beyond the blockading ships, Joshua Penny hoisted sail and headed toward the south fork of Long Island. The two men followed a devious route, around and through the archipelago of islands that mark the eastern limits of the sound. They had to proceed cautiously, since units of the Royal Navy on torpedo alert might or might not occupy the islands at the moment.

They managed the trip without incident, and early the next morning, with the sun still a hairline on the eastern horizon, they arrived at their destination (probably Three Mile Harbor). After lowering sail and making fast, the two men bade each other good day and parted company.

Later that day—it was 21 August 1813—the master of a Sag Harbor sloop who had regular business dealings with the blockaders and who was not above a little spying when it came his way informed the British that one of his neighbors, the same Joshua Penny, had been heard making boastful remarks about attacking the British fleet with torpedoes. The news quickly made its way to Hardy in the *Ramillies*, which was at that point lying off Gardiner's Island. Hardy thought the story so important he immediately sent his first lieutenant into Sag Harbor in broad daylight to find out where Penny lived. The goggle-eyed American militia guardsmen from the local fort stood back in amazement at the sight of a large and determined enemy officer striding purposefully down the main street of town in full uniform with sabre jangling. They knew it was folly to challenge him. If anything untoward happened to Hardy's first lieutenant, the commodore's guns could easily wreck the village. When the British officer had satisfied himself as to the precise location of Joshua Penny's house, he had himself rowed back to his ship. That night he returned again, this time with a squad of marines, who pulled the hapless Penny out of bed, dragged him down to the docks, and wrestled him into one of the *Ramillies*'s boats, tearing his shirt as they did so. On board ship they unceremoniously clapped him in irons, thrust him into a dark hole with no light, and put him on bread and water. All the while the prisoner protested his innocence.

Within a day Hardy received a formal demand for Penny's release from the local militia commander, a Major Benjamin Case. The letter noted that the prisoner was a native-born citizen of East Hampton township and a noncombatant; therefore, the British could not legally hold him as a prisoner of war.

Hardy's reply is astonishing, for its shows just how much information his spy network had been able to glean, and how thoroughly familiar the British were with any number of details of both military and civilian activities:

Sir:—I have the honor to acknowledge the receipt of your letter . . . requesting the release of Joshua Penny. . . . I now beg leave to inform you I had received certain information that this man conducted a detachment of boats, sent from the *United States* squadron, under the command of Com. Decatur, now lying in New London, from that port to Gardiner's Island on the 26th of July last, for the express purpose of surprising and capturing the captain of H.B.M.'s frigate *Orpheus* and myself, and having failed in that undertaking, but making prisoners of some officers and men belonging to the *Orpheus*, he went with the remaining boats to Three Mile Harbor. The next account I had of him was his being employed in a boat contrived for the purpose, under the command of Thomas Welling, prepared with a torpedo to destroy this ship, and that he was in her at Napeng Beach when this ship and the *Orpheus* were at Fort Pond Bay last week. He has also a certificate given him on the 18th of this month, by some of the respectable inhabitants of East Hampton, recommending him to Com. Decatur as a fit person to be employed on a particular service by him, and that he has for some time been entered on the books of one of the frigates at $40 per month; add to which, this notorious character has been recognized by some of the officers and men of this ship as having been on board her two or three times with clams and fruit—of course as a spy to collect information of our movements.

Having been so well acquainted with the conduct of this man for the last six weeks, and the purpose for which he has been so employed in hostilities against his Britannic Majesty, I cannot avoid expressing my surprise that the inhabitants of East Hampton [Township] should have attempted to enforce on you a statement so contrary to fact. I therefore cannot think of permitting such an avowed enemy to be out of my power, when I know so much of him as I do. He will, therefore, be detained as a prisoner of war until the pleasure of the commander-in-chief is known. . . .

I have the honor to be sir, your most obedient, humble servant,

Thomas M. Hardy
Captain of HM's
Ship *Ramillies*

It is apparent that by the end of summer Hardy had put together a spectacularly effective intelligence-gathering system that covered both shores of the sound and reached all the way into Decatur's account books!

The letter is a masterful performance, overpowering in detail and calculated to teach an important lesson to the large, dangerous audience of farmers and mariners that surrounded his squadron on every shore. To underscore his control of the situation and to send a clear message to anyone still tempted to try some new tricks on his ships and men, Hardy enclosed with his letter a copy of another letter, which he had written to the local justice of the peace.

Sir:—I have received positive information that a whale boat, the property of Thomas Welling and others, prepared with a torpedo for the avowed purpose of destroying this ship, a mode of warfare practiced by individuals from mercenary motives, and more novel than honorable, is kept in your neighborhood, and from the very good information I obtained from various sources, there is no doubt that these persons will soon be in my power. I beg you to warn the inhabitants of the towns along the coast of Long Island, that wherever I hear this boat or any other of her description has been allowed to remain after this day, I will order every house near the shore to be destroyed.

I have the honor to be, sir, your obedient servant,

Thomas M. Hardy
Capt.

All in all, it had been quite a summer on Long Island Sound for Thomas Masterman Hardy. It had begun with his publicly announced disapproval of attacks on civilians in the Chesapeake, and it was ending with a wholesale threat to destroy any village that did not toe the line.

The summer had been difficult, but he had done his duty and done it well. He had tightened the blockade and kept Decatur locked up in New London. He had kept the peace, and the British had not killed even one American, military or civilian. As he turned over temporary command of his squadron to Captain Oliver of the *Valiant* and prepared to take his prisoner Joshua Penny to headquarters in Halifax, he could reflect that the season for torpedoes and submarines was fast coming to a close. Such clandestine underwater activities required warm, dark nights, and a New England winter would soon put a stop to those adventurers and their damned Yankee barnacles.

The *Ramillies* was already well on its way to Nova Scotia when word was released from Washington that President Madison had ordered two British prisoners of war to be held hostage for the safe return of Joshua Penny. This announcement from the Executive Mansion was proof, if proof was needed, that Hardy had touched a nerve.

5

Autumn 1813

Old England versus New England—"a torpedo from New York"—escape from the Acasta— Robert Fulton—the Canadian war

THE single overriding question concerning the war in Long Island Sound relates to Hardy's behavior. Why was he so patient? Why in the face of such constant irritation and provocation was he so restrained? Even the dangerous proclivity of civilians to attempt the destruction of his ships—and their abundantly demonstrated ability to do so—failed to rouse him to anything beyond momentary indignation. In contrast, a completely different style of British peacekeeping held sway only a couple of hundred miles south in the Chesapeake Bay. There, in very similar geographical circumstances—an enclosed body of water surrounded on all sides by American farmers and seamen—Admiral Sir George Cockburn was carrying on a series of raids against the civilian population that were of such a nature that his name was to live on for generations in the Chesapeake as a synonym of terror.

Why was Hardy's rule so benign? The simple answer, which is true but incomplete, is that he was by nature temperate and judicious. But the more significant reason for British forbearance in the north derived from national self-interest. The cabinet in London did not much care what happened to Americans in the southern states, but they were desperately solicitous of New Englanders and were prepared to go to considerable trouble to placate them. The reason for all this currying of favor was that Britain depended upon New England to feed Wellington's army in Spain, which would have starved were it not for the farms of Massachusetts and Connecticut.

It was well known that New England businessmen were far more interested in profits than patriotism, and the trade in foodstuffs was an open secret. American merchantmen loaded with grain were shuttling back and forth between their home ports and Cadiz and Lisbon, providing the bulk of the food required by the British troops fighting Napoleon in the Peninsula. To allow passage through the blockade, British agents provided the American grain ships with special licenses that protected them from seizure if stopped at sea. Carrying such enemy "protections" was a treasonable offense, but the merchants of New England winked at the practice, as did their elected officials.

Trading directly with the enemy was, of course, strictly against the law, but no law prohibited trading with Britain's allies, so New Englanders needed no further subterfuge to justify the business. Everyone knew that the day after the Americans delivered their cargoes to Spanish and Portuguese customers in Cadiz or Lisbon, the food was consigned to Wellington's quartermasters. But since the Iron Duke was busy fighting Napoleon, and Congress did not care about Napoleon one way or another, no one paid much attention.

Wellington was not the only British recipient of New England's bounty. The British army in Canada also relied heavily on food supplies that crossed the border from Vermont. This dirty little secret represented a very different situation from the trade with the Iberian Peninsula, for it meant that American farmers were profiting by supplying troops who were fighting American soldiers. The fact that nothing was done to curtail this patently treasonable business reflects the most serious political problem confronting the United States during most of the war, namely that the governments of the New England states did little to stop their less scrupulous citizens from actively supporting the British cause. The treason struck right to the heart of the nation. There was even talk of secession in New England. While the notion never got beyond the talking stage, the threat of secession was always present, and the government in Washington had to juggle with the possibility throughout the war.

New England's treasonable inclinations were not universal. The opinions of those in the legislature and in the counting houses of the capitals did not necessarily reflect those of the common citizens. In Connecticut, for instance, a tight oligarchy of seven or eight families, almost all of whom disapproved of the war and were friendly to England, ran the political system. But along the Connecticut coast, where the war impinged on everyday life, the overwhelming sentiment was in favor of the national government and against the British. One of the ironies of that very ironic war is that Hardy's forbearance, designed to placate the pro-British oligarchy, actually benefited the anti-British common citizens.

The summer came to an end on Long Island Sound with a tantalizing glimpse of still another example of the new weaponry that was threatening to change the practice of naval warfare in this little corner of the war. A fortnight after Hardy's departure for Nova Scotia a dispatch from New London described "a torpedo from New York" that was chased by several British boats for a distance of nine miles. The article went on to describe how the mysterious craft managed to escape only by frequent diving. That the news report labeled the vessel a "torpedo," rather than reserving that term for the bomb it might be carrying, reflects the novelty of the word and the understandable confusion of journalists trying to describe an entirely new kind of weaponry that was defining itself as it progressed, and was making itself known only in unpredictable and secretive fragments.

The significant fact that the newspaper report was able to identify the home base of the submarine—"a torpedo from New York"—suggests that the writer had been fed the story by someone familiar with the details. The evidence points to a mysterious Mr. Berrian, who operated out of that city and who probably leaked the story to a New London source because he was trying to interest Decatur in his project. The records hold very little information about Berrian, undoubtedly because the name was a *nom de guerre* invented to protect his identity, a common practice among those shadowy characters involved in the underwater war. Engaging in such unsportsmanlike warfare carried a certain social stigma, and of course there was always the danger that British agents in America might use equally unsportsmanlike methods to stop those involved in the development of such tools of destruction.

This newest torpedo, or more precisely, semisubmersible, appears to have been very different from the little submarine employed by "the gentleman from Norwich." That vessel, like Bushnell's original 1776 model, was similar to a diving bell and had only a minimal capacity for lateral travel. This newer craft clearly had the ability to move along almost as quickly as the English longboats which were powered by a dozen oarsmen.

The newspapers reported that the vessel was a heavily timbered craft about thirty feet long, covered with iron plates. Even on the surface she rose only eighteen inches above her waterline, according to the papers. Below her shot-proof deck a crew of twelve men turning two hand-operated propellers could push her for short distances at a speed of just under four knots.

She was likely undergoing sea trials when the British sighted and chased her. Having escaped capture, she did not appear again in 1813, but she would return the following summer.

Each of the four instances of unorthodox naval warfare we have come upon so far was the work of a different man or group: Scudder's *Eagle*, the one-man submarine of "the gentleman of Norwich," Elijah Mix's torpedo, and Mr. Berrian's thirty-foot semisubmersible. Each was the work of civilians acting on their own initiative. Whatever else America might be turning into, it was already the land of entrepreneurs in 1813.

Torpedoes remained in the news. The New York *Post* reported that a floating bomb "simple in its mechanism and powerful in its effect" had been tested and "found to exceed the most sanguine expectations of the inventor." This device, the article explained, was a purely defensive weapon, a pressure-sensitive bomb tethered to the sea bottom and used to protect the entrances to harbors and the like. Today we would call it a sea mine.

In Boston, the home of Federalist politics and pro-British sentiment, a newspaper viewed with alarm the whole idea of torpedoes:

> It is high time to calculate the cost which the innocent merchant as well as coaster will have to pay for such ingenuity; should a single ship be destroyed in this way there will not be an American vessel, of any description, that should come within the power of the enemy that will escape destruction; nor will *our towns, which are at present respected,* escape the general wreck. So far as the war has progressed, WE *have been spared from its most sanguinary effects:* let the machines be successfully

employed, and *"the dogs of war,"* will then in reality be let loose upon us, crying *"Havoc and confusion."*

Meanwhile, the British fleet outside New London, now under the temporary command of Captain Oliver of the *Valiant*, continued to grow. The *Endymion*, 50, and *Statira*, 38, said to be a precise match for the trapped *United States* and *Macedonian*, permanently joined the forces off Gull Island. By early September *Niles' Register* could report there were now no less than four 74s in Long Island Sound. In the same report, editor Hezekiah Niles hinted at still more secret new weapons to come, namely, "some large gallies, or barges, to carry heavy guns, [that] are building at New London to cruise in the Sound, and meet the barges of the enemy."

No such galleys were ever built, or at least no trace is to be found of them. They were, like as not, products of Decatur's fertile imagination, little fictions fed to the press to bedevil the British, possibly based on some preliminary designs he was receiving from New York.

The constant threat of torpedoes continued to hang over the fleet in spite of the increasingly cold weather, forcing the English to adopt certain defensive procedures. As early as July Hardy had instituted a policy of running a cable along the bottom of the *Ramillies* every two hours and of deliberately changing anchorage often enough to discourage underwater attack. Now, in addition, the fleet set out guard boats, which rowed slowly around each ship throughout the night, maintaining a watch.

The function of these guard boats was twofold. First, of course, was the defensive need to maintain a watch against attack. But the second problem was probably just as significant to the officers on duty: to guard against desertion by their own men.

The Royal Navy recognized and accepted the widespread desire of British seamen to escape to America, and no one even bothered to hide the fact. An indication of just how endemic the temptation was, and how clearly the officers understood it, is that when the obligatory Royal Navy court-martial was convened to investigate the loss of the *Macedonian*, it concluded its report by expressing its admiration to the crewmen for not deserting to the American side after they were captured! The almost universal expectation on the part of British officers was that their men would surely desert if given half a chance.

Because of the narrow confines of Long Island Sound, it was never possible for a British blockader to be more than ten miles from shore, and usually they were much closer. Thousands of British tars worked in constant sight of the neat farms and small villages that lined the coast. These villages could only remind the men of home and their former lives, for the Americans who lived on either side of the sound were almost all transplanted English, and they and their fore-bears had brought an English style, English customs, English law, and most important of all the English language to this new land. It was sometimes heartbreakingly familiar to homesick Englishmen.

A lonely tar, roughly used and ill treated by the hated service for which he sweated, could not be blamed for daydreaming of finding some way to cross the few miles of water that separated him from freedom. His desire to leave the tyranny of navy life for good and start an entirely new life in a land where he could never be hunted down and punished for his action, where the king's authority meant nothing, was perhaps overwhelming.

Such dreams were common in the blockading fleet. To ensure that they did not come true, the guard boats maintained as tight a vigil on the ships they guarded as on the dangers they guarded them from. Just in case the men at the oars might entertain similar dreams of escape, a trusted officer or midshipman commanded each boat. But no precaution is foolproof, and on the night of 19 September 1813 the inevitable happened. Between midnight and one o'clock a guard boat from the *Acasta* came in for a relief crew. By prearranged plan, when the officers and crew left the boat—leaving two men behind who were privy to the conspiracy to hold the boat to the gangway—twelve sea-men, including the sentinel on watch, jumped into the boat and pushed off silently into the dark. Since they left no one behind to sound the alarm, the officers did not immediately perceive the con-spirators' design. They quickly rowed under the stern of the frigate, thus avoiding her guns.

When the *Acasta* finally raised the alarm, just as the conspirators began to pull away from her, the remaining sentinels on board fired upon the men in the boat, but without effect. The escapees answered with three cheers and rowed away, disappearing into the night. The *Acasta* fired off a couple of rockets to try to locate the deserters in the pitch black, but it was too late. The boat was gone.

The men could see nothing. Having rowed to within the sound of waves washing up on Fishers Island, and not knowing with certainty where they were, they threw out the anchor and waited for the dawn.

They were still far from safe, and in the blackness every ear strained to hear the sound of an oar in a row lock or the voices of a search party. If recaptured at this point, the men all knew they risked a sentence of death by hanging or, even worse, a ceremonial flogging around the fleet, which almost always resulted in a far slower, more agonizing death.

An hour later, when light had increased just enough so that they could make out their hands in front of their faces, the deserters rowed down the south side of Fishers and rounded the eastern end of the island. Now hidden from the *Acasta* by the hills on the island, they turned north and pulled for the village of Stonington, four miles distant.

The sun was fully up when they reached the harbor. They identified themselves, and the local citizenry immediately welcomed them with cheers and handshakes, escorting them up to York's Tavern and installing them in a comfortable place by the fire. For many of the tars, this landfall was the first time they had stepped ashore in years. After a large breakfast—it was Sunday morning—the Englishmen sold their boat, "a fine twelve oared barge with sails," as the newspapers reported, along with the armaments therein, which consisted of six muskets, ten cutlasses, two pairs of pistols, and an ample magazine. With the money, they traveled overland to New London and a new life. For fourteen new immigrants, their servitude to king and country was at an end.

In November, after almost three months without torpedo activity, a report in the Norfolk (Virginia) *Herald* brought the subject back to the forefront. Elijah Mix, the man who had come so close to damaging the *Plantagenet* in July, now made a public demonstration of his newest-model infernal machine.

His target was a four-hundred-ton hulk that lay stranded in twelve feet of water near the shore at Portsmouth, Virginia. Mix, who was in a skiff anchored two hundred yards below the hulk, dropped his new, improved floating bomb in the water on the flood tide. As it was caught by the current and carried toward the target, he paid out a line attached to the explosive; and after calculating the velocity of the tide on an object the size and weight of his torpedo and concluding the precise moment when it must have been carried under the stern of the hulk, he jerked the line. The action triggered a devastating explosion, and to the wonderment and satisfaction of the gathered witnesses the spray and smoke shot thirty feet into the air, while fragments of the wreckage were scattered in every direction.

On examination, Mix found that the torpedo had made a hole in the side and bottom of the hulk sufficiently large for a ship's yawl to row through. "Dreadful indeed would be the havoc on board a man of war in such a situation," concluded the newspaper account, savoring the awesome prospect. "Not a solitary being would be left alive to tell the tale."

Dreadful indeed.

On the same day that Elijah Mix was proudly demonstrating his new, improved torpedo in Virginia, Captain Thomas Masterman Hardy was sailing south once more from Halifax to rejoin the blockade. With him he brought a proclamation from Sir John Borlase Warren, K. B., Admiral of the Blue and commander in chief of the North American Station, which announced a new definition of the blockade that would bring it significantly closer to New London and ensure the continued incarceration of Decatur and his squadron.

The wording of the proclamation raised certain diplomatic problems for the cabinet in London, namely, how to include a large part of the New England coast within the blockade without calling attention to that fact. The British eagerness to avoid upsetting New England is reflected in the precise definition of the revised blockade:

> All that part of Long Island Sound, so called, being the sea-coast lying within Montuck Point, or the Eastern point of Long Island and the point of land opposite therto, commonly called Black Point, situate on the sea-coast of the main land or continent, together with all the ports, harbors, creeks and entrances of the East and North Rivers of New-York, as well as all other ports, creeks and bays along the sea-coast of Long Island and the state of *New-York*, and all the ports, harbors, rivers and creeks, lying and being on the sea-coasts of the states of *East and West Jersey, Pennsylvania*, the lower countries on the *Delaware, Maryland, Virginia, North and South-Carolina, Georgia*, and all the entrances from the sea into the said river of *Mississippi*. . . .

Although the blockade had added seventy-five miles of coastline north of New York, nowhere in this precisely drawn description do the names "Connecticut" or "New England" ever appear.

Hardy also brought south with him from Halifax his summertime nemesis, Joshua Penny, still protesting his innocence of any dealings with torpedoes. The British apparently decided in Halifax that making Penny a free man was wiser than turning him into a martyr, and of course they had the question of hostages to consider. Another possibility is that two months of misery in the dank, cold prisons of Halifax might well have given Penny reason to mend his ways. (If such was the British hope, the man did not fulfill it. Immediately after his return, Joshua Penny took a position as "personal pilot" to Stephen Decatur— hardly the move of a guiltless bystander.)

Undoubtedly a letter written only days before in London, presently en route to Admiral Warren in Halifax, would have interested both Hardy and his prisoner:

> Sir—I have the command of my Lord's Commissioners of the Admiralty to transmit to you herewith for the information of the Officers employed upon your station, a Book which was published in America in the year 1810, by Mr. Fulton respecting the use of torpedoes invented by him.
>
> J. W. Croker

Enclosed was a thin book of slightly over fifty pages entitled simply *Torpedo War and Submarine Explosions*.

The figure of Robert Fulton ghosts fitfully through the history of the blockade of New York. He is the *éminence grise* of the War of 1812, writing letters, proposing projects, pulling strings, addressing presidents, cajoling prime ministers, and keeping secrets from them all. A clever theorist, a practical visionary, an astonishingly original idealist whose influence was felt at every level, Fulton had strong beliefs and startling insights that echoed through the corridors of power on two continents.

He is principally remembered today as the first man to develop a practical steamboat, although he himself considered that success one of his lesser achievements. He was born in Pennsylvania in 1765 and studied as a boy under a Quaker schoolmaster. Although Fulton never held any particular religious beliefs, his early exposure to the practical idealism of Quakerism may have influenced his own later idealism, which, to put it mildly, was highly idiosyncratic. As a young man he showed considerable promise as a portrait artist, and in 1787 he traveled to London to study under the tutelage of his fellow Pennsylvanian, Benjamin West, who had recently been elevated to president of the Royal Academy.

But art was to prove only a stepping-stone to Fulton's greater interests in life. The world was entering a new historical epoch that would in time come to be called the Industrial Revolution, and England was at the epicenter of the change. This bright, sensitive young man soon found himself caught up in the ferment of new ideas generated by the emerging technologies. One of those ideas was navigation canals, and Fulton witnessed an England busy building waterways from one end of its island to the other, using waterborne barges to move people and goods with unaccustomed ease at greatly improved speed and at significantly lower cost than ever before. Fulton was quick to grasp the underlying driving force of the new movement: that a single technological development, even a minor one, quite often had within it the potential to bring about profound changes and improvements in all sorts of seemingly unrelated industries and activities.

An improved mechanical ratchet, for example, might lead directly to a new kind of canal lock, which might in turn open up to exploitation a hitherto neglected region of the country encouraging commerce and industry and bringing the benefits of prosperity to thousands of farmers, traders, and craftsmen. And all that from an improved ratchet. As an optimistic American, fascinated with new ideas and idealistic about the prospects of progress, Fulton eagerly espoused the new industrial philosophy and turned his full attention to a life of invention.

In 1797—after ten years in England—he traveled to France, which was undergoing a very different kind of revolution, to spread the gospel of navigation canals. It was while in France that Fulton hit upon his great idea, the idea that would color all his thinking and govern his activities throughout the rest of his life. The idea developed through conversations with his close friend Joel Barlow, the American minister in Paris. The two men spent weeks comparing revolutionary France to their own native revolution back home, and Fulton's great idea arose quite naturally out of his idealistic view of democratic revolution as transmuted by his experience with navigation canals. The idea was simplicity itself: *world peace through world trade*, that is, eliminate wars by eliminating trade barriers, thus bringing the benefits of industry and prosperity to all. The concept seems enlightened but hardly startling today, but in 1798 it was truly revolutionary.

In spite of Adam Smith's brilliant arguments in favor of free trade in *The Wealth of Nations*, no eighteenth-century country with any muscle would even dream of opening up its markets to outsiders. The only economic concept recognized at the time was the mercantile system. In that crude form of capitalism, government worked hand in glove with business interests to organize a tightly controlled monopoly, maintaining a closed circuit of raw materials, manufacturing, and finished products and fiercely guarding against outside infringement. The great nations maintained powerful military machines to protect their markets and to conquer new ones.

How, wondered Fulton, might one overthrow this monopolistic beast and bring the benefits of cheap goods, plentiful employment, and a richer life to all? One day in Paris the answer came to him with all the pristine clarity of Paul's vision on the road to Damascus: *destroy the power of the world's navies!* Fulton reasoned that closed mercantile systems could exist only because navies protected the sea-lanes and the market harbors. Therefore, all you had to do to abolish the monopolies was to break the power of the navies: the rest of the system would fall apart of its own accord. The concept was all quite obvious to Fulton except for one small detail—how was he to destroy the navies? Fulton needed several more months of discussion with Barlow to find the key that would complete the equation: *destroy mercantilism by destroying navies, and destroy navies . . . with submarines!* Silent, invisible underwater vessels that could strike without warning. No navy in the world could protect itself against attack from such boats.

The concept was breathtakingly simple, at least to Fulton.

Where did he get his ideas on submarines? Certainly he didn't invent them out of whole cloth. The history of underwater craft can be traced all the way back to ancient times. Alexander the Great is said to have descended below the surface of the water in a diving bell. James I is reported to have traveled briefly under the Thames in London in a submarine vessel invented by the Dutchman Cornelis Jacobszoon Drebbel. But Fulton's ideas concerning underwater warfare were almost assuredly sparked by conversations with his friend and fellow dreamer Joel Barlow, and Barlow had close ties to David Bushnell, the man who invented a practical submersible and a waterproof explosive to go with it in 1776. It is even possible that Barlow introduced Fulton to Bushnell. Whether they ever met or not, Bushnell unquestionably served as an inspiration for Fulton, although it is clear that Fulton's first submarine, which he eventually named the *Nautilus*, was a very different boat from Bushnell's *Turtle*.

Flushed with the grandeur of his bold design for world prosperity, Fulton was soon deeply embroiled in the intricacies of his new scheme, setting up a studio in Paris, drawing up plans, and consulting specialists in every phase of boat building. As the twenty-one-foot *Nautilus* began to take shape, he was also perfecting the rest of his plan. He recognized that a submarine alone was not the answer. Like Bushnell, Fulton would also need an underwater explosive device, which would require a quite distinct technology. His mind turned to the waterproof bombs that Bushnell had once called "torpedoes."

Fulton could contemplate with utter equanimity the fact that the first victims of his idealistic new brand of warfare would be the officers and men of the Royal Navy. He held no personal animosity toward Great Britain. Quite the contrary, many of his closest associates and greatest admirers were British. But like many men of intellectual genius, Fulton was remarkably detached from day-to-day concerns. What counted most was the ideal. No one could deny that Britain ran the world's largest mercantile empire and protected it with the world's largest navy. Therefore, if he was ever to topple the outdated economics of monopoly, he reasoned, the Royal Navy was the obvious place to start. Besides, he was in France, and France was at war with Britain. He fell to work with renewed vigor and messianic energy.

Fulton established himself with French ministers and admirals and spent weeks—months—discussing his novel system of naval warfare with them. The French were at first cool toward his ideas; but as the Royal Navy's blockade continued to choke off France's access to its overseas markets and totally block trade with its Caribbean colonies, French interest and financial support become every day more available.

In the summer of 1800 Fulton tried out the newly completed *Nautilus* in open water off Le Havre. At one point, during a storm, she remained submerged for more than six hours with Fulton and his crew on board. In the following year he continued his tests off Brest. At no time did he come into contact with ships of the Royal Navy, but reports concerning his activities filtered in from British spies in France and had a profound psychological effect on the British. In 1802 Lord Stanhope cleared the galleries of the House of Lords, that he might in secret inform the lords that a new naval invention had been "brought to perfection by a person in France as to render the destruction of ships absolutely sure . . . and that there was no way of preventing it."

With admirable common sense, the king's ministers recognized that the best defense against this unnamed person (everyone knew it was Fulton) was to persuade him to sell his plans and his talents to Britain. A secret emissary was infiltrated into Paris to lay the proposal before Fulton. After some hesitation he accepted. Fulton must have been uneasy about shifting his allegiance to the one navy he most wanted to destroy; but Napoleon had grown increasingly skeptical of the young American idealist's ideas, and Fulton sensed he had nothing to gain by remaining in Paris. Clandestinely he made his way out of revolutionary France and across the channel to England.

Back in Great Britain, Fulton laid aside his plans for his submarine and concentrated on torpedoes. He and his infernal machines were well in place by 1804, when Napoleon collected a large fleet of landing craft on the channel coast for an invasion of England. The British attempted to discourage the invasion by making a raid on Boulogne with a boatload of Fulton's torpedoes, and although they apparently caused little or no damage, the effect on enemy morale was significant. Lord Melville reported:

> . . . I have the satisfaction to tell you that by information from France which I have this morning received, the alarm created everywhere by the operations at Boulogne exceeded everything we have supposed. The pannick has been conveyed from Boulogne by the seamen and soldiers there to the other ports, particularly Brest, and the pannick has laid hold of the army intended for the invasion at every place from whence it was intended to come. It may require further consideration how far something should not be done to keep up and increase the pannick.

In short, Fulton's torpedo raid quite possibly played a highly significant role in Napoleon's failure to invade England in the summer of 1804, helping to save Britain from the greatest threat since the Armada.

The date 15 October 1805 marks the high point of Fulton's work with the British navy. On that day, in front of a group of dignitaries gathered at Prime Minister William Pitt's estate near Dover, Fulton demonstrated how his torpedoes could actually sink a ship. The target vessel was the Danish brig *Dorothea*, anchored just offshore, and the demonstration was so spectacularly successful—Fulton recalled later

PLATE I.

Robert Fulton's drawing of the destruction of the *Dorothea*, which took place before an invited audience of officials in October 1805. Such demonstrations of the effectiveness of Fulton's torpedoes led eventually to the passage by Congress of the Torpedo Act of 1813, which encouraged American citizens to use such weapons against the blockading British fleet. (Fulton's *Torpedo Warfare and Submarine Explosions*)

that the *Dorothea* exploded "like a shattered eggshell"—that Pitt was eager to buy the weapon and proceed with it. The wiser sea lord, Earl St. Vincent, disagreed, pointing out that Britain already had command of the seas and, therefore, had the most to lose if such weapons became commonplace. It was in Britain's best interests, noted St. Vincent, to take the moral high ground and to condemn torpedoes as "uncivilized," in the hope that such a stance might deter others from adopting such dangerous weapons.

Six days later Horatio Nelson, with Hardy at his side, rendered moot the question of torpedoes when he destroyed the French and Spanish fleets off Cape Trafalgar. Britain no longer needed Fulton or his infernal machines.

Soon thereafter, having pocketed £15,000 for his services to the crown, Fulton sailed home to America with plans for a steamboat to be called the *Clermont*. Before he left London, he had his portrait painted by his old friend and mentor, Benjamin West. In the background West painted in an image of Fulton's proudest achievement, the exploding *Dorothea*.

Steamboats and torpedoes, it was all of a one for Robert Fulton, although he placed quite different values on the two projects. In a letter to Barlow about the steamboat Fulton wrote, "I will not admit it is half so important as the torpedo system of defense and attack."

Even as he busied himself with the *Clermont*, Fulton continued to promote his unorthodox schemes for free trade through underwater mayhem. Thomas Jefferson, himself an inventor and keen promoter of democratic ideals, was a great supporter of Fulton and helped him reach the power brokers and other influential men in the new city of Washington. In 1810, in an attempt to influence Congress and the Navy Department, Fulton wrote, illustrated, and published a treatise entitled *Torpedo War and Submarine Explosions*, a clear, complete exposition of his economic, political, and military beliefs and insights. It failed to win Fulton the congressional votes he needed to build an underwater military service to protect the American coast, but its calm, reasoned enthusiasm would eventually lead to several developments, not the least of which was the Torpedo Act of 1813, already described.

Fulton sent copies of *Torpedo War* to Lord Stanhope and others in England and France. Three years later, with the political situation in the world vastly changed, the Admiralty sent the book back across the Atlantic to Admiral Warren in Halifax. And so it was that the idealistic vision of a world given over to prosperity and perpetual peace became required reading for all his majesty's officers on the North American Station.

Although it was such a little conflict, the War of 1812 has an almost global quality to it. Before it was over, American and British armies would face each other at both ends of the Mississippi as well as deep in the jungles of Florida and on the plains of Bladensburg. American and British ships would battle off the coasts of Chile and Java and South Africa. What happened in one place often had profound repercussions great distances away. It is typical of the global nature of the war that the next link in the chain of events that eventually led to the tiny Battle of Stonington took place five hundred miles west of the Connecticut coast on the Canadian frontier just north of Niagara Falls.

At the inception of the war the most baffling problem facing the British cabinet concerned the immense size of the United States. America was a great sprawling emptiness with no perceptible center, no vital core, no jugular open to attack. How did one go about conquering such a place? The British turned to the Duke of Wellington in Spain for help, and he wrote with clinical detachment, explaining that the only way to deal with an enemy as geographically amorphous as the United States was to surround the place.

Specifically, Wellington recommended a three-pronged naval campaign that would establish control of the St. Lawrence River leading into the continent from the east, control of the Mississippi River leading into the continent from the south, and control of the Great Lakes, which connected the two. Control of the Great Lakes, he wrote, was the indispensible first step toward victory over America.

A brief glance at a map confirms that the keys to control of the Lakes are the narrow straits that connect them. (In today's military jargon the straits would be called choke points.) If the British could establish dominance at just four points—the Niagara River, Detroit, Michilimackinac, and the Sault Ste. Marie—they would have control of a great blue necklace of water stretching over a thousand miles inland to the headwaters of the Mississippi itself. Afterward, all that would be necessary would be to establish contact with a Royal Navy group moving up the river from New Orleans and finally, with the help of the blockading fleet at sea, totally encircle the great sprawling giant called the United States and slowly, like an anaconda with its victim, begin to squeeze the life out of it.

Following Wellington's advice, the British made control of the Lakes a matter of first importance, and in consequence, war along the Canadian frontier quickly took on a particularly bitter quality. The weather was a brutalizing factor, alternating insensibly cold and devastatingly hot and buggy. The British use of Indians as shock troops guaranteed that massacres, scalpings, and similar terrifying practices became the norm. The remoteness of the region, the difficulties in transporting food and clothing and weapons, and the problems of providing shelter made life difficult for both sides. Then, just before Christmas 1813 the burning of Newark, Ontario, added still another layer of bitterness to an already vicious colonial war.

As of 10 December 1813 the most important American foothold in Canada was Fort George, near the village of Newark on the western bank of the Niagara River, twenty miles north of the falls. The American commanding this vital beachhead was Brigadier General George McClure, a political hack who owed his rank and elegant uniforms to cronies in Albany.

On the day in question McClure was in a panic. His state militia troops had reached the end of their enlistments and were deserting him and returning to their homes in upstate New York, directly across the river. McClure found himself holding Fort George with only seventy regular troops and about a hundred Canadian Volunteers under the command of a turncoat named Joseph Wilcocks, lately of his majesty's colonial forces and now a lieutenant colonel in the U.S. Army.

To add to McClure's woes, the cold north wind off Lake Ontario had already dumped eight inches of snow on the area, with more falling every hour. And now Wilcocks informed McClure that British forces were moving in on him from the west. Fort George, designed to defend against the east only, lay open to their attack.

General McClure could see only one recourse—to abandon Fort George and head back across the river to the safety of New York State and Fort Niagara, the twin of Fort George visible on the other bank. Wanting to leave the British nothing he made plans to blow up Fort George and burn down the neighboring village of Newark (today known as Niagara-on-the-Lake). The partisan leader from nearby Buffalo, Dr. Cyrenius Chapin, pleaded with McClure not to burn Newark, which was of no military value. He argued that the British would surely take revenge on American villages for such an action, but McClure was adamant.

That afternoon McClure and his turncoat aide Wilcocks supervised the total destruction of the little village, walking torch in hand through the neat gridiron of streets, systematically and methodically setting fire to a hundred and fifty houses, barns, and stables and making sure the owners did not get a chance to douse the blaze. By early evening four hundred innocent civilians, women and children for the most part, were made homeless in the dead of winter.

The British troops in the west, galvanized by the sight of flames at Newark, hurried forward and appeared in the village earlier than expected. McClure and his men had to retreat across the ice-clogged river so quickly that they never managed to destroy the defenses of Fort George, or even its barracks. In spite of all McClure's plans, the British army had shelter that night. Only the civilians were left homeless.

Burning Newark was a pointless, stupid act, and the American press roundly condemned McClure. The British were outraged and demanded revenge. They gave their Indian allies full rein, and with righteous fervor they rampaged together across the Niagara frontier, burning, butchering, scalping, and destroying half a dozen villages and towns (including Buffalo, as Dr. Chapin had prophesied). The British also stormed Fort Niagara, where sixty-five American soldiers, many of them wounded and in hospital, met death by the bayonet.

McClure's totally unnecessary brutality escalated the level of violence in the war, and a direct linkage of cause and effect would lead from the burning of Newark on 10 December 1813 to the attack on Stonington exactly eight months later.

6

Winter 1813–14

Elizabeth Stewart, spy master—the
"blue lights" scandal—Demologos—*a challenge*
between commodores—Cockburn to New London—
Britain runs low on cash

THE same cold weather that swept down on the Great Lakes was also making itself felt in New London, where the people met the familiar challenge of on-coming winter much as they continue to do today, by repairing and refitting storm doors and painting and sealing shutters. In an era without insulation the principal protection against the cold was a lavish use of fuel, and each house in town had cords of wood stacked up beside the door.

In the more affluent homes, servants polished the silver for the seasonal galas, soirees, and other festivities. These parties had little to do with the advent of Christmas—it would be another generation before Charles Dickens turned that day into the most loved of Christian festivals—but winter meant parties simply because the people had almost nothing else to do in those dreary months when roads were impassable, no crops would grow, and life outdoors was both dangerous and uncomfortable.

In New London during that winter of 1813–14 not everyone was welcome at the parties. Stephen Decatur, who under other conditions would undoubtedly have been considered a notable catch for a socially ambitious hostess, would receive few invitations and would accept none of those he received. The majority of New London's citizens still held him personally responsible for the blockade and were not prepared to forgive him for it. Fitful and angry, the stiff-necked Decatur kept to his ships.

Notable that winter was a shift in spirit, a growing disillusionment with the war, a sense of frustration with its lack of progress, emotions that gave rise to angry denunciations of the government in Washington. The same anger triggered a perverse burst of Anglophilia in many. It became difficult to differentiate between Americans who professed a certain admiration for things British and Americans who actually wanted Britain to win the war.

Much of this discontent could be traced to the so-called "peace party," an informal amalgam of malcontents, Tories, and disaffected merchants angry at the disastrous effect the war was having on business. These alienated types were beginning to make themselves felt in various parts of the country, although the primary center of disaffection continued to be New England. Most peace party members were quite open about their sympathies, reckoning that they were well within their rights as American citizens to complain about the government, and even to argue against it, as long as they did not actively join in schemes to subvert it. But in any such group there were bound to be some whose level of enthusiasm rose beyond complaining to a level of disloyalty that required a much stronger word.

As Hezekiah Niles wrote glumly, "It is truly distressing to observe the prevalence of treasonable practices in the United States," adding, "We have perhaps, more persons in this country so 'well inclined' to the enemy that they think it no harm to 'aid and comfort' him. . . ."

In New London, a natural magnet for both active and passive forms of pro-British sentiments was a woman of considerable standing in the community, Mrs. James Stewart, née Elizabeth Coles. She was a native of the town, the daughter of a respected merchant, and the elegant entertainments she hosted at her mansion near Mill Pond were known for their generally Anglophilic character. Mrs. Stewart's royalist sympathies were common knowledge, but even the most fervent patriot could forgive her because she was the wife of the recent British consul in New London, the same James Stewart whom federal officials had so unceremoniously ordered out of town for suspected espionage.

Mrs. Stewart and the children and servants had remained behind, but the absence of her husband did not keep her from maintaining a significant social presence in town.

For several years the Stewarts had been known as a genial and charitable couple, and it was remembered that during his years in residence as the king's agent in New London the pair never seemed to be in want for funds, which was a little surprising since his total income from the British government during that period never exceeded £300 a year. But then Stewart was known to be a clever fellow with a nose for business, and the townspeople generally assumed that with his imaginative turn of mind and his native wit he undoubtedly used his position to develop supplementary sources of income, some of which might well involve a degree of sharp practice. Rumors did circulate, for instance, concerning certain protections that Stewart allegedly sold to line his own pockets.

Upon the outbreak of war, one of the last duties of the British minister in Washington as he prepared to return to England was to provide Stewart—who was staying behind as agent for prisoner exchanges—with twenty blank documents, all duly signed and bearing the seal of the king's minister. These official state papers were called protections and were in effect maritime passports, which when filled in with the proper names and information would allow the sea captain who possessed one to pass through the blockade without hindrance. The protections were intended for the exclusive use of American ships bound on activities favorable to British interests, principally the supplying of food to Wellington's army in Spain; but of course such a piece of paper would be worth a fortune to an enterprising privateer trying to run the blockade. Such a sea captain, if stopped by a British patrol ship, had only to flash his protection and off he would go, scot free.

Did each one of James Stewart's twenty protections go to a deserving captain aiding the British cause against Napoleon, or did Stewart sell them to the highest bidder and pocket the proceeds? No one in New London society in 1813 knew the answer to that question for sure, but enough rumors circulated along Bank Street to fuel suspicions. Since the British government also held strong suspicions on the subject, we can assume that if he had engaged in any underhanded dealings involving the protections, Stewart knew how to hide the embarrassing details. The only indirect suggestion of his guilt in this and perhaps other matters is the grand manner in which the Stewarts lived on an annual income of three hundred pounds.

This is not to say that James Stewart was not useful to his nation, nor, indeed, that he and his American wife were not instrumental in furthering the British cause. After the abrupt departure of Mr. Stewart, Mrs. Stewart took over his position as spy master, and she and her agents made New London the conduit for an almost endless stream of American intelligence reaching the entire fleet.

Long after the war Elizabeth Stewart was able to obtain a pension for herself and her husband (in spite of the unsettled question of the protections) on the basis of letters from Captain Hardy and others attesting to the "very important and correct information of the enemy's movements" she was able to convey to the British naval forces lying off her native city. A typical example of her work involved the incident of the "blue lights."

Toward the end of November 1813 Stephen Decatur learned from his sentinels at Fort Trumbull and Fort Griswold that the blockading fleet was shrinking in size and number. Apparently the British were finally tapping the excessive supply of ships off New London for other points along the coast. Whatever the reason, Decatur realized that he might now have a chance to escape his prison up the Thames.

With studied casualness, he abandoned his fortifications at Allyn's Hill and moved his squadron south until it stood off Market Wharf in New London itself, only two miles from the sea. Decatur made personal visits to the two guarding forts, ostensibly to inspect the armaments at each position but in fact to supervise the return of cannon to the ships—an activity his men performed as secretly as possible at night to avoid observation. Each morning he checked the enemy forces. From the top of the battlements at Fort Trumbull, Decatur could see a single ship-of-the-line off Gull Island, accompanied by two frigates and a lesser ship. Beyond them he had a clear view south of Montauk Point and could see that the area was free of enemy ships. This was a considerable relief, for it meant that should he get clear of the Thames he had a good chance of making it to the sea.

Decatur's confidence grew. If the British squadron remained at its present size and a particularly dark night presented itself—highly likely, given New England's weather at that time of year—he had a fighting chance of getting himself back into the war.

The prospect was glorious: the open sea, British merchantmen ready for the taking, and, most important of all, the Admiralty forced to deploy at least three more 74s with their requisite accompaniment of frigates and sloops of war to guard those thousands of miles of sea-lanes!

On 12 December an overcast sky and lack of a moon guaranteed the total darkness Decatur needed. After sunset he sent urgent messages to the forts, ordering his sentinels to rejoin their ships. Still later, when the sky was sufficiently dark to hide the squadron's actions from curious eyes on shore, Decatur signaled to raise anchors and unfurl sails.

The *United States* lowered two guard boats to lead the way. As the squadron started down the Thames, each of the three ships was on its own. No signal lights would keep the *United States*, *Macedonian*, and *Hornet* in visual contact. Each captain was concerned with only one goal—to get through the blockade. Later, perhaps weeks hence, if all went well and they made good their escape, the ships would rendezvous at some distant point, perhaps in the Azores or off the Orkneys or the coast of Brazil. Each captain had already committed to memory the precise meeting plans agreed upon. But at this moment the important thing was simply to get away—to break out of the trap that had held them all for five full months of frustration.

It is difficult for us today, who have spent our entire lives habituated to the pervasive presence of electric light, to understand the depths of the darkness that Decatur could rely upon to hide his ships. With no moonlight, and with a cloud cover obscuring even the faint light of stars, the darkness was almost absolute. New London had no street lights. The town cast no glow on the clouds overhead. The feeble candles in the taverns and homes were hidden behind window shutters at this time of year. Once past Fort Trumbull, Decatur and his ships would be swallowed up by the black, the absolute pitch black.

Moving a large sailing ship down a river was cumbersome and difficult under the best conditions of full daylight and required enormous skill. At night the difficulties multiplied. The topsails had to be alternately backed and filled to keep the ship in the fairway. Each of the three harbor pilots—one to each ship—had to make exquisite judgments about precisely when to point the yards into the wind so that the ship might be allowed to drift with the tide. A wrong guess could spell disaster, and even a minor shift of wind direction, if undetected, might cause the whole expedition to fail.

The oarsmen in the guard boats peered blindly into the night, trying to identify points of land by the sound of waves lapping the shore. The little squadron inched down the channel, each man praying silently that they not touch a shoal or run into a bar or experience any other catastrophe that might put them at the mercy of the British.

At the mouth of the river the lighthouse opposite Avery Point was darkened, a victim of the siege. As the guard boats rounded the point, a whispered word from the after watch caused one of the officers to turn his head back toward Fort Trumbull, where he saw the one thing he most dreaded seeing. From a position well below the fort some person unknown was displaying a small but unmistakable blue signal light.

A yellow light in the darkness might have caused some anxiety, but it would probably have meant nothing—a farmer searching for a stray cow perhaps, maybe a drunk returning home, or a window opened to provide fresh air to a sick child. But a blue light could mean only one thing: a signal. A signal for what? The answer was obvious. To the south, out in the blackness of Long Island Sound, the British lay at anchor, and Hardy's squadron, forewarned, would be waiting. The hopelessness of the situation became even more evident when Decatur and his men detected a second blue light on the other bank of the Thames, near Fort Griswold. An angry, embittered, miserable commodore ordered his ships back up the Thames.

Mrs. Stewart and her people had earned their pay that night.

The following morning a still shaken Decatur contemplated New London from his quarterdeck and formulated fresh plans. He would shame this smug, self-righteous community of traitors. He would alert the patriots and awaken them to the invidious serpent in their midst. He would use the power of the press to root out the traitors and create a fear in their camp where too little fear existed.

Later that week, as a result of a private discussion with the local newspaper editor, the following appeared in the New London *Gazette*:

It will astonish every American who has one spark left to kindle into a flame the love of his country, when we state as a fact for which we vouch—that on Sunday evening last when the report was current our squadron would put to sea the next morning—in the course of the night blue lights were raised on the heights, both at Groton and on this side of the entrance of our harbor; evidently designed as signals to the British fleet; this has excited the highest indignation and the most decisive measures have been taken to detect and bring to condign punishment the traitorous wretches who dare thus to give the enemy every advantage over those great and gallant men, who in the war with Tripoli, and in the present contest, have surrounded the American stars with a lustre which cannot be eclipsed.

If Decatur had hoped that New London would rise up as a body to strike down the traitors in their midst after the editorial appeared, the townspeople quickly disabused him of such fantasies. New Londoners were angry enough, all right, but not at any supposed traitors. They were distressed that anyone might give their town a bad name, and angry citizens twice accosted the editor in the street, chastising him for publishing such poison. A few days later and a little farther up the coast a Rhode Island newspaper set the record straight on the matter of blue lights by reporting, "We were unwilling to believe that any of our citizens could be guilty of so gross an outrage on the laws of their community; and are happy now to have it [in] our power to state on the authority of a respectable paper published in Norwich that the statement was TOTALLY INCORRECT. It appears that on the night of the 12th inst. blue lights *from the enemy's ships* were discernable from our guard boats; *but none were seen proceeding from the land.*"

In other words, it never happened.

It quickly became a game of "whom do you believe?" A good many people found it reasonable to assume that an experienced naval officer was having hallucinations—or was perhaps lying—while unidentified people who were not present at the location were telling the truth when they denied the blue lights.

Undaunted, Decatur wrote to Secretary of the Navy William Jones, releasing the letter to the press. Most newspapers across the country quickly copied it:

New London, December 20, 1813
Some few nights since, the weather promised an opportunity for this squadron to get to sea, and it was said on shore that we intended to make the attempt. *In the course of the evening two blue lights were burnt at both the points at the harbor's mouth as signals to the enemy, and there is not*

a doubt that they have, by signals and otherwise, instantaneous information of our movements. Great but unsuccessful exertions have been made to detect those who communicate with the enemy by signal. The editor of the New London Gazette, to alarm them, and in the hope to prevent the repetition of these signals, stated in that newspaper, that they had been observed, and ventured to denounce those who had made them in animated and indignant terms. *The consequence is that he has incurred the expressed censure of some of his neighbors. Notwithstanding these signals have been* REPEATED, *and have been seen by twenty persons at least in this squadron, there are men in New London who have the hardihood to affect to disbelieve it, and the effrontery to avow their disbelief.*

Again, the response from the local citizenry was one of derision and ridicule. Decatur deserved chastisement, they claimed, not the city that he had single-handedly put in jeopardy.

Even Decatur could see that he was not doing his cause any good. By attacking New London he was only reinforcing the anger that so many in the town already felt toward him. But he was adamant. If he had only words to fight with, then he must use them as best he could.

Right after Christmas he tried a new tack, addressing himself not so much to his unwilling hosts as to the fleet of blockading ships outside the harbor. Decatur deliberately broke security and made a highly secret meeting public. He leaked a story to the newspapers— which he knew went directly to the blockading fleet—reporting on a series of meetings that he and his fellow captains had just concluded in New York and New London concerning an amazing steam vessel of war designed by the eminent scientist and inventor, Robert Fulton.

Again, he chose to publicize his thoughts in the form of an open letter to the secretary of the navy:

New London January 3, 1814
We the undersigned have this day examined the model and plans of a vessel of war, submitted to us by Robert Fulton, to carry twenty-four guns, twenty-four or thirty-two pounders, and use red hot shot, to be propelled by steam at the speed of from four to five miles an hour, without the aid of wind or tide. The properties of which vessel are: That without masts or sails she can move with sufficient speed; that her machinery being guarded she cannot be crippled; that her sides are so thick as to be impenetrable to every kind of shot—and in a calm, or light breeze, she can take choice of position or distance from an enemy. Considering the speed that the application of steam has already given to heavy floating bodies, we have full confidence, that should

such a vessel move only four miles an hour, she could, under the favorable circumstances which may always be gained over enemies' vessels in our ports, harbors, bays and sounds, be rendered more formidable to an enemy than any other kind of engine hitherto invented. And in such case she would be equal to the destruction of one or more seventy-fours, or of compelling her or them to depart from our waters. We therefore give it as our decided opinion, that it is among the best interests of the United States to carry this plan into immediate execution.

> Stephen Decatur
> Ja. Jones
> J. Biddle

Not a submarine this time from Mr. Fulton, but a huge, wallowing, unsinkable defensive catamaran, designed to lurk safely in harbor until the wind died down. Then, with the blockading fleet totally immobilized and swinging helplessly at anchor, this extraordinary new ship would fire up its engine and steam out to meet the hapless foe. With absolute control of his ship's own movements, the captain could choose a safe position where the enemy guns could not return fire. At his leisure he could then supervise the complete destruction of his defenseless enemy with broadside after uninterrupted broadside.

The construction of such a machine, which Fulton named *Demologos*, literally, the voice of the people, actually began in New York two months after Decatur's letter. The vessel's primary mission was to lift the blockade of New London, and while it never fought in combat—the war was over before it was ready—it remains the first steam warship in history and was the subject of much nervous argument in London and wherever the Royal Navy served. By publishing his letter, Decatur hoped to distress his British foes. He succeeded. But their distress did him little good. Mrs. Stewart and her friends saw to it that the blue lights kept him in port throughout the entire winter.

During the same week when Decatur was trying to deal with the blue lights, an incident took place aboard the blockading flagship *Ramillies* that was to lead to a curious and revealing exchange of correspondence between Decatur and Hardy.

Nicholas Moran was the master of an American merchant sloop captured by the *Endymion* in one of her periodic sweeps of civilian shipping. After his capture Moran was entertained aboard the *Ramillies* while the British made arrangements for him and his crew to return to shore. During a conversation that took place in Captain Hardy's cabin, Captain Hope of the *Endymion* asked Moran contemptuously whether Decatur in the *United States* was trying deliberately to avoid confrontation, implying that the *Endymion* might be happy to go head to head with Decatur's flagship.

Hardy volunteered that the duel he would like to see was one between his own squadron's *Statira* and the *Macedonian* in Decatur's group. He reminded the company that the *Statira* and *Macedonian* were virtually identical sister ships, and that such a contest might provide an interesting opportunity to compare the seamanship, tactical enterprise, and gunnery skills of the two navies. Then Hardy, undoubtedly conscious of the Admiralty's strict rule forbidding single-ship actions with the American navy (the British had suffered too many embarrassing defeats in such actions), politely laughed off his own suggestion, protesting that he could never suggest such a challenge, but that the idea intrigued him.

Only hours later Nicholas Moran was once again on American soil a free man and was relating his story to customers of Brown's Tavern in New London. At a neighboring table a tall man in civilian clothes appeared particularly interested in Hardy's comments and questioned the ship's master at length on the details of the encounter. The tall man was in fact Stephen Decatur, and having identified himself and cleared up a last few details to his satisfaction, he returned to the *United States* with a plan for action.

The following morning he sent Captain Biddle of the *Hornet* under a flag of truce to the *Ramillies* with a remarkable challenge addressed to Hardy.

After recapping Hardy's own suggestion of a combat between the *Statira* and the *Macedonian*, Decatur added a new level to the notion by bringing in Captain Hope and the *Endymion*. As the message explained to Hardy,

> The *Endymion*, I am informed, carries twenty-four pounders and mounts fifty guns in all; this ship [Decatur's ship, the *United States*] also carries twenty-four pounders and mounts forty-eight guns, besides a twenty-four pound carronade, a boat gun.
>
> The *Statira* mounts fifty, the *Macedonian* forty-seven, metal the same [that is, the total weight of cannonballs fired in a single broadside by either ship was the same], so that the force on both sides is as ideally equal as we could expect to find.

> If Mr. Moran's statement be correct, it is evident that captain Hope [of the *Endymion*] and captain Stackpoole [of the *Statira*] have the laudable desire of engaging with their ships the *United States* and the *Macedonian*. We, sir, are ready and equally desirous for such a meeting forthwith.
>
> The only difficulty that appears to be in the way, is from whom the formal invitation is to come. If, sir, you admit Moran's statement to be correct, the difficulty will be removed, and you will be pleased to consider this as an invitation. . . .

By careful wording, Decatur has turned Hardy's suggestion for a duel between two frigates into a far more complicated challenge involving four ships, and still made the invitation sound like a totally British idea.

What was Decatur's motive in delivering this challenge? Conceivably he was convinced of the superiority of his two ships and their crews, but more likely he considered his present circumstances so desperate that it was worth sacrificing one ship if it somehow allowed the other to make her escape.

Captain Biddle returned to the American squadron with the news that an answer would be forthcoming from the British the following day. The crews of the two American frigates were assembled on deck, and when the proposition for action was submitted to them, they received the news with cheers.

The following morning an officer from Hardy's squadron brought the British answer in the form of two letters, one from Hardy and, enclosed within it, a letter from Captain Stackpoole of the *Statira*.

Hardy's letter showed that he had not risen to Decatur's bait:

> I beg to inform you I have no hesitation whatever in permitting captain Stackpoole in the *Statira* to meet the *Macedonian*, as they are sister ships carrying the same number of guns and weight of metal. But as it is my opinion that the *Endymion* is not equal to the *United States*, being 200 tons less, and carrying 26 guns on her main deck, and only 32 lb. carronades on her quarter deck and forecastle, I must consider it my duty (though very contrary to the wishes of captain Hope) to decline the invitation on his part.

As Theodore Roosevelt was to point out many years later, the true difference in weight of metal between the two ships was 3 percent— hardly a sticking point.

However, the original offer was still open, and Captain Stackpoole's letter showed admirable zeal and commitment to action:

It will afford [the *Statira*'s] captain officers and crew the greatest pleasure to meet captain Jones in the *Macedonian* to-morrow, the next day or whenever such a meeting may better suit his purpose, let him only be pleased to appoint the day and place; say six or ten leagues south of Montaug Point, or further if he pleases. My only objective for selecting this distance from the shore is to avoid any interruption. . . .

Having set the terms, Stackpoole could not resist a flourish of smarmy patriotism:

> In accepting this invitation, sir, it is not to vaunt, or, in the most trifling degree, to enhance my own professional character. . . . The honor of my king, the defence of my country, engaged in a just and unprovoked war, added to the glory of the British flag, is all I have in view.

Decatur clearly had no reason to accept a two-ship duel. Even if the *Macedonian* proved successful, she was hardly likely to leave the battle in fit shape to go to sea. And what if she should take the *Statira* as prize? What port could she bring her into, with the whole American coast under siege? Bring her back to New London? That solved nothing.

Reluctantly, Decatur had to admit the British had outfoxed him, or at least outmaneuvered him in a comedy of manners. In all likelihood, Hardy regretted starting the negotiations, and the best that either commodore might do at this point was to leave the other side a face-saving way out of the situation. Decatur withdrew his proposal, pleading current orders as his excuse. But he could not let Stackpoole's self-righteous moralizing go unanswered. He closed his letter to Hardy:

> Whether the war we be engaged in be just or unprovoked on the part of Great Britain, as capt. Stackpoole has been pleased to suggest, is considered by us as a question exclusively with the Civilians, and I am perfectly ready to admit both my incompetence and unwillingness to confront captain Stackpoole in its discussion.

> I am, sir, with the highest consideration and respect,

> Stephen Decatur

This surprising willingness of the two commodores—in defiance of strict orders—to engage in battles of honor, wagering the lives and welfare of their crews as collateral, and betting thousands of dollars (or pounds) worth of their nations' shipping into the bargain, is the stuff of Arthurian legends, and an indication of how different the mores of 1814 were from our own time's.

Inevitably, the challenge of the two commodores found its way into the public prints, which provided another example of the cultural gap separating us from that earlier era. In an editorial comment on the proposed confrontation an American journalist concluded, "Should a match be made up between the *Macedonian* and the *Statira*," he wrote, "we should expect to see some of the scenes of the Battle of Issus re-exhibited; and *Statira*, like her namesake, the proud daughter of Darius, after courting a match with the Macedonian, consent to be espoused by the victor when he shall have brought her into captivity by conquering the arms which protected her." What writer today could expect readers to recognize that the Macedonian referred to was Alexander the Great and that the *Statira* was named after one of his Persian wives?

While Decatur was trying his best to get out of New London by stealth and guile, and Hardy was making sure—also by stealth and guile—that the American did not succeed, other events crowded in and competed for the attention of the people living at the eastern end of Long Island Sound.

In the second half of January the citizens of New London learned the doleful news of McClure's treachery on the Niagara frontier and the subsequent bloody revenge of the British forces. On the heels of that distressing story came the terrifying news that Rear Admiral Sir George Cockburn, the man known as the monster of the Chesapeake, had arrived off New London on board his flagship *Sceptre*, 74, in company with the *Victorious*, 74, two frigates, and a pair of sloops.

Everyone in America knew about Cockburn, the very devil incarnate whose raiding parties had spread fire, rape, and destruction from the Delaware to Georgia. For months, as the people of New London read the dreadful reports and gruesome details from Havre de Grace and Hampton and Cumberland Island, they had contrasted Cockburn's brutal behavior with the judicious control maintained by Hardy, congratulating themselves upon their good fortune. But now the dreaded Cockburn was off New London, and everyone feared the worst. What could he want? Once again the more nervous members of the citizenry prepared to move out of town. But when the admiral's formidable flotilla off Gull Island showed no signs of animosity, the people returned their luggage, still packed, to the attic.

Stephen Decatur had no idea what Cockburn's presence might signify, but clearly with three 74s now standing at the mouth of the Thames, as well as four frigates and an assortment of lesser craft, it was not in his interests to attempt an escape. On 27 January he retreated once again toward Norwich.

Cockburn's visit, as it turned out, was purely a formality. He simply wished to talk to his old friend Captain Hardy; and the whole visit might have lasted only a day or two had not one of his 74s inadvertently run aground on the south side of Fishers Island, forcing him to postpone his return to the Chesapeake a few extra days until his men could float the ship off and effect necessary repairs.

What did Cockburn and Hardy talk about during this cold week in January off the Connecticut coast? No record of their conversations exists, but they would have been interesting talks. The two men were old shipmates. They had served together as midshipmen in the *Hebe*, and later Hardy was Cockburn's first lieutenant in the *Minerve*. Both had been favorites of Nelson. Cockburn outranked Hardy, but that would not have mattered on a personal level. Attaining the rank of captain took risks and hard work, but once achieved, one needed only time and luck to make admiral. Hardy could be certain that if he managed to keep himself alive, he would eventually rise to Cockburn's level and possibly beyond.

The two men held remarkably similar commands. In many ways the Chesapeake and Long Island Sound were identical naval theaters. Each was a closed seaway of roughly the same size with access to the Atlantic. Each contained a myriad of rivers and bays and islands. Each commander had to deal with the same problems: potential desertion of his own men, potential treachery from civilians, and a lineup of problems that were as much diplomatic as they were military.

Yet how differently they had each handled their situations— Hardy with measured restraint, and Cockburn with an energy and passion that had made his name synonymous with terror all along the coast. In all fairness, Cockburn was hardly the villain the American press made him out to be. True, the troops under his command had run out of control and committed deplorable atrocities during the raid on Hampton, Virginia, but that was an exception. He had conducted all his other activities in the Chesapeake with a scrupulous regard for the rules of war as then practiced. Cockburn fought roughly, but then that is the way wars are apt to be fought.

As old naval hands the two men would have had much to talk about, much gossip to exchange. There was the matter of their commander in chief, Admiral Sir John Borlase Warren. His name was being mentioned in Parliament with considerable regularity these days, and almost always in a derogatory manner. Was he on the way out? The Admiralty disliked controversy.

The news from Europe would also have excited the commanders. Finally, in the early months of 1814, England and her allies were on the brink of winning their twenty-year war with Napoleon. Such a victory would undoubtedly change things on the American side of the Atlantic. Britain was conducting a blockade with only eleven ships-of-the-line, but with Boney out of the way the Admiralty could afford to send over another fifty, another seventy-five ships-of-the-line to crush the Yankees and strangle their commerce. And what about Wellington's battle-hardened troops from the Peninsula—just what might they do against raw and untrained American militia!

Of course other, more complex questions about the American war were less tractable to simplistic answers. Neither Hardy nor Cockburn was likely to understand questions that were too subtle for their bluff, direct natures. What, for instance, was England to do about its great Midlands factory towns—Birmingham, York, Manchester, and the like—suffering terribly for lack of American raw materials . . . the very raw materials that were rotting on the wharves the Royal Navy blockaded? What to do about a war the government did not want and that could do England no good and was being fought so far away and over such an immense area that it could not be won . . . even if England wanted to win it? What to do about the fact that after twenty years the British people were heartily sick of war, and so were the Lombard Street bankers who had financed it?

What these two old salts understood was war, and they had seen it from every side. They understood, as perhaps only a British naval officer of the time might have the sophistication to understand, that war involved everything. After food for the troops and gunpowder for the cannon stretched a long list of factors—diplomatic, economic, military, and even cultural—that were crucial to the waging of war.

Take the matter of cash. It was a basic commodity in any war, but along the American coast Britain was running out of it, and the problem threatened the whole conduct of the war. The issue was complicated and is, to modern eyes, bizarre. The British government was accustomed to paying for its war supplies—food, armaments, transport—with notes drawn on the Bank of England. Vendors and suppliers could present these notes to the bank or its agents and obtain the going rate, paid out in currency and bills. If the Chancellor of the Exchequer did his sums right, and his people kept a careful eye on outgo and income, financing something as big as a war was usually possible with only a minimum of fiscal discomfort for a considerable length of time.

But the war with France had gone on for twenty years, and just toward the end of it, when the Bank of England was stretched about as far as it could go and every note of credit had to be handled with the most consummate delicacy, the Americans declared war. America might not be a large or powerful enemy, but it was a vital supplier of goods to the British war machine. But the declaration of war changed everything. Yankee ships' captains delivering grain to Cadiz who were once quite happy to accept paper for their cargoes now demanded gold and silver. As belligerents, they had little use for notes on the Bank of England. Specie became the only accepted medium of exchange, and England had almost none to give.

To get around the problem, British purchasing agents sought out other producing countries—Brazil, Argentina—that would accept their notes, but it was too late in the year, the harvest was poor, and the countries could not deliver. With hungry troops fighting in Spain, Britain had no choice but to accede to Yankee demands. Suddenly a disproportionate percentage of Britain's dwindling gold reserves was flowing directly into the pockets of the very Americans with whom the British were at war.

In war zones the Royal Navy routinely used small amounts of gold to buy information and fresh produce for the crews—gold was obviously the best currency to use—but as bullion reserves dwindled, the Admiralty issued less and less gold and tried to get along on local cash, which was difficult to obtain but cheaper than gold.

Both Hardy and Cockburn were aware of the lack of gold in their war chests, and they may even have been aware of the cause. But certainly, as they bid each other good-bye, they were not aware that one of the Royal Navy's most serious headaches on the North American Station was a whopping cash-flow problem.

* * *

In March 1814, somewhere in the mid-Atlantic, the *Viper*, an American privateer out of Baltimore, spotted an unidentified schooner on the horizon and set off to catch her. The wind stood to the *Viper*'s advantage, and within a short time the chase was over, and the schooner lay under the guns of the privateer. The *Viper*'s captain went immediately on board to talk with the captain of the captured vessel and examine her cargo.

Her papers identified her as the *Rosa*, registered as a Spanish vessel, with a crew as polyglot as they come—it might have included sailors from almost every country facing the Atlantic as well as the Mediterranean. Her captain gave vague answers concerning her last port of call and her destination, raising the curiosity of the privateer captain. Had the *Rosa* any papers? Any bills of lading? Any receipts? No. Such circumstances were known, of course. Small merchant ships often carried on business in an informal manner. Perhaps she was what she claimed to be, simply a schooner trading between the Azores and the Canaries, blown off course by the winds of late winter.

If such, she was of no value to the *Viper*. America was not at war with Spain. If he brought the *Rosa* into an American prize court and she turned out to be what she claimed to be, she and her crew would be free to go, and the *Viper* would have gone to a great deal of time and expense for nothing.

What the captain of the *Viper* needed was proof of some British connection. Was the cargo British? Did she have a British protection? Was she carrying British secrets? The Americans searched the hold, the cabins, and the afterdeck. They opened sea chests and interrogated the crew. Wooden ships have many hiding places, but if something is hidden, a determined investigator, with time and patience, will almost inevitably find it. At last the American captain came up with what he needed. Hidden among the other ship's papers was a letter with a draft on an English bank enclosed. And along with it a letter from the British commander in chief in Bermuda addressed, "To Captain Talbot of H. M. Ship Victorious, or the senior officer of His Majesty's Ships off New-London."

The captain of the *Viper* was delighted. A prize, by God! These bits of paper would prove the *Rosa* to be a legitimate prize in any court. He threw an appraising eye over the schooner and tried to estimate her value at auction: ten thousand dollars? Twenty? Whatever the schooner and her cargo brought, his percentage as captain would be substantial.

The letter itself, which American newspapers eventually published, brought up a familiar name:

February 17, 1814

The government of this island, as well as the commercial interests, experiencing considerable difficulties by the want of cash; and Mr. Stewart, who was lately his majesty's consul at New-London, being now here, having offered to procur money from the United States, I am desirous, in order to aid the views of government, as well as to promote mercantile operations, that every facility should be given to the plans of the abovementioned gentleman, in obtaining the supplies of cash he undertakes; and for this purpose, I have to request, that, agreeably to his arrangement, you will be pleased to receive on board his majesty's ship, under your command, whatever sums of money may be carried alongside by persons whom he will engage; and that you will also forward the same by any of his majesty's ships, from time to time, coming to this island; or in the event of a large sum being ready, to send a sloop of war purposely with it. The vessel bearing this letter, you will likewise suffer to remain under your protection, if she should not be permitted to go into New-London.

I have the honor to be, sir, your most obedient humble servant.

John Borlase Warren

James Stewart. The former British consul in New London, known to friends and neighbors as a clever fellow with a nose for business. That nose had now led him to St. George's, Bermuda, where he was busily involved in victualing the Royal Navy and at the same time running a long-range smuggling business designed to raise American dollars for the use of British naval forces in their war against the United States.

The letter mentioned no word about his principal contact in New London, but then the addressee would know perfectly well who that was. Mr. Stewart had a wife, who was doing even more to further the British cause than he.

7

Spring 1814

A shift in British war aims—the Yankee *goes raiding—Jeremiah Holmes, torpedoist—"Torpedo Jack" and the raid on Pettipaug—Cochrane takes command—the 18 July directive*

BY far the most important event in the spring of 1814—at least from the British point of view—was the total, final collapse of Napoleon. After endless years of war in Europe, the West Indies, and North Africa, Bonaparte was finally crushed, deserted by his people, and banished to the Mediterranean island of Elba, there to live out his years, as it was supposed, in rueful contemplation of his fall from grace.

In London a jubilant prime minister and his cabinet, buoyed up by the victory, could at last spare the time to deal directly and at proper length with that nettlesome and unsought-for little war with America. Given the euphoria of the moment, we should not be surprised that almost as soon as the cabinet looked closely at the situation, it came to the conclusion that the pesky conflict on the other side of the Atlantic need not be considered a total waste of time—that on inspection, the situation offered opportunities that might be turned to considerable benefit to the United Kingdom and its colonies.

There was, for example, the matter of the border with Canada. A considerable number of ministers felt that Britain had definitely given away too much in the Treaty of Paris that closed the Revolutionary War. A little skilled reworking of that 1783 agreement might do wonders for the future of Canada and guarantee a less troublesome America. The foreign minister quickly decided on a new policy calling for the complete withdrawal of the United States from the Great Lakes, the limiting of America's northern border to the Ohio River, and the establishment of an Indian buffer state in the northwest territories. In addition, a sizable chunk of northern Maine would be transferred to the Maritime Provinces so as to improve access to the Canadian interior.

Further inspection of the Treaty of Paris quickly brought forth the suggestion that it might be prudent to guarantee British access to the Mississippi, before the Americans began moving west into the Louisiana Purchase and threatening the territory claimed by England's Spanish allies.

The *Times* of London, always the most bellicose and anti-American of papers, took the next logical step and suggested the actual recolonization of the American states. Rather than chipping away at bits and pieces, suggested the editors, why not send across Britain's brave warriors and jolly tars in sufficient numbers to reconquer the thirteen colonies in their entirety, returning to the simpler and grander imperial design that existed before the Treaty of Paris?

Industrialists in the Midlands saw considerable merit in the notion, not least because it would once again allow England to put a limit on the ambitious growth of competition centered in New England. The investment potential intrigued the City bankers. But the Foreign Office, foreseeing in recolonization the same headaches that had led the American colonies to revolt in the first place, was a little more realistic and, therefore, skeptical. Still, no one could deny that the prospect offered enormous promise, if Britain could overcome the inherent problems.

So it was that in the heady aftermath of a glorious victory the cabinet found itself shaping an entirely new set of war aims. Britons, once content to put the damned war behind them, now saw it as an opportunity to punish a dangerous and overweening America and to compensate a grossly ill-used Britain. All that remained to do was to put the plan into action.

For a full year and more the ministers had dithered over a peace conference with the Yankees, at one moment demanding one and in the next breath finding vague excuses to put it off. But with victory assured and with a clearly defined set of goals in hand, the prime minister ordered his foreign secretary to set the diplomatic machinery in motion. The American negotiating team, led by John Quincy Adams and Henry Clay, which had been cooling its heels first in London and latterly in St. Petersburg, packed bags for Gothenberg, Sweden, the venue that the parties had finally agreed upon.

Any of Britain's military leaders stationed in America could have told the cabinet that the prospects for winning the war looked a good deal brighter 3,500 miles away in London than they did up close. In Canada, Britain had lost an important naval battle on Lake Erie to Oliver Hazard Perry and was no closer to taking control of the Great Lakes than it had been twelve months earlier. To the south, Andrew Jackson, aided by short supply lines and intelligent leadership, was using the war with Britain as an excuse for stealing Florida from the Spanish. Even in the quiet backwaters of Long Island Sound, the Connecticut Yankees along the coast were once more out in force to bedevil the blockading fleet.

These tough, practical men of the sea had discovered that the war provided a delightful way of exercising their deep-felt patriotism while simultaneously turning a profit. The combination was irresistible.

At the Hornet's Nest on the Mystic River a group of these canny mariners invented a new outlet for their acquisitive energies: a system for hunting down and capturing British smugglers. As part of its plan to obtain American cash, the Royal Navy had encouraged a vast number of smugglers from Britain to cross the ocean to sell goods to Americans. Whole fleets of seagoing entrepreneurs from Cornwall, Yorkshire, and the Hebrides had heeded the call, lured by the vision of a smuggler's paradise: a large, ready market unprotected by revenuers, with a power no less than the Royal Navy itself to secure the entire operation. These newest recruits to the war were the precise counterparts of the Mystic River men, and what the American group now proposed was a sort of counterblockade in which they would play the part of the revenue service.

A group led by Lemuel Burrows formed a syndicate and for six hundred dollars purchased a large, forty-two-foot-long barge mounting twelve oars and named the *Yankee*. She had the look and lines of a Royal Navy barge, a similarity that the new owners enhanced by mounting a brass cannon in her bow and covering up her telltale name. Burrows was to be the captain, but since it was to the Americans' advantage to be mistaken for a British boat, a recently arrived Englishman living in the area was selected to play the part. He was got up in something like a lieutenant's uniform—dark blue jacket and brass buttons—and rode in the position of command. This Englishman, who went by the name of Peter Washington, was probably one of the emigrés who had escaped from the *Acasta* to Stonington the previous fall.

For much of that spring the *Yankee* cruised the eastern end of the sound and adjacent waters in search of prey. The crew took her as far east as Martha's Vineyard, where they captured traitorous American supply boats sailing under license to the British fleet, and as far west as the Connecticut River, where they were fired upon by the militia, an uncomfortable turn of events that only proved how convincing was their disguise.

Standing off toward Long Island to escape the musketry, they spotted a sail coming up on Plum Island and made for it. The quarry turned out to be the English sloop *George*, loaded with salt and bearing papers from New London to New Haven. The *Yankee*'s crew, complete with make-believe captain, had no trouble boarding her. While "Peter Washington" examined her papers, other crew members entered the hold and examined the bags of salt spread from gunwale to gunwale. Suspecting that they were seeing something less than what was in fact there, the men thrust swords and ramrods into the salt and quickly met with obstacles, which turned out to be bales of silk and calico, bundles of blocked tin, and boxes of medicine. The captain of the *George* sheepishly admitted that she was in fact a smuggler that had just taken her cargo from a prize anchored at Gardiner's Island and was preparing to sell it at New Haven.

On learning this information, the crew of the *Yankee* revealed their true identity and, taking command of the *George*, put about for the Mystic River, where the goods were hurriedly transshipped several miles upstream to Head of Mystic to prevent any attempt at recapture. The cargo was eventually sold at auction for a little more than $6000, ten times the purchase price of the *Yankee*.

On another cruise the *Yankee* overhauled a schooner, loaded with what appeared to be corn and flour, off Fishers Island. Her captain produced papers that showed her to be an American blockade runner, so the *Yankee* let her pass, only to learn a week later that another freebooter off Newport, practicing the same trade as the *Yankee*, had stopped the same schooner and discovered she was in fact a British smuggler. The Newport crew eventually realized some $30,000 from the capture.

While the crew members of the *Yankee* were amusing themselves catching smugglers, another group, led by Jeremiah Holmes, was involved in a more complicated enterprise. Their endeavor promised not only many thousands of dollars in prize money but might also make possible the final escape of Decatur's squadron.

On 8 March 1814 Decatur made a third attempt to steal past the blockaders and was again foiled by blue lights. It became clear that if he really wanted to get out he would require some more effective means of making his escape. When a local sea captain previously unknown to him named Jeremiah Holmes approached the *United States* and requested an audience with the commodore, Decatur was immediately receptive.

After introducing himself and providing bona fides of his identity and trustworthiness, Holmes described his business. Holmes's strong belief in secrecy clearly impressed Decatur, as did his story. Over the winter Holmes had established a partnership with a New York businessman named Ryker, who had been one of Scudder's partners in the *Eagle* syndicate the previous summer. In spite of the difference in spelling, this Mr. Ryker was likely the same as the Captain Riker who skippered the *Eagle*, but as noted, checking the details of such clandestine operations is virtually impossible. Despite the failure of the *Eagle* to sink the *Ramillies*, Ryker was eager to try again. He had now designed—or caused to be designed—a torpedo that could work independently of the attacking vessel. He and Holmes had agreed to give it a try at New London, with Ryker putting up the money for all expenses and Holmes running the operation. Holmes was aboard the *United States* that evening to alert Decatur to the plot, so that he would be ready to take appropriate action in case the torpedoists were successful. Not surprisingly, Decatur was eager to hear the details.

Early in March Holmes and some members of his crew, including the man he had chosen as his armorer, Zebulon Woolsey, journeyed overland to take delivery of their new torpedo boat at the Mott and Williams boat yard in New York. The boat was a single-banked galley of sixteen oars, and the reason for its considerable size became evident when Mr. Ryker produced the torpedo itself.

It was a cumbersome thing, quite unlike the compact designs of Mr. Fulton. It consisted principally of a thirty-foot hollow cylinder fashioned of tin plate, about seven inches in diameter. It looked at first glance like a water conduit; but it contained seventy-five pounds of superfine gunpowder, and it floated on buoys. Near one end a crossbar about twelve feet in length with hooks at either end perforated the cylinder. The crossbar contained the firing mechanism.

As Mr. Ryker explained to Holmes and his armorer, the torpedo was designed to be used in conjunction with the tides, much like the one demonstrated so effectively by Elijah Mix in Virginia. The launching boat was to position itself four hundred yards uptide of the target and to let the torpedo out on a line in such a way that the tide carried it to the target. Once there the hooks on the crossbar would, it was hoped, catch on some line or protrusion, and the force of the tide on the cylinder would eventually turn the torpedo at an oblique angle tripping a spring and causing the bomb to explode.

Holmes and his men gingerly placed the disarmed torpedo in the center of their barge, covered it with rags and cordage to disguise it as best they could, and set sail for New London. If caught by the British with the torpedo the men knew they would almost assuredly be executed. As a precautionary measure, they detached the buoys from the infernal machine so that they could more quickly drop it over the side if they were approached by the enemy.

Once back in New London, Holmes hid the barge up the Thames, not far from the *United States*, and informed Decatur of his return. The commodore was enthusiastic. Late at night the entire torpedo crew made their way in small groups to the *United States*. Once assembled, they discussed the situation at length with Decatur and his officers, going over every aspect of the operation in minute detail. Afterward they rowed down river and out into the sound and practiced for the next three nights the difficult art of torpedoing. The plan called for Holmes and his men to detonate the bomb and disappear as quickly as possible while Decatur, taking advantage of the confusion, sailed out to freedom.

On the night when they finally decided they were ready, no 74s were anchored off the Thames, so they decided to attack a frigate. The one they targeted—probably the *Endymion*—was lying off the

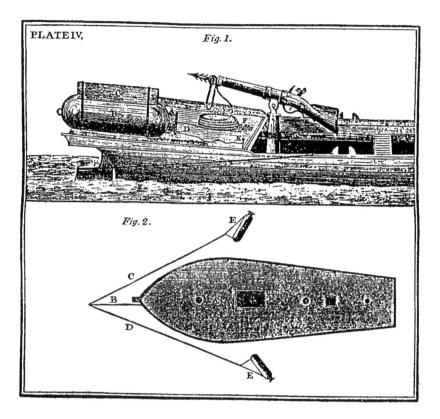

PLATE IV,   *Fig. 1.*

Fig. 2.

Two of Fulton's suggestions for employing his torpedoes. Fig. 1 shows a torpedo attached to a harpoon. In Fig. 2, two floating torpedoes (EE) attached by a line (CD) are swept by the tide toward an anchored ship. When the ship's cable (B) catches the line, the torpedoes are forced against the hull on either side and made to explode either by contact or by a clockwork device. This was the method used to blow up the *Dorothea* and was similar to the method employed by Jeremiah Holmes in his attack on the British squadron. (Fulton's *Torpedo Warfare and Submarine Explosions*)

west end of Fishers Island. From the beginning, the attack did not go well. First, they misjudged the tide and arrived too late, so by the time they were paying out the torpedo from the boat, the tide had turned to flood. Then they realized that the line attached to the floating bomb was too stiff to work freely, and it fouled on something hidden on the sea bottom. When they tried to free it, they succeeded only in pulling the torpedo underwater, where it too got caught. Raising it without danger of explosion was impossible. The men worked frantically throughout most of the night to try to free the torpedo; but after several hours of fruitless effort they finally gave up, cut the line, and abandoned the weapon, rowing disconsolately back to shore.

The next day the crew sailed the boat back to New York for a second torpedo, and within a week Ryker supplied them with not only a second bomb but a third one as well. Once more they returned as quickly as possible to New London.

By now a 74 had once again taken up station there. Holmes thought the ship was the *Ramillies*, but in fact Hardy had been called away, and the command of the blockade was now in the hands of Captain Capel of the *La Hogue*, 74. That night of 24 March the Americans targeted his ship.

Holmes' barge passed silently past Eastern Point and around the dark shape of the *La Hogue*, coming up to the northwest of her and dropping anchor. This time the men caught the tide, and the rope was properly flexible. After paying out the torpedo for a considerable distance, and feeling the gratifying pull of the tide directing it toward the ship-of-the-line, Holmes ordered the anchor raised. The oarsmen attempted to row eastward toward the land, so as to swing the torpedo against the ship. The wind was fresh from the northwest, and the tide was strong in ebb. These conditions so deceived the men in the boat that in passing across in the darkness they unwittingly drifted down so near the targeted ship's bows that they could clearly make out the sails furled on her jibboom.

Realizing their danger, they hauled the boat up to windward and anchored, all the time trying to haul in on the torpedo. They pulled the bomb up near the *La Hogue*'s bow, where the hauling line caught in the anchor cable. A sudden strain on the crossbar tripped the detonator, and the torpedo exploded at exactly 2:45 in the morning, shattering the night's silence, sending a huge column of water into the air, and soaking a half dozen terrified sailors on the *La Hogue*.

In an instant a storm of musketry poured down from the ship's deck on every side, without effect. Captain Holmes and his crew were already desperately pulling for shore. Shouted orders from the quarterdeck sent signal lanterns running up into the rigging as an alarm to the rest of the squadron. The deep boom of the ship's guns added to the alarm. For some reason the British did not set off any Congreve rockets. Perhaps the *La Hogue* had none. Rocket light might have revealed the culprits, who by this time were well out of range of hand weapons.

Decatur, waiting to hear that the 74 was disabled and at least temporarily out of operation, heard an excited version of the failed attack, and realized that he had run out of luck and lost his last chance to escape. The British would now be so thoroughly alarmed and on their guard against such attacks that there was no possibility of another attempt.

Three weeks later a disconsolate Decatur ordered the *United States* and *Macedonian* moved upriver as far as the depth of water would allow, and he had the frigates dismantled. He announced that he and his officers and crew would go by land to New York to take over the frigate *President*, while Captain Jones and his officers and crew of the *Macedonian* went to join the fleet in the Great Lakes. Captain Biddle of the *Hornet* would remain, left in charge of a full quarter of the entire U.S. Navy.

A direct offshoot of Jeremiah Holmes's attack on the *La Hogue* was the highly successful British attack on the shipping at Pettipaug Point on the Connecticut River. Immediately following the explosion of the torpedo the British sent out boats in search of the culprits who, as we have seen, managed to escape. But one of the British boats managed to find a small skiff with a single person in it, and the officer in charge ordered him brought back to the ship. The prisoner immediately proclaimed his innocence, but the lateness of the hour and the fact that the man was rowing with muffled oars were enough to make Captain Capel suspicious. He ordered the American clapped in irons and threatened with death for his part in the aborted action. To extricate himself from a highly compromising situation, the mysterious captive, whom the British sailors promptly dubbed "Torpedo Jack," offered to pilot a fleet of British barges up the tricky Connecticut River channel at night to Pettipaug, a haven for privateers and blockade runners. The British knew all about Pettipaug and had long desired to attack the place. They jumped at the opportunity.

One night a week later a British raiding party of about 220 men, guided by Torpedo Jack, moved up the Connecticut River past Saybrook and as the day dawned arrived off Pettipaug. The American militia had got wind of the raid and was already mustered on shore, prepared to do battle with the boats. The British commander, who had the men and weapons to defeat the militia if it came to a fight, offered to spare the town and its wharves if the militia would not interfere with his planned destruction of the shipping. The citizens of Pettipaug eagerly accepted the offer and stood by quietly as the British, in a matter of minutes, set fire to seven privateers, twelve large merchant ships, and ten coasters. The fires raged through most of the day, and the clouds of black greasy smoke were visible for miles in the clear March air. This raid was the most destructive single attack on American shipping during the entire war.

When the news of the Pettipaug raid reached the nation, it provoked a storm of calumny directed at the citizens of the town. Their civic irresolution was seen as spineless cowardice in the face of the enemy. To be fair, the Americans were heavily outgunned and outmanned and probably cannot be faulted for acceding to British demands. But even if they were not guilty of cowardice, the people of Pettipaug might be surprised to learn that in the twentieth century their village—now known as Essex—proudly celebrates the British raid with a patriotic annual parade.

Once the cabinet in London had decided to put fresh pressure on the United States, events followed quickly on one another.

The first step was to remove Admiral Warren from command of the American Station. There were several convenient reasons for the move, including complaints from Canada that Warren's captains were impressing local fishermen and were not doing enough to protect them from privateers. On the other side of the Atlantic, on the floor of the House of Commons, members complained that the Royal Navy, for all its numerical superiority, was not able to control the number of American privateers swarming across the shipping lanes and infesting the Irish Sea in such numbers that the insurance rates at Lloyd's were going through the roof.

Admiral Warren's replacement was Vice Admiral Sir Alexander Cochrane, a tough and experienced campaigner with a strong anti-American bias well suited to making life difficult for the Yankees. When he arrived in Bermuda the new commander let it be known that he would not limit his activities to the sea but would embark on land actions as well. He announced that three to four thousand marines would soon be joining his command, to supplement the navy's ten to twelve 74s and their complement of frigates and smaller craft. Up to this point, the British had used marines only sparingly in the war, but the large number envisioned by Cochrane could only mean more attacks on shore stations and manufactures. The newspaper account of Cochrane's arrival added that he planned to bring with him to the American coast "a strong body of riflemen and battering artillery, Congreve rockets, shrapnel shells, with all the ammunitions &c. necessary to give effect to these engines of destruction."

Cochrane quickly and clearly showed that he would use every means at his disposal to make life difficult for the Americans. On 2 April he signed a proclamation designed to panic the southern states—a veiled invitation to every slave in America to throw off his or her shackles and escape to freedom:

> WHEREAS it has been represented to me, that many persons now resident in the UNITED STATES, have expressed a desire to withdraw therefrom, with a view of entering into his majesty's service, or of being received as free settlers into some of his majesty's colonies,
> *This is therefore to give notice,*
> That all those who may be disposed to emigrate from the UNITED STATES, will with their families, be received on board his majesty's ships or vessels of war, or at the military posts that may be established upon or near the coast of the UNITED STATES, when they will have their choice of either entering into his majesty's sea or land forces, or of being sent as FREE settlers to the British possessions in North America or the West Indies, where they will meet with all due encouragement.

Cochrane's proclamation walks a very fine line that is not easy to perceive today, but that would have been clear to any reader, slave or free, at the time he wrote it. In the code of the early nineteenth century private property was sacrosanct, and slaves, of course, were property. Cochrane, as an officer of his king and as a gentleman, could not openly encourage property to run away from its owners, even if he was fighting the owners. His proclamation, which never mentions conditions of servitude, skirts the dilemma with admirable subtlety, managing to encourage slaves to desert their masters without ever quite suggesting they should. The only giveaway is the capitalization of the word FREE in the penultimate phrase.

Cochrane had a disagreeable surprise for the northern states as well. In April he extended the blockade north from Black Point to the Canadian border, including in it for the first time the entire coast of New England.

Around this time an English newspaper in a sanguinary mood noted, "Twenty-five thousand troops are forthwith to be transported to America; and already, the public mind is prepared for the exertion of all our strength, in bringing back that froward people to unconditional submission." A later story corrected the figures: the twenty-five thousand troops were only the ones embarking for Quebec. Another ten thousand were bound for Halifax. These men were all battle-tested veterans of the Peninsula campaign, trained under the command of Wellington himself, and could be expected to give a good account of themselves, particularly against the demonstrated incompetence of the American militia.

In less than two months after his arrival in Bermuda, Cochrane had brought a new tension to the war. He had threatened to use a new kind of force, a new style of aggression not seen heretofore. He had made sure the Americans understood he had the men and equipment to wreak havoc on their coastline. All he really needed now was some sort of excuse to increase the pressure, some justification for the mayhem he planned to unleash. It arrived from an unexpected quarter.

On 15 May 1814, on the Canadian frontier, a small body of American troops crossed Lake Erie to Long Point on the Ontario side and destroyed the flour mills, distilleries, and some private homes near the village of Dover. The U.S. government had not authorized the raid and the officer commanding it was afterward court-martialed and censured. But the British army commander in Canada, General Sir George Prevost, had no time for explanations or excuses. Here was private property—the very bricks and mortar upon which civilization rested—wantonly destroyed, egregiously abused, and he must put a stop to it.

Prevost knew how to give lessons to Yankees. When they burned the village of Newark, he retaliated by sending Indians to butcher and scalp whole villages of men, women, and children. The same astonishingly disproportionate reaction would characterize his response to the burning of property near Dover.

He wrote first to his field commander, General Drummond, noting wistfully, "I cherished the hope that the severe although just retaliation inflicted for the destruction of the Village of Newark would have detered the Enemy from reverting to similar acts of Barbarity." As he addressed himself to the attack on Dover, one can almost feel his gorge rise: "Such horrors cannot be suffered to remain without notice or unrevenged."

Still shaken with outrage, he wrote the next day to Cochrane in Bermuda, suggesting that the navy should "assist in inflicting that measure of retaliation which shall deter the enemy from a repetition of similar outrages."

Prevost's letter took six weeks to get from Montreal to Bermuda, but as soon as it arrived, Cochrane wasted no time in putting it to use. On 18 July 1814 he issued orders to all the ships in his command, from the St. Croix River on the Canadian border to the St. Mary's on the Florida frontier, directing general retaliation along the entire coast. His wording left no doubt as to the vengeful nature of the attacks he wanted carried out:

> You are hereby required and directed to destroy and lay waste such towns and districts upon the coast as you may find assailable. You will hold strictly in view the conduct of the American army towards his Majesty's unoffending Canadian subjects, and you will spare merely the lives of the unarmed inhabitants of the United States. For only by carrying this retributory justice into the country of our enemy can we hope to make him sensible of the impropriety as well as of the inhumanity of the system he had adopted. You will take every opportunity of explaining to the people how much I lament the necessity of following the rigorous example of the commander of the American forces. And as these commanders must obviously have acted under instructions from the Executive government of the United States, whose intimate and unnatural connection with the late government of France has led them to adopt the same system of plunder and devastation, it is therefore to their own government the unfortunate sufferers must look for indemnification for their loss of property.

As later events would show, Cochrane's order of 18 July 1814 was the immediate cause of the Battle of Stonington. He would never have issued that order had not Prevost pleaded for help, and Prevost, in turn, would not have asked for help if the attack on Dover had not been the sequel to the attack on Newark. So the Battle of Stonington, when it finally occurred in August 1814, could trace its origins, in a direct paper trail, to the burning of an equally obscure village in Ontario eight months earlier and hundreds of miles away.

8

Summer 1814

Hardy contemplates a raid on Portsmouth—
conquest of Passamaquoddy—smuggler to the
king—Hardy sails southwest

IN June 1814 Thomas Masterman Hardy lay at anchor in the *Ramillies* off St. George's, Bermuda. He had only recently arrived at the headquarters of the North American Station after an extensive scouting expedition along that part of the New England coast added to the blockade by order of Admiral Cochrane.

Now Hardy sat preparing his report to Cochrane and simultaneously forming plans for what promised to be the most daring and devastating amphibious attack of the entire war—the storming of Portsmouth, New Hampshire, and the destruction of one of America's first ships-of-the-line, the *Washington*, currently under construction in the shipyards there.

Ramillies, Bermuda
16th June, 1814

Sir:—In obedience to the directions contained in your letter of the 14th April I proceeded in His Majesty's Ship under my command off Boston, where I found the *Nymph* and *Junon*. As I was of the opinion that a Ship of the line would create a considerable alarm by appearing off Portsmouth, I judged it best to leave the *Ramillies* cruizing off Cape Anne,

111

where she remained in charge of Lieutenant Truscott, who is a most zealous attentive officer and first Lieutenant of this Ship, and proceeded off Portsmouth in the *Nymph* with the *Junon* in Company.

The British had been aware of the *Washington* from its inception, along with her sister ships, the *Independence* and *Franklin*, which were concurrently under construction in Boston and Philadelphia, and had followed their progress with keen interest from the first debates in Congress. Building a capital ship normally took around three years, from the laying of the keel to the commissioning; but under wartime duress the Americans were cutting corners and pushing ahead at an impressive rate, and Cochrane was anxious to know just how soon he might have to face this new kind of American threat. He understood perfectly well that the addition of one of these ships to the American navy would not materially shift the balance in the Atlantic, but since a 74 was the equivalent of perhaps three frigates, neutralizing it if at all possible was clearly in the British interests. To thwart such an eventuality the Americans had gone to considerable lengths to provide the *Washington* with suitable protection.

> By the chart and sketch of Portsmouth which accompanies this letter, [Hardy continued,] you will perceive that the entrance to the Harbor is particularly well defended and the different Batteries appear very strong in front, but I do not think that any of them are protected in the rear. The Battery on Pearces Island is not more than 400 yards from Navy Island . . . and . . . the ground on which it stands is much higher than any part of Navy Island.

The destruction of the *Washington* was precisely the sort of bold, dashing project dear to Cochrane's heart, and Hardy undoubtedly looked forward to the possibility of a little fun and games on his own part after all his months of arduous guard duty off New London. Not incidentally, he would certainly have looked forward to the opportunity to earn some worthwhile prize money into the bargain.

> I am therefore of opinion that the only mode of destroying the ship now building would be by landing a sufficient number of Troops on the Eastern Shore near Godfrey Cove, where there is a good anchorage and is about four miles from Navy Island, but we should have to pass Spruce Creek, which I understand is dry at low water, and has a soft, muddy Bottom. From the information that I have been enabled to gather from the Fishermen, there are 500 United States troops at Portsmouth, and on the 27th ultimo there were collected 5000 Militia. . . .

The United States frigate *Congress* was laying close to Navy Island, and appeared perfectly ready for sea, but I was informed that a few men were wanting to complete her complement.—If a shack had not been built over the ship on the stocks, I could have assertained her exact state of forwardness—from the information I received, I am convinced however that she is not planked higher than the Bends, and only part of her decks are laid.

I have the honor to be

Sir,

Your most obedient

humble servant,

TM Hardy, Captain

The *Washington* with its $235,861 price tag, represented a significant portion of the entire federal budget, and if Hardy had been allowed to carry out his plans to attack Portsmouth, and if the raid had succeeded (which is likely), it would have dealt a serious blow to the American war effort. Even more important, it would have had a devastating psychological effect on the American people, and particularly on the citizens of New England, most of whom were only half-heartedly behind the war to start with.

But the raid never took place. It seems the cabinet in London had more significant schemes on its mind than the mere destruction of a ship-of-the-line.

The previous April the foreign secretary, Earl Bathurst, had pondered the means of implementing a policy of limited recolonization. While his ambitions fell short of the *Times*'s wholesale demands for a reconquest of all the former colonies, he was eager to regain for Britain certain specific parcels of land, generally with an eye toward strengthening the defenses and resources of Canada.

The first step was to discredit the Treaty of Paris, to cast doubt on the validity of the instrument by which, in 1783, Britain and America established who owned what in North America after the Revolution. Once the authority of the treaty was in question, Bathurst could then pick and choose locations, from New Orleans to Michilimackinac Island, that could give Britain permanent strategic advantages on the continent.

To attain his ends, Bathurst needed to find some piece of American soil where the United States's right of occupancy was not entirely clear. Eventually, after careful study of the Treaty of Paris, the clerks in the Foreign Office came up with a candidate. The spot was called Moose Island, an obscure bit of real estate, measuring about two miles by four, at the northeastern corner of the United States in Passamaquoddy Bay. The island contained a decent harbor, called Eastport, with a permanent population of about 1500 people, and lay between Campobello Island, belonging to New Brunswick, and the coast of Maine, which was at the time a province of Massachusetts.

Given its location, Eastport was, not surprisingly, primarily a smuggling port. Throughout the war revenue runners from both England and America filled the harbor, getting along easily enough with each other and finding it a convenient place to do business. Bathurst was not interested in who lived there. They could be Red Indians or Frenchmen for all he cared. He was primarily interested in using the place as a justification for the recolonization of other locations, or alternately as a bargaining chip that might prove useful to the English negotiators at the upcoming peace talks, which had now been switched from Gothenburg to Ghent and were to begin in August.

On 28 April 1814 Bathurst sent messages in secret code to Cochrane in Bermuda and to General Sherbrooke in Canada, apprising them of the plan to take Moose Island. Cochrane received Bathurst's letter in the same week he received Hardy's plans for the suggested attack on Portsmouth. Much as Cochrane might have wished to send Hardy off to destroy the *Washington*, he had no choice but to postpone that intriguing project and put Hardy in charge of the navy's involvement in the Moose Island operation instead.

The conquest of Moose Island is worth examining in considerable detail. It demonstrates with what seriousness Britain entertained the idea of taking back at least part of the United States. It also shows the remarkable efficiency of the British armed forces and their ability, even when operating at great distances over an enormous area, to carry out the nation's foreign policy. But just as important, the taking of the island gives us an opportunity to see the inner workings of the system, the mechanics by which the British got things done. Perhaps most interestingly, it provides an opportunity to observe Captain Thomas Hardy up close in his last military action prior to his attack on Stonington. The precision and efficiency of the Moose Island operation contrast so markedly with the vague, inconclusive nature of the Stonington adventure, which was to follow a month later, that the

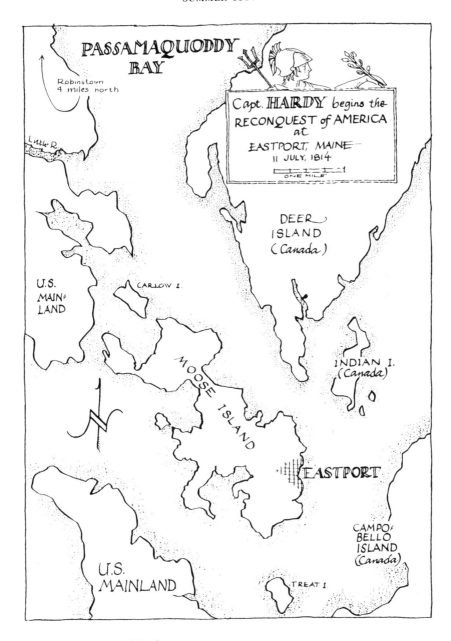

Map Three: Moose Island

difference helps shed light on some of the puzzling questions that remain about the second event.

On 22 June Captain Hardy set sail from Bermuda in the *Ramillies*, accompanied by two troop transports carrying the 102nd Regiment, along with a highly specialized vessel, the bomb ship *Terror*, designed specifically to attack land targets. On 7 July, off the coast of Nova Scotia, Hardy rendezvoused with the sloop *Martin* carrying Lieutenant Colonel Thomas Pilkington, who took command of the 102nd, and two transports carrying artillery. Captain Senhouse of the *Martin* had been specially selected for the assignment because of his intimate knowledge of the Bay of Fundy and of the area's generally treacherous waters.

The next day the augmented squadron set sail for Eastport, and on the morning of the 11th the brig *Borer*, Captain Rawlins, joined the group off Grand Manan Island. Hardy sent the *Borer* through the Quoddy Passage to anchor near the ferry lane between Moose Island and the mainland, effectively cutting off any possible American retreat. Then with the troops ready to land, and favored with a fair breeze, Hardy ordered the *Terror* to take up position. He then sent the *Martin* into Eastport with a message addressed to the army commandant of Fort Sullivan, who had just awakened to the unwelcome news that a large enemy force of nine ships was standing offshore.

The message to Fort Sullivan is representative of Hardy at his most characteristic: cool, blunt, but providing his enemy with an honorable way out. Still, the commandant could not mistake the mailed fist inside the velvet glove. The opening sentence reads either as empathy for a fellow warrior or as a polite but imperious demand.

> On board His Majesty's Ship Ramillies, off Moose Island July 11, 1814
>
> Sir:—We are perfectly apprized of the Weakness of the Fort and Garrison under your Command, and your inability to defend Moose Island against the Ships and Troops of His Britannic Majesty, placed under our directions.

Just in case the Americans were not prepared to jump at Hardy's face-saving hint that they should think in terms of surrender, his second sentence took on a threatening tone and closed with an abrupt ultimatum.

We are induced from the humane considerations of avoiding the Effusion of Blood and from a regard to you, and the Inhabitants of the Island, to prevent if it is in our power the distresses and Calamities which will befall them in case of Resistance—we therefore allow you five minutes from the time this summons is delivered to decide an answer.

The final sentence, couched in the most genteel phrasing, makes the threat manifest.

In the event of your not agreeing to capitulate on liberal terms, we shall deeply lament being compelled to resort to those coercive measures which may cause destruction to the Town of Eastport and which will ultimately insure our possession of the Island.

With due attention to the accepted social forms, but in stark contrast to the reality of the situation, Hardy signed with the obligatory "Your most obedient humble servant, T. M. Hardy."

Upon reading this note, the commandant, Major Perley Putnam, promptly turned down the suggestion of surrender. But minutes later, when the British calmly began to disembark an enormous number of soldiers into barges, the terrified inhabitants, who had no desire for a fight, prevailed upon him to change his mind. Reluctantly, he gave in to the inevitable. As he scrawled his reconsidered capitulation, he must have been grateful that Hardy had given him a phrase or two to plagiarize:

Fort Sullivan July 11, 1814

Gentlemen:—Conformibly to your demand, I have surrendered Fort Sullivan with all the public property—This I have done to stop the Effusion of Blood and in consideration of your superior force.

I am, Gentlemen, with respect,
Your most obdt servant,
Perley Putnam
Major, Commanding

Once again, Hardy had brought off another of his bloodless victories. Within minutes of the capitulation—certainly in less than an hour—he and his army counterpart arranged a very official and lawyerly agreement that would help clarify any later argument over suzerainty of Moose Island:

Articles of capitulation for the surrender of Moose Island, agreed to between Sir Thomas Hardy commanding the Naval Forces and Lieutenant Colonel Pilkington commanding the Land Forces on the part of His Britannic Majesty and Major Putnam, Commandant of Moose Island, on the part of the United States—11 July 1814

Article 1st

The officers and troops of the United States at present on Moose Island, are to surrender themselves Prisoners of War, and are to deliver up the Forts, Buildings, arms, ammunition, stores and effects with exact Inventories thereof, belonging to the American Government, and they are hereby transferred to His Britannic Majesty in the same manner and possession as has been held heretofore by the American Government.

Article 2nd

The Garrison of the Island shall be prisoners of War until regularly exchanged. They will march out of the Fort with the honors of War, and stack their arms at such place as will be appointed for that purpose— The officers will be permitted to proceed to the United States on their parole.

Article 3rd

Every respect will be paid to private property found on Moose Island belonging to the inhabitants thereof.

Hardy, Pilkington, and Putnam then signed and approved this paper, and by the end of the morning the victors had checked the lists of personnel and of all ordnance and stores that the Americans had delivered. These lists indicated that the armaments of the fort consisted of four long 10-pounders, one 18-pound carronade, and four field pieces. The garrison consisted of six officers and about seventy-five men, twelve of whom were sick.

The British superiority in men and material was almost ludicrous. By the end of the morning they had disembarked their entire cargo of fifty or sixty cannon, as well as a thousand troops plus another two thousand women and children. (The British planned to stay, and nothing stated their intentions more clearly than the simultaneous arrival of the soldiers and their families.) The troops spent the rest of the day trying to find where to house this crowd. The officers, returning to the *Ramillies*, undoubtedly broke out a bottle or two in celebration of a job well done.

The majority of the people of Eastport seemed singularly unmoved by the momentous happenings taking place around them.

When the American flag was struck and replaced with the Union Jack, there were even some cheers and huzzahs in the crowd. A locally important figure reportedly observed, "Now we shall get rid of the tax gatherers, and the damned democrats will get it."

The next day, the British had to take care of more details, the most important of which was to define the new status of Moose Island precisely, not as American property under British control but as British property plain and simple. To make this point clear, the British commandant in New Brunswick addressed a letter to the most prominent American official in the area, General John Brewer of the Washington County militia in nearby Robinstown on the mainland.

> St. Andrews,
> July 12, 1814

> Sir—I am directed by his excellency maj. gen. sir John Sherbrook, to make the following communication to the inhabitants of Robinstown and elsewhere on the main land:—

> That the object of the British government is to obtain possession of the islands of Passamaquoddy Bay in consequence of their being considered within our boundary line:—That they have no intention of carrying on offensive operations against the people residing on the continent, unless their conduct should oblige us to resort to the measure; and in the event of their remaining quiet, they will not be disturbed either in their property or persons.

> I have the honor to be your most obedient and humble servant.

> J. Fitsherbert
> lt. col. com.

As prescribed, General Brewer then sent a copy of this letter to Governor Strong in Boston, and the country at large learned of the conquest of Eastport by the end of the week.

The promise contained in Lieutenant Colonel Fitsherbert's letter—that the British had "no intention of carrying on offensive operations against the people residing on the continent"—was an outright lie. The false promise may explain why Hardy, as the senior officer of the expedition, did not put his name to the letter. Six weeks later General Sherbrooke and General Gosselin came down from Nova Scotia with nearly four thousand troops and a fleet of twenty-four ships, entered Penobscot Bay, took possession of Castine, and sent troops against Belfast and Hamden. The British captured Bangor and Machias. Thus the Maine coast from Penobscot Bay to Passamaquoddy Bay passed under British rule and was formally annexed by a proclamation issued by Sherbrooke. The pretext for the annexation of Moose Island—that Great Britain had not ceded the Passamaquoddy area in 1783—did not apply to the Penobscot, and the invasion is indicative of how seriously the British took the idea of recolonization.

The *Times* could barely control its delight at the seizure and was quick to start counting the gain in economic terms:

> This . . . tract of country [is] double the extent of the surveyed part of the district of Three Rivers. This too, like the western territory, was shamefully ceded to the United States in 1783, as a present that was never looked for; but which it is hoped will be attended to in the next treaty of peace. The district we speak of is the most valuable in the United States for fishing establishments; and has a coast of 60 leagues abounding in excellent harbors, from whence much lumber is sent to Europe and the West Indies.

An incident that marred the otherwise orderly and clockwork nature of the invasion involved the customs house receipts. As soon as the British landed, the collector of customs, a worthy federal official whose name has unfortunately not come down to us, hurriedly attempted to sequester his stamps and official papers, and, in particular, the unsigned treasury notes in his possession, which had a face value of $9000. While he busied himself with these particulars a traitor from the mainland, John Rodgers from Kennebec, seized the collector by the collar and held him until a British officer arrived. Together they tried to compel the collector to sign over the bonds, but he resolutely refused, claiming grandly that "hanging would be no compulsion." His bravery won the day, and the British eventually allowed him to leave the island with his bills intact.

The entire operation was quickly over except for the official annexation of the island, and Hardy and Pilkington took care of that detail on 14 July by posting a proclamation.

ROYAL PROCLAMATION

By captain Sir Thomas Hardy, Bart. commanding the naval forces, and lieut. col. Andrew Pilkington, commanding the land forces of his Britannic Majesty in the bay of Passamaquoddy.

WHEREAS, His Royal Highness the Prince Regent of the United Kingdoms of Great Britain and Ireland has been pleased to signify his pleasure that the islands in the Bay of Passamaquoddy should be occupied in the name of his Britannic Majesty, and the said islands having been surrendered to the forces under the orders of vice admiral the hon. sir Alexander Cochrane, K. B. and his excellency lieut. gen. sir John Sherbrooke, K. B.

This is to give notice to all whom it may concern that the municipal laws established by the American government, for the peace and tranquility of these islands, are to remain in force until further orders.

All persons at present in these islands are to appear before us on Saturday next, at 10 o'clock in the forenoon, on the ground near the school-house, and declare their intention, whether they will take the oath of allegiance to his Britannic majesty; and all persons not disposed to take said oath, will be required to depart from the islands in the course of seven days from the date hereof, unless special permission is granted to them to remain for a longer period.

The citizens of Eastport were then shown a copy of the oath they would be asked to take:

FORM OF OATH

I, _____ , do swear that I will bear true faith and allegiance to His Britannic Majesty King George III of the United Kingdom of Great Britain and Ireland, his heirs and successors, and that I will not directly, or indirectly serve or carry arms against them or their allies by sea or land—so help me God.

GOD SAVE THE KING.

During the night following the posting of the proclamation, a stealthy hand replaced it with another message:

Whereas, since the conquest of this island by his Britannic majesty's forces under the command of Sir Thomas Hardy and lieut. Col. Andrew Pilkington, it appears, by a proclamation published by virtue of their authority, that the citizens of this place are to chose either an eternal allegiance to his majesty George the 3d (from whose yoke our fathers freed us) or an abandonment of their property on this island; it becomes their duty seriously to consider whether they will renounce forever the rights and privileges of American citizens, or accept the terms of the oath of allegiance for themselves, their heirs and successors, or like good men, and true to their country and honor, refuse such oath of abject submission, and appeal at once to the virtue and generosity of the American people for reparation. If the oath be taken, you cannot dare to stand by the side of your bleeding country in the hour of her distress; but you and your children forever must be considered the subjects of Britain. Never let it be said by your children, *our fathers basely sold what their fathers bravely won.* If you do not take the oath, you are still freemen and honorable Americans and can meet your fellow citizens with a pure heart. If you do take the oath, you will be considered degraded in their eyes forever.

"A day, an hour, of virtuous liberty,
Is worth a whole eternity of bondage."

A TRUE AMERICAN

Early risers the following morning duly made note of the True American's stern message, and crowds gathered to read it and guess as to its author. The authorities at first assumed Hardy's proclamation was drawing the crowd, but as soon as they discovered their mistake, a trooper removed the offending document and replaced it with a copy of the original.

Three days later, on the Saturday morning appointed, two-thirds of the people of Moose Island swore allegiance to the king. The first to do so was the local representative to the Massachusetts legislature in Boston, a man named Weston, whom the British promptly rewarded with an appointment as one of his majesty's justices of the peace. The deputy collector of revenues, a man named Corney, with none of the patriotic fervor of his recent superior, took the oath and simultaneously accepted the commission as chief customs collector for the crown.

The British shipped the five hundred or so who opted for "virtuous liberty" out to Portland the same day, and a newspaper report from Portland soon after gave out the doleful news to America.

Portland, July 28. Last evening arrived at this port a British cartel boat, with 5 officers who were taken at Eastport at its late surrender. We have conversed with Major Putnam, who informs that he left there on the 16th inst. Previous to his departure the British had landed 60 cannon and upwards of 1500 troops—a large quantity of rockets were also landed and every preparation was in requisition to complete its fortifications and render it a safe rendezvous for their shipping and to form a grand military arsenal. Two transports arrived on the 16th supposed to have troops on board. Houses, meeting-houses and every vacant apartment was appropriated as barracks for the soldiers.

So began the only invasion of American soil by a foreign power until the Japanese occupation of Attu and Kiska Islands in the Aleutians in World War II.

The conquest of Moose Island is notable for several reasons. In the first place, the invasion was a combined forces operation, involving both land and sea elements, with the potential for confusion of the command structure and poor communications that always threaten such exercises. Moving a large number of sailing ships through unfamiliar waters is never simple. Any number of problems could arise, with disastrous results. But the whole operation went off like clockwork, and the right people with the right equipment were at the right place at the right time, in large part because of the careful, by-the-book planning of Thomas Masterman Hardy.

The fact that the victory was accomplished without the firing of a single gun—not even a pistol—and that the only persuasion employed was reason and good sense spiced with a few threats, is characteristic of Hardy. His foresight had closed off any chance of retreat—or hope of reinforcement—early in the day. His simple but utterly compelling message to Major Putnam forestalled any chance of unnecessary and wasteful heroics. The terms of surrender were precise and unequivocal. The letter to the American authorities on the mainland, signed by Fitsherbert, but undoubtedly approved by Hardy and possibly written by him as well, was equally clear and unambiguous.

A piece of land, the property of a proud sovereign nation, had been annexed by another without confusion, without resistance, and, it bears repeating, without the loss of blood.

There was nothing brilliant about the conquest of Moose Island, but there was a simplicity, a humanity, an admirably workmanlike quality to it that was the hallmark of Thomas Masterman Hardy.

One additional fact is probably also worth noting. Eastport made no attempt to defend itself, any more than had Pettipaug, and the British had reason to believe that New Englanders would always bow to force.

Of all the people who played a part in the tangled affairs that led eventually to the Battle of Stonington, surely the most shadowy, the most ephemeral and curious, must be James Stewart, his majesty's erstwhile consul in New London.

Stewart was one of those charming types so typical of the Regency period, displaying the manners of a courtier, the scruples of a highwayman, and the social buoyancy of a cork. In an age that admired audacity, he was among the most audacious, constantly overreaching his station, always in some kind of hot water for misappropriation of funds or abuse of trust or some other malfeasance or misconduct, yet always ready with some faintly spurious excuse that more or less explained the impropriety, or at least mitigated the consequences and smoothed over the more outrageous excesses.

Stewart's readiest defense lay in the presumption that he was a gentleman, and that the charges leveled against him simply could not be taken seriously and were painful for a man of such gentility to bear. As one traces through the checkered trail of papers left in the Admiralty and Foreign Office by this minor diplomat, one finds repeated accusations and suspicions concerning his character and motivations but never any proof of guilt—or innocence, for that matter. His hurt tone and bruised sensibilities are everywhere, but his promised defense never appears.

At the time of his expulsion from New London, he was already under a cloud as far as the Foreign Office was concerned for his alleged mishandling of the valuable merchant-shipping protections with which he had been entrusted. He was later to assert that when he left New London he took with him all the papers that explained any seeming mishandling of the protections. Unfortunately, after leaving New London aboard the *Atalanta* bound for Halifax, he was shipwrecked and lost all his papers, including his commission and his money. Doubtless he lost the exhibits that would have exonerated him on the matter of the missing protections as well.

The story of the shipwreck comes from a petition Stewart presented many years after the war in one of his attempts to obtain a pension. Another application for favors filed much closer to the time in question—in 1815—alleges that after leaving New London in 1813 on an unspecified vessel, he was captured and robbed by an American privateer in the West Indies. The results would have been very much the same as the disaster on the *Atalanta*—his papers, commission, and money all lost to him forever. It is difficult for even the most charitable observer to accept both disasters, particularly since either one would have served the purpose; but such confusions and contradictions are typical of James Stewart's accounts of his career, which are almost invariably self-contradictory as well as self-serving.

Despite the confusion about whether he lost his papers to a privateer in the West Indies or in a shipwreck in the North Atlantic, what happened next is well documented. As Stewart described in his 1829 petition, he "tendered his services to the Right Honorable Sir John Borlase Warren [commander in chief of the North American Station] to procure money and fresh provisions for His Majesty's forces."

Thus we find Stewart in Bermuda early in 1814 as a victualer and sometimes banker for the Royal Navy. (Admiral Warren had moved his headquarters south from Halifax. Bermuda was not only warmer, but it also kept the admiral away from General Prevost, who was always demanding action in favor of his Canadian troops.) Virtually every important ship on the station stopped at Bermuda for orders and refitting. Stewart's job was to handle the victualing of these ships. Not surprisingly in the early nineteenth century victualers ranked right with ships' pursers as the most villainous and infamous figures in the entire Royal Navy. In the time-honored tradition of war profiteering and general waterfront skulduggery, the victualer had any number of ways of cheating to improve his profits—short-weighting, mislabeling, adulterating, passing off rotten or weevil-infested foodstuffs as fit rations (the sailors did not mind maggots, but weevils were far too bitter for most tastes). For all of Stewart's protestations, his was really not a gentleman's occupation.

By March, when Admiral Cochrane replaced Warren, Stewart was attempting to enlarge his activities. When the new commander of the fleet ran his eyes over a recently copied order, his sharp eyes caught an apparent "mistake" whereby James Stewart was appointed victualer for the entire fleet, including those portions of it stationed off New London, the Chesapeake, and as far south as the Mississippi. Cochrane quickly countermanded the order with a crisp, no-nonsense series of memos.

Undaunted, Stewart's inventive mind came to his rescue and gave him an idea for an entirely new way to serve king and crown. To his position as victualer he proposed to add that of banker. The scheme was complicated but well thought out. As victualer to the fleet in Bermuda, he was obliged to accept treasury bills in payment for his supplies. As long as he dealt with British merchants, these bills were virtually the same as cash, and Stewart's plan was to open up a retailing operation and exchange his treasury bills for British goods—fashions and fabrics, furniture and books and medicines—that he would then smuggle into the United States and sell for cash. He would then sell the American cash to the Royal Navy, which needed it to buy food from American farmers. The navy would of course pay him in treasury bills. The margin between what he spent in treasury bills for smuggling merchandise and what he managed to get back from the navy in treasury bills in exchange for his dollars and cents would be his profit, which was likely to be enormous and would, of course, supplement the considerable profits he was already amassing as victualer.

To implement his scheme, Stewart conceived the idea of sailing north to New London in a ship loaded with contraband goods and of establishing a permanent base on some island off the coast. There he would carry out his trading in a businesslike way, accompanied by his wife and children, whom he had not seen for over a year.

Cochrane eagerly approved Stewart's idea, arranging for him to catch a ride north with Rear Admiral Sir Henry Hotham, who was scheduled to sail on the last day of July for New London.

James Stewart was undoubtedly a happy man when he stood on deck of the *Forth* on 31 July 1814 and watched the sailors high in the rigging setting the sails for the trip to New London, 750 miles to the northwest. He was going home and would soon be in the fond embrace of his wife and seven children again. And he was once more deeply involved in just the sort of shady business at which he excelled, an enterprise that added a new dignity to the smuggling trade and made it, for once, a position fit for a gentleman.

Hardy's invasion of northern Maine sent shock waves throughout the United States. To the New England states, the conquest of Moose Island marked the first overt British action directed against their area, and to the nation as a whole it signaled a new determination on Britain's part to win the war on favorable terms.

The prospects were chilling. For New Englanders, lulled by the gentle cosseting of a Britain that needed their foodstuffs, Hardy's land grab was a terrifying whiff of the true power of the enemy that up until now had limited itself to the Canadian frontier and the southern states. Boston newspapers, finding it increasingly difficult to maintain their resolutely pro-British stance, sputtered in anxious confusion as they tried to justify Hardy's attack and calm their readers simultaneously.

After Eastport, what? Hardy, having left a permanent garrison of eight hundred troops in Passamaquoddy to guard England's newest possession, sailed westward with his squadron down the coast, spreading alarm before him. All of New England watched anxiously. Every harbor, every vulnerable place, every inhabited island along his course made preparations for his arrival.

Boston was in a panic. As the capital of New England, Boston was a prime target for attack. The moral and economic effect of its capture or destruction would be catastrophic. Although Boston was one of the principal shipbuilding centers on the coast, Bostonians knew that their city and its harbor were virtually defenseless because Governor Strong had for two solid years opposed the war in every way open to him, refusing to make even the most cursory efforts to guard his state against attack from the sea. Unfortunately, the British knew of Boston's weakness. In a desperate effort to strengthen fortification, militiamen hurriedly readied and manned two forts in Boston harbor, Fort Warren on Governor's Island and Fort Independence on Castle Island. Elsewhere along the coast citizens hurriedly armed little Fort Lily, at Gloucester, and strengthened and garrisoned Fort Pickering, near Salem, and Fort Sewell, at Marblehead.

As the *Ramillies* and her attendant vessels swept west toward the short New Hampshire border, the American Brigadier General Montgomery ordered every tenth man in his brigade to repair to Portsmouth for its defense. He personally took command there, deliberately deploying the men so as to make their presence highly visible from the sea. He wanted Hardy to see every soldier and to make him imagine thousands more were waiting just out of sight. General Montgomery was under no illusions as to the importance of Portsmouth. He and his men were not there to defend the city but to protect the USS *Washington*.

When Hardy's squadron passed by Portsmouth in the last days of July, the commodore undoubtedly examined the coast in minute detail. He would have seen dimly the bulk of the *Washington* still obscured by the overarching building house, and he would have noticed Montgomery's militia. Being human, Hardy undoubtedly entertained the idea of organizing a dash into Portsmouth, a lightning strike to destroy the *Washington*. A raid would have been an audacious move, and Hardy, for all his quiet reserve, was still a man who understood the meaning of glory.

By any dispassionate calculation, Hardy was far and away the most effective officer on the North American Station. For fifteen months he had blocked Decatur and neutralized two large frigates along with a sloop of war. With one quick, decisive move he had just started the reconquest of the United States. To add the destruction of the *Washington* to such a list of achievements would have been a tempting thought. But the commodore eventually turned his mind away from dreams of glory and profit to the more prosaic issue of preparing his squadron for the passage around Cape Ann.

Instead of a raid on the *Washington*, which would have dealt the Americans a devastating blow, what lay in Hardy's immediate future was a totally pointless attack upon an unimportant little village in Connecticut of no strategic significance whatsoever.

Back in the summer of 1813 an association of New York City business leaders, known as the Common Council and dedicated to furthering the industry and development of the city, became acutely aware of how much the welfare of their city was tied to that of the far smaller community of New London, down at the other end of the sound. Decatur's incarceration in the Thames had turned New London into the linchpin of the blockade of New York; therefore, in the judgment of the Common Council, helping rid New London of its blockading squadron would benefit New York. In this spirit of neighborly concern the council furnished several hundred dollars to a Mr. Berrian to construct a torpedo boat specifically designed for use against the British off New London.

The pseudonymous Mr. Berrian first tested his specially designed vessel in a trial run in the sound at the end of the summer of 1813; but as we have seen, the enemy discovered him and he was only just able to avoid capture. With the return of warm weather, and fully confident of his craft, which he named the *Turtle* in honor of Bushnell's Revolutionary War original, Mr. Berrian was ready for more serious action.

A journalist's description of the *Turtle*'s departing from New York gives a pretty good idea of its overall appearance and capabilities: "A new invented torpedo boat resembling a turtle floating just above the surface of the water, and sufficiently roomy to carry nine passengers within, having on her back a coat of mail, consisting of three large bombs, which could be discharged by machinery, so as to bid defiance to any attack by barges, left this city one day last week to blow up some of the enemy's ships off New London. At one end of the boat projected a long pole, underwater, with a torpedo fastened to it, which as she approached the enemy in the night, was to be poked under the bottom of a seventy-four, and then let off. . . ."

On 26 June 1814 the *Turtle* was heading toward Gardiner's Bay to attack the blockading fleet when she was ignominiously washed ashore by a gale at Horton's Point, near Southold, Long Island. One member of the crew who attempted to swim to shore during the storm drowned, but the others survived by staying with the vessel until it grounded. By that time the British had spotted the *Turtle*, and barges from the frigate *Maidstone* and sloop *Sylph* were sent in to destroy it. The crew, with the help of local farmers and militia, frantically tried to dismantle the craft to protect whatever secrets it might have contained. They managed to remove the spiral wheel by which the boat moved, as well as the rudder and crank, but when British marines came on shore, the Americans were forced to retreat.

Several British officers made their way to the strange craft and examined it warily, cautiously checking for any live explosive devices. Then they began carefully sketching it and measuring its dimensions. She was twenty-three feet long with a breadth of ten feet. Her top was arched like a turtle shell and immensely strong. She had the scantling of a 100-ton ship, which supported wooden top planking eight inches thick that was in turn cased over with half-inch plate iron. Lieutenant Bowen of the *Maidstone* reported that she was "so strongly and well constructed that a shot cannot penetrate, or can anything grapple with it."

Bowen's report, which generally confirmed and augmented the American newspaper accounts, stated that the semisubmersible drew six feet of water, leaving only one foot of boat exposed above the surface. This ironclad deck was painted a dirty white to camouflage it. According to the British, the *Turtle* had a crew of twelve, rather than the nine reported by the American journalist. While the newspaper story suggested a torpedo boom of some sort, Lieutenant Bowen reported that she was designed to tow five floating torpedoes, each on its own lead. He was unable to explain how the crew would use these weapons against enemy ships.

The British had been acutely aware of the *Turtle* for some time and had kept a close eye on its construction in New York. They were convinced that it was the brainchild of Robert Fulton and referred to it as such. More likely, while the torpedoes it carried might have been Fulton's, the boat itself was another man's design. At the time Berrian was busily constructing the *Turtle*, Fulton had more than enough to handle, developing not only his steam-powered catamaran but another submarine as well.

After gleaning all the information possible from the beached *Turtle*, Lieutenant Bowen ordered an explosive charge placed on board, and moments later with a loud bang the *Turtle* disappeared into splinters.

As Captain Burdett of the *Mainstone* reported, "To Lieutenant Bowen I am again indebted for the very skillful manner in which he performed this most desireable piece of service, which probably has

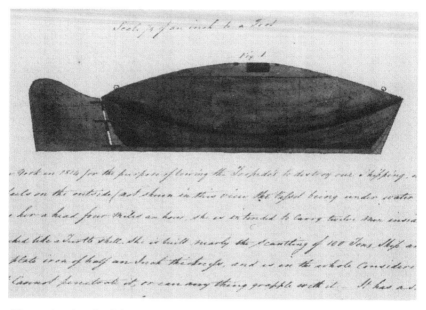

Watercolor sketch of the American submersible washed up on a Long Island beach on 26 June 1814. British Lieutenant Bowen's rendering is maddeningly short on details, probably because the Americans had been able to remove elements of the propulsion system and torpedo apparatus prior to the arrival of the enemy. (Public Record Office, London)

saved the lives of many gallant and valuable subjects of His Majesty in this treacherous mode of warfare."

The two watercolor sketches of the *Turtle* now in the British Public Records Office are a unique reminder of that long-ago conflict. The destruction of the semisubmersible on Horton Beach marks the end of torpedo warfare in the War of 1812. She was the final entrant in a strange, motley parade of gimcrackery and genius, the last of a line of terror-craft created out of a potent but dangerous mixture of Yankee ingenuity and lust for prize money.

Almost every modern reader is struck by the apparent anachronisms of submarines and torpedoes in the War of 1812, but in fact the true anachronisms in that war were not the submarines but their targets, the great sailing ships, the stately but unwieldy ships-of-the-line, which represented a technology that reached back to the Roman triremes and was about to disappear. Even as the smoke cleared from the wreckage of the *Turtle*, a hundred miles due west in New York Robert Fulton was completing his first steam gunboat (the same one that Decatur endorsed in his letter to the secretary of the navy), which would in a stroke render obsolete any ship of war that depended solely on wind power. Along with his steam gunboat, Fulton was still very much involved with undersea war as well. His plans for a radically different kind of submarine, the *Mute*, were already in the hands of the Navy Department. This craft was to be a completely different kind of submarine, and it prefigured the familiar modern subs by abandoning the clumsy torpedo (which, as noted, was simply a mine) and employing a waterproof cannon that could fire underwater—much as a modern torpedo—directly from the attacking vessel into the target.

America's leading role in the development of submarines over the past two centuries is a long and curiously intense participation, as if the United States had some special need for the weapon unperceived by the other naval powers of the world. The list of America's underwater pioneers stretches from Bushnell to Fulton to Holland (who built the first modern submarine) to Lake (who sold the kaiser his first U-Boat . . . built in New Jersey!) to the first nuclear-powered submarine (christened *Nautilus* in homage to Fulton)—a straight, undeviating line of Yankee involvement, Yankee commitment. The development of the terrifying Trident submarines, each one carrying five times the total explosive power of World War II, is only the most recent expression of a long tradition.

The fact that the Tridents are built within sight of New London, and their crews are trained in the same waters where so much early submarine history transpired in the War of 1812, adds an almost poetic subtext to the American tradition.

9

Early August 1814

*The death of Midshipman Powers—Stonington
is selected for destruction—the first Battle of
Stonington in 1775—meeting at Ghent—America's
darkest hour*

IN the first week of August 1814 there was a decided increase in British naval activity on Long Island Sound, and those who lived along its shores experienced a corresponding increase in general anxiety. Although Admiral Cochrane's draconian orders "to destroy and lay waste" were still secret from the general public, the details of Hardy's action at Eastport were enough to make Americans nervous.

More enemy vessels seemed to arrive every day. The activity on the water intensified. More barges scurried back and forth with messages. More vessels loaded and off-loaded supplies close to shore, in plain sight of land.

An eerily prescient news item under a dateline of Stonington, (Con.), ran in *Niles' Weekly Register*. "This harbor is frequented by the enemy," it began gloomily. "We daily expect an attack." In fact the article overstated the situation. No British vessels had anchored in the harbor, but enough "neutral" Swedish vessels were trading with the Americans while working openly with the blockading fleet to make everyone uneasy. No evidence exists that the British even contemplated an attack on Stonington at that early date, but the people who lived in the village, who in truth had done little to warrant a British attack, still felt anxious.

The villagers were intensely aware of their own vulnerability and conscious of what a tempting target their village made. The boatyards in Lambert's Cove almost always included merchantmen or privateers that would make valuable prizes for anyone willing to come in and get them. In addition, just as the buildup of the blockading fleet was reaching its peak, fate provided the British with an excuse—if they wanted one—to attack the village.

On 30 July 1814 an unnamed American privateer disguised as a merchantman stood in from the sea and, rounding Montauk Point, headed for the north shore of Long Island. In all probability she was returning from a cruise and was bound for her home port. Captain Paget of the *Superb*, 74, anchored in Gardiner's Bay, dispatched a barge to investigate. The barge was under command of an eighteen-year-old midshipman named Thomas Barratt Powers.

On coming alongside the privateer, the midshipman was confronted by about fifty sailors—almost the entire crew—standing at the gunwales, heavily armed and in a fighting mood. Powers immediately realized that he was outnumbered and outgunned, and adopting the accepted etiquette of the sea, he removed his hat as a token of surrender.

One member of the crew—later reports claimed he was a Dutchman—acting without orders, leveled his musket and shot Powers through the head. The captain of the privateer, fearing retribution from the British navy, immediately changed course, brought the dead midshipman into Stonington harbor, and ordered his crew to turn the body over to the militia. That night, under cover of darkness, the privateer slipped out of the harbor and resumed its previous course, keeping its home port a secret from the British.

Meanwhile, in Stonington, the Reverend Ira Hart, chaplain of the 30th Regiment, arranged for the burial of the midshipman with full military honors. After a ceremony replete with muffled drums, a guard of honor, and a final volley of musketry in salute, the village sent a message to Captain Paget aboard the *Superb*, informing the British of all that had occurred. For a day or so no one was sure whether the British believed Stonington's protestations of innocence in the midshipman's death, or whether they might take the opportunity to revenge themselves upon the village.

In due course it became clear that Captain Paget held Stonington blameless, and eventually he and his officers subscribed the money to erect a monument over Powers's grave. The marker stands in the Stonington cemetery to this day, inscribed with a poem dedicated to the fallen youth:

The spirit fled, yet 'ere it bounded free
To the fair regions of eternity,
His earthly stay had been so pure, so chaste,
That nature smiled to view her heavenly grace.
His life departed, yet 'ere that expired,
That life, that virtue warmed & glory fired,
The brightest ray of earthly honor gleamed,
And round his parting breath in radiance beamed,
Brightly it shone til life's last ebb was given,
Then upward fled, with fame to plead his cause in heaven.

Who, one wonders, wrote such florid lines, replete with all the ritual code words of gallantry and morbid sorrow customary to the age? Was the verse from a favorite source long since forgotten? Was it left to the minister or even the stonecutter to find something appropriate to the young man's resting place? Or, and this is most likely, was the poem the work of one of Powers's messmates? Poetry was still a common form of expression at that time, and a saddened and anonymous wordsmith thousands of miles from home might have found a tiny immortality on a remote Connecticut gravestone.

The death of Midshipman Powers was no more meaningful or meaningless than a hundred other incidents that happen every day in the course of a war. What significance it might hold comes only from its proximity in time to the little battle that was about to take place in Stonington. It is evidence that the people on both sides of the battle could share the anguish of a young man dead before his time and had no reason to hate one another. In many ways the Battle of Stonington—and the whole War of 1812, for that matter—was a conflict without enemies.

Over the weekend that followed the death of Midshipman Powers, three enormous ships-of-the-line, accompanied by frigates, brigs, and attendant small craft, entered the sound. Rear Admiral Sir Henry Hotham, until recently Captain of the Fleet under Cochrane in Bermuda, and now overall commander in charge of the northern arm of the fleet, was making his first appearance on the American coast.

By Sunday, 7 August, the enemy's vessels visible in Gardiner's Bay included two 90-gun ships, four 74s, four frigates, and a brig, in addition to the vessels off New London. The force was clearly more powerful than necessary if its only purpose was to maintain the blockade.

That week, Royal Marines landed at Montauk and ordered the farming families living there to move ten miles west, taking with them only what they could carry. Was Montauk to be the next annexation? Nobody could say, but undoubtedly something was in the air. As the Connecticut *Courant* reported, "The late movements of the enemy have excited apprehensions that some important expedition is in contemplation."

What, in fact, was in the air was a massive attack upon the entire coast of the United States, or at least as much of it as the British could practicably threaten, precipitated by Admiral Cochrane's order of 18 July. Cochrane had already joined Cockburn in the Chesapeake for the attack on Washington, scheduled for two weeks hence, and that raid was to be the forerunner of any number of other incursions, depending only on the arrival of men and supplies from Europe. So far only enough troops had arrived to handle the Washington adventure, but the British were already building barracks in Bermuda to house twenty-five thousand more soldiers, due any day from the Peninsula. Cochrane had also instituted a search for American pilots for every major harbor and river from Maine to Georgia to be placed on the navy's payroll so that he might have the ability to strike anywhere that suited his purpose.

That same Sunday, 7 August, in the midst of the naval buildup and the nervous speculations of those on shore, Admiral Hotham hoisted his broad pennant on the frigate *Forth* and, after crossing the sound and anchoring off New London, sent in a message to the authorities demanding that they release Mrs. James Stewart and her children forthwith into the custody of Mr. James Stewart, who was at that moment on board his frigate.

Not waiting for a reply, Hotham ordered the *Forth* back to Gardiner's Bay, where he was busy with the hundreds of details involved in taking over a new command. He was also anxious to discuss matters with his predecessor, Captain Sir Thomas Masterman Hardy, who had lately arrived from Maine aboard the *Ramillies* and now awaited a meeting with the admiral.

In due time, an answer to Hotham's demand concerning Mrs. Stewart arrived from the New London authorities.

> Military District No. 2
> New London
> 7th August 1814

Sir:—I have received your letter of this date, and regret that it is not in my power to comply with the wishes of Mr. Stewart in relation to the removal of his family.

Your letter on this subject shall be immediately transmitted to the Government of the United States, and it will give me great pleasure to have it in my powers to communicate a decision favourable to Mr. Stewart.

> I am Sir,
> very Respectfully
> your obedient Servant
> T. H. Cushing
> Brig. Genl.

Cushing's note makes it clear that as early as 7 August the British were fully aware of the local-versus-national government complications involved in Mrs. Stewart's situation.

On both that Sunday and the following Monday, 8 August, Hotham held important meetings with Thomas Hardy. Protocol might have dictated that the meetings take place on the commanding officer's vessel; but since the *Forth* was a frigate, and Hotham was using her only as a convenience until he should transfer his flag to the *Superb*, it is likely that the two men arranged to hold their meetings in the relatively greater comfort of the *Ramillies*.

There is no record of their discussions, so that what follows is to some extent speculative. But the subsequent actions and statements of the two men make it likely that their talks would have followed along the lines suggested here.

These meetings were not simply discussions between an admiral and one of his captains. Hotham outranked Hardy, but as with Hardy's discussions with Cockburn, the junior officer was in many ways the admiral's equal, possibly even superior. He was, after all, the anointed, the keeper of the flame. There was, moreover, a practical as well as mystical side to the deference that Hardy could command. Thanks to his closeness to Nelson he had become the beneficiary of certain social advantages, and even admirals took note of a man who had taken tea privately with the king of England.

One of the first topics of conversation would have been Hardy's new orders, which would have arrived from Bermuda in the *Forth*. He was relieved of all responsibilities in the north and ordered to proceed to the Chesapeake and to report to the commander in chief. Hotham, due to his closeness to Cochrane, would have been thoroughly conversant with the planned attack on Washington and would have explained as much to Hardy, perhaps speculating on the possibility that Hardy would be replacing Cockburn. (Subsequently this proved to be the case, but it was after the attack on Washington.)

Doubtless they discussed the increase in military activity along the coast—the greater size and number of ships, the greater number of troops and support elements—the whole shift of war-making activity brought about by the fall of Napoleon. It would have been inevitable, at this point, to touch upon Cochrane's order calling for a wholesale attack on the civilian populations along the coast. This would have been the first time that Hardy had heard of it, and how deeply such an order would have gone against his grain we can only imagine.

They would also have discussed Hotham's new position as commander of the northern blockade, particularly as it related to Long Island Sound, the area that Hardy had so long overseen. Undoubtedly Hotham would have numerous questions—particularly concerning the nature of torpedoes and submarine defenses.

Hotham might well have suggested that while Cochrane's order to attack the coast was designed to aid the upcoming Canadian offensive, the squadron in the sound had its own reasons for initiating such actions, harrassed as it was for all these months by maritime guerrillas. Cochrane's order was tailor-made to curb the notorious activity of the torpedoists. Did Hardy know where the torpedoists operated from? Did the conspiracy have a center?

Hotham would have pointed out that Hardy, straight from Passamaquoddy, was precisely the man best suited to strike the first blow against those misguided and dangerous terrorists. It was only appropriate that the commander who had maintained a fair and evenhanded control over the area for almost two years, despite the uncivilized horror of torpedo warfare, should strike the first blow under Cochrane's order. Not incidentally, Hotham might have suggested that the bomb ship

Terror, which had accompanied the *Ramillies* south from Maine, would be a particularly fortuitous addition to the attacking force.

Was Hotham issuing an order? In a way, perhaps. In another way, no. Inevitably, an order would eventually pass from Hotham to Hardy, couched in the familiar decorous phrases of naval etiquette, but the reasonable assumption is that Hotham would give Hardy the right to decide what the order was to be. Hardy, after all, knew the territory, and Hotham did not. The conversation would in all probability have broken off at this point to allow Hardy to consult his intelligence sources and to put together a reasonable plan of attack.

And now we can imagine Hardy alone, making his decision. Cochrane's order is explicit. Attack. And so Hardy is forced to take a step totally out of keeping with his character.

He examines the charts—the beautifully engraved charts published in London forty years earlier under the title of the Atlantic Neptune—and considers his options. He can definitely identify only three places with torpedo activity. One of them is New York City, the home of Mr. Robert Fulton. But New York is an impossible target— perhaps the best defended harbor in the world.

Then, at the eastern end of the sound, there are Sag Harbor on Long Island and the Hornet's Nest up the Mystic River in Connecticut. He quickly discards the possibility of attacking Sag Harbor. No torpedo incidents connected with the whole of East Hampton Township had occurred since he threatened to destroy the place following his capture of Joshua Penny the previous year. Destroying Sag Harbor after it had so assiduously followed his orders would be inherently unfair.

The Hornet's Nest was undoubtedly a more legitimate target— Hardy's spies would at least have heard rumors of Jeremiah Holmes and his confederates—but the location was well defended, and the chance of stranding his attacking vessels—particularly the deep sailing *Terror*—in the shallows was very real.

New London? Hardy could vividly remember the *Eagle*, the stories of the mysterious gentleman from Norwich, the nearly successful attack on the *La Hogue*. There was a certain justice in selecting New London as a target. But Hardy could also remember the public promises he had made just the week before he chased Decatur up the Thames, promises not to attack unless specifically so ordered. Could he, in all honor, claim such an exigency at this point? Not really.

Besides, New London as a target presented complications. James Stewart's family lived there, and Hotham had already made overtures to get them back. Strike New London as a candidate.

The list lengthened, as did the objections to each location. Saybrook and Pettipaug were both known for their blockade running and privateering, but each was heavily fortified or otherwise difficult to get at. Groton Long Point was inoffensive. Black Point was not even a target. Watch Hill was unapproachable, and Weekapaug had nothing to do with the war. The Pawcatuck River was inaccessible because of the shallows of the bay at its mouth.

The village of Stonington, more by default than for any logical reason, became a more and more likely target. It was not known for torpedoes, but it had a tenuous relationship to its guilty neighbor, the Hornet's Nest. Both communities were part of the same township. As a practical matter, Stonington was simply easier to attack than any other place. It stuck out into the sound like a jetty, with water on three sides. The village might have some defenses, but they could hardly be very effective, given the vulnerable location.

If the issue had been his alone to decide, Hardy would probably have rejected an attack on Stonington as more trouble than it was worth. But Cochrane's orders were clear. He wanted any sort of diversion to help General Prevost's army in Canada. "You are hereby required and directed to destroy and lay waste such towns and districts upon the coast as you may find assailable." Orders were orders, and on that basis an attack on Stonington was as good as an attack anywhere else.

The following day, Monday, 8 August, Hardy presented his plans to Hotham, who endorsed them with enthusiasm. Hotham called in his secretary and dictated the order to lay waste the village of Stonington. If Hardy had any doubts about the raid, he kept them to himself and went about the business of organizing the attack for Tuesday.

Hardy was probably aware that there were two different Stoningtons—the township, which was big and the village (or borough), which was small. The town, which at the time was about twice the size it is today, contained several different communities, including Milltown in the north (birthplace of Jeremiah Holmes), Head-of-Mystic at the top of the river, and the community the British called the

Hornet's Nest at the mouth of the river (where Jeremiah Holmes lived). In addition there was the Borough of Stonington on Stonington Point. Although an integral part of the township, forming the largest single community within it, the borough was a separate political unit governed by a warden and burgesses elected by the villagers. In 1814 it consisted of a little over a hundred homes, with a population of about eight hundred people, most of whom were involved in fishing, shipbuilding, and trading. It was the highly vulnerable borough, rather than the much larger town, that Hardy proposed to attack.

Unbeknownst to Hardy, the village he had slated for destruction had already experienced a British attack in a previous war. That was in 1775, when Stonington had successfully defended itself against the British frigate *Rose* in the early days of the American Revolution. The proud memory of that incident was to prove of decisive significance in the action to come.

Like most communities on the Connecticut coast, Stonington was made up almost entirely of English stock, the descendents of the Protestant Levelers, Diggers, Baptists, and Fifth Monarchists who had formed the heart of Cromwell's revolution and had come across the sea to build a new life as far away as possible from royal authority. Those first settlers were an unquestionably revolutionary breed, the first real democrats of the modern era. After a century and more in the New World, the burning religious conviction that had animated the first migrants may have cooled, but their equally strong belief in personal freedom thrived. When the revolt of the American colonies against Great Britain finally erupted in 1775, the citizens along the coast of New England, including those in Stonington, were among the first—and the most fervent—to take up the cause of revolution.

By early summer of 1775, a year before the signing of the Declaration of Independence, the major portion of the British army in North America lay under siege in Boston, imprisoned by a ragtag army of Yankees under the patrician command of George Washington. The siege was so secure that the city was experiencing a severe shortage of food, with both military and civilians limited to starvation rations. To alleviate the situation, the British navy dispatched Captain James Wallace, of the frigate *Rose*, 20 guns, to scour the Rhode Island and Connecticut shorelines for provisions.

Wallace set sail with two other vessels under his command, the *Swan* and *King-fisher*, and quickly established himself as the terror of Long Island Sound. His little squadron blockaded New London harbor for a time and sank or captured any number of American craft by gunfire and acts of piracy. Wallace preferred to attack offshore islands, where the militia presented less of a threat. By late summer his squadron had grown to nine vessels, thanks to several prizes, and with these he made a grand attack on Fishers Island and carried off a large herd of cattle, more than a thousand sheep, and other provisions. Similar raids followed on Gardiner's Island and Plum Island.

A few miles to the east, the farmers on Block Island were well aware of Wallace's depredations and feared for their own livestock. Early in August they shipped their cattle across Block Island Sound to Stonington, herding the animals ashore and putting them to pasture at Quanaduck Cove, just north of the village.

Wallace learned of this shipment from local Tories, and on 30 August 1775 he brought the *Rose* off Stonington Point and sent in a barge, demanding the Block Island cattle. Without hesitation, the villagers refused. (This was the part of the story the villagers most cherished—the forthright refusal of brave men to bow to authority.)

Captain Wallace then ordered one of his tenders to seize the cattle and anything else the crew could find. In response, the local militia hastily assembled and marched down to Brown's wharf, where the enemy was attempting to land. As it happened, the militia were armed with Queen Anne muskets, considerably more accurate than the normal issue and almost as good as rifles at long distances. They were able to inflict severe casualties and forced the landing party back into the boat.

An outraged Wallace realized that further landings were not possible, but he was determined to punish the insolent colonists. He warped the *Rose* to a position where her broadside faced the village; and setting springs on the anchor cables to stabilize his ship, he ordered a methodical, deliberate cannonading of Stonington that continued without pause throughout the rest of the morning and into the late afternoon.

In the light of Captain Hardy's subsequent attack thirty-nine years later, it is interesting to tally the damage inflicted by Wallace. In the course of the action, virtually every house was hit, some suffering considerable damage. There was only one human casualty, a

Jonathan Weaver, Jr., who was wounded but later recovered. Considering the intensity and duration of the barrage, one might have expected greater destruction, until we remember that Wallace's gunners were limited to heavy iron shot. Such cannonballs can be devastating against wooden ships, battering holes in their thick hulls and causing them to sink. But wooden houses, of course, cannot sink.

Wallace called off the bombardment the following morning—possibly because he could see how ineffective it was. But he was not yet ready to give up on the Block Island cattle, so his squadron hovered off the point for several days before finally sailing away empty-handed.

The *Rose*'s unsuccessful raid on Stonington marked the first time in the Revolution that the colonists repulsed a Royal Navy force, and the memory of the attack and the brave response to it was a treasured story, told and retold often enough in the village to take on the aura of legend. The anniversary of the raid, and the glorious defense put up by the villagers, was celebrated every year with sermons in the church and proud toasts in the tavern. It had been, all agreed, Stonington's finest hour.

One can only wonder whether Hardy, had he known the story of the *Rose* and of Stonington's proud defiance, might have selected a different target.

On 8 August, the same day that Hardy and Hotham agreed on plans to attack Stonington, a far more significant meeting got underway in Ghent, Belgium. At one o'clock in the afternoon a team of British diplomats, after months of delays and cancellations, finally sat down with their American counterparts at a table in the Hotel des Pays Bas to discuss terms for a possible peace between the two nations.

Ever since the fall of Napoleon on 31 March, the London press had been intoxicated with Britain's success in Europe and heady with euphoria. With every passing day the editorialists grew more bellicose toward the United States, more vindictive in their demands that America be punished, and increasingly insistent that Britain must gain some tangible reward for having been victimized by the odious Yankees.

The vituperation in the papers reached new levels of abusiveness, even by the standards of the English press. The *Times* habitually referred to President Madison as a liar and impostor. The *Post* said of him that he was "a despot in disguise; a miniature imitation" and miserable tool of Bonaparte, claiming that Napoleon actually wrote

Madison's Annual Message to Congress. The *Sun*, only four days before negotiations opened in Belgium, made reference to "that contemptible wretch Madison, and his gang."

Far more serious than the personal attacks on political leaders were the demands, often reflecting the opinions of cabinet ministers and others in power, that America must be kept in its place and any future American expansion must be severely limited and in some cases reversed. We have already seen something of these plans to curtail the growth of the United States in Hardy's attack on Moose Island and in the programs for Indian buffer states in the Great Lakes region. If Britain had met only half of these goals, the United States today might well be only a quarter its present size and the history of the world, particularly in the twentieth century, vastly different.

Lord Castlereagh, the minister generally considered one of the more moderate figures in the government relative to the United States, believed strongly that the peace treaty should incorporate the goals demanded in the press. His secret instructions of 28 July to his negotiating team, on the eve of their departure to Ghent, included a long list of specific territorial concessions to be demanded of the United States. As an example of his determination in this regard, and his utter faith in the efficacy of Britain's military might, Castlereagh's instructions, which he wrote long before any word could possibly have reached London of Hardy's success at Passamaquoddy, specifically list that area of Maine as unquestionably British and not subject to negotiation.

At Ghent the Americans realized almost as soon as they sat down at the table that the reason for Britain's repeated delays in agreeing to a conference was Castlereagh's determination to establish a strong military and territorial superiority before beginning any negotiations, so that his people might be able to deal from strength.

The Americans, who had started the war with a list of grievances concerning everything from impressment to unfair business practices, quickly came to understand that they were in such a weak position that they could not possibly win their way on any of their complaints, and that the best they could possibly hope for was to negotiate a return to the *status quo ante bellum*, in which both parties would agree to simply ignore the war and pretend it had never happened. The British, on the other hand, made it clear that any negotiating must start with a recognition on both sides of the *uti possidetus*, that is to say that the possession of territory, including territory taken in the course of military action, was to be considered permanent. Since the negotiations were likely to last for months, and since the British forces were on the offensive on every front, a distinct British victory, both military and diplomatic, was almost assured.

The day before the Battle of Stonington, 8 August 1814, was for Americans perhaps the darkest day in the entire war up to that point, and one of the darkest days in the history of the United States. With the destruction of Washington only a fortnight away, with the plans for the conquest of New Orleans and the opening up of the Mississippi approved and moving forward, with Wellington's battle-hardened veterans on the move in Canada, and with the American negotiators facing a powerful and implacable enemy on the other side of the table, the future of the young United States looked particularly bleak.

10

The Battle:
9 August 1814

*Hardy's squadron off Stonington—his message to
the "unoffending Inhabitants"—"We shall defend
this place"—bombshells, stink pots, and rockets*

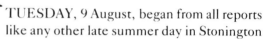

TUESDAY, 9 August, began from all reports
like any other late summer day in Stonington
Borough. On the harbor side of town, west of Water Street, men were
busy at the docks and wharves and worksheds with the endless task
of painting, pitching, and repairing their sailing vessels. The village's
two public schools were closed so that the students could help with
the harvest. At York's Tavern on the common, guests were finishing
the morning meal and making plans for the day ahead. Along the wide,
elm-shaded main street, women hung out the washing and gossiped
with neighbors.

Most of the hundred and twenty or so homes, schools, and business structures were crowded into the northern end of the peninsula
that formed the limits of the village. The southern half, leading down
to the point, was relatively undeveloped and only sparsely populated.

The only indication that day that a state of war existed in the
land was the occasional sight of one of the twenty or so militiamen
under the command of Lieutenant Samuel Hough. They were on duty
in the borough simply as a precaution. Everyone was aware of how
vulnerable Stonington was, but hardly anyone really expected an at-

146

tack. The two 18-pounders provided by the federal government to defend the borough were at that moment locked away in the armory near the common, along with what was thought to be an adequate supply of gunpowder.

Five hundred yards south of the armory on a bare rise of ground overlooking the harbor mouth stood a low breastwork, about four feet high. Here the villagers would deploy the cannon in case of danger.

Nothing unexpected marked the day until around three o'clock in the afternoon, when anyone who happened to look south would have noticed an unaccustomed sight. A small squadron of enemy vessels appeared to be working its way up Fishers Island Sound from the direction of New London. Enemy ships were a common enough sight, but to see oceangoing vessels in Fishers Island Sound was highly unusual. The sound was known for its dangerous shallows and unpredictable channels, and only the most experienced captains, sure of themselves and their ships, dared to cross it without the aid of a pilot. Invariably, the British kept their ships on the southern, deep-water side of Fishers Island and ventured into the sound proper only in barges and similar shallow-draft vessels. The little squadron now approaching from the west was proceeding slowly, presumably to allow time to take repeated soundings.

The largest vessel was a frigate, quickly identified by those familiar with the blockading fleet as the *Pactolus*, 38 guns. The squadron also included a brig, the *Dispatch*, 20 guns, and a bomb ship, which could easily be distinguished by her characteristic lack of a foremast, and her main mast stepped back to allow room in the bow for her powerful mortars.

The presence of the bomb ship was particularly worrying. Bomb ships, as the villagers well knew, never participated in sea battles but were designed and built exclusively for use against land targets. These vessels were the newest and most destructive in the Royal Navy, incorporating the most advanced ordnance technology. They usually carried two sea mortars, great squat guns that could hurl two-hundred-pound explosive shells and firebombs into enemy fortifications. The guns were so powerful and developed such a strong recoil that the hulls of the ships had to be specially braced and strengthened to withstand the terrible pounding. The British had only eighteen bomb ships in their entire navy and had given them names appropriate to their destructive nature, such as *Infernal*, *Thunder*, *Sulphur*, and *Hecla*. The one now moving up from New London was the *Terror*, which the villagers knew had been with Hardy in Maine.

The British vessels could be bound only for Stonington. The other possible target, Westerly, Rhode Island, could be reached only by crossing Pawcatuck Bay, which was too shallow even for fishing smacks and certainly couldn't handle the deep draft of a bomb ship. But why Stonington? The village had done nothing to warrant such notice from the blockading fleet.

Undoubtedly, some of the villagers wondered if the visit might have something to do with the unfortunate business of Midshipman Powers, so recently buried in the Stonington cemetery. Had someone in the Royal Navy made a dreadful mistake and, deciding the villagers were responsible for the young man's death, come to punish them for their wicked deed? The idea was possible but unlikely. They had behaved in an entirely proper manner in that sad little incident and had cooperated fully with the officers of the *Superb*.

Were these ships the prelude to an invasion? Was Fishers Island Sound the next Passamaquoddy, and Stonington the next Eastport? Again, the idea was unlikely in the extreme. Invasions required a lot more hardware—troop transports, ships-of-the-line, and the like. If the British were to invade, they would require a larger squadron than this one.

Doubtless, one image, one common memory arose independently in every mind: the memory of the attack by HMS *Rose* on Stonington in 1775. The similarity between the present circumstances and that earlier moment of pride and valor was simply too close to escape anyone's notice. The same enemy, the same number of vessels, and even the same month, thirty-nine years later.

Amos Palmer, chairman of the committee on public safety, ordered the armory unlocked and the 18-pounders moved out and installed in the breastworks. A squad of militia men under the direction of Lieutenant Hough quickly organized a team of horses and hitched them to the guns' field carriages. About five o'clock the three British vessels anchored off the point, and the *Pactolus*'s crew lowered a barge. The village leaders gathered in a knot at the point and watched the approach of the barge, which was now displaying a large white flag of truce.

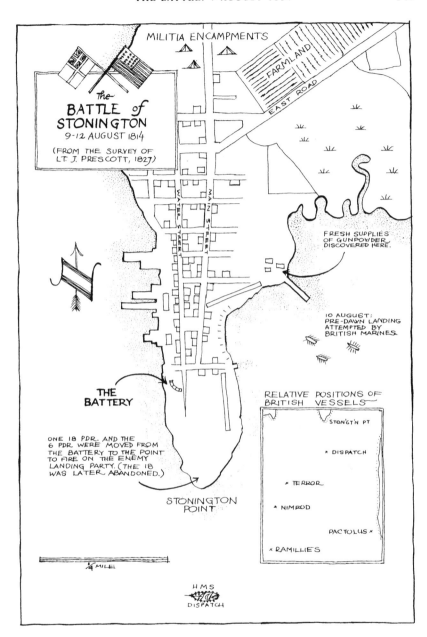

MILITIA ENCAMPMENTS

FARMLAND

EAST ROAD

The
BATTLE of
STONINGTON
9-12 AUGUST 1814

(FROM THE SURVEY OF
LT. J. PRESCOTT, 1827)

FRESH SUPPLIES
OF GUNPOWDER
DISCOVERED HERE.

10 AUGUST:
PRE-DAWN LANDING
ATTEMPTED BY
BRITISH MARINES.

THE
BATTERY

RELATIVE POSITIONS OF
BRITISH VESSELS

STON'GT'N PT

ONE 18 PDR. AND THE
6 PDR. WERE MOVED FROM
THE BATTERY TO THE POINT
TO FIRE ON THE ENEMY
LANDING PARTY. (THE 18
WAS LATER ABANDONED.)

× DISPATCH

× TERROR

× NIMROD

STONINGTON
POINT

PACTOLUS ×

× RAMILLIES

¼ MILE

H M S
DISPATCH

Map Four: Battle of Stonington

One of the magistrates suggested that it would be improper to allow the British to actually set foot on shore, so a boat was obtained, and with two magistrates on board—Captain Palmer and Dr. William Lord, the village physician—along with Lieutenant Hough, they set off to meet the enemy barge.

The two boats came alongside each other just offshore. A British lieutenant in full uniform identified himself and inquired solemnly whom he was addressing. On learning that Palmer and Lord were elected officials of the borough, and that Lieutenant Hough represented the Connecticut Militia, the British officer handed a letter to Captain Palmer, who opened and read it, along with Dr. Lord.

> His Britannic Majesty's
> Ship Pactolus. 9th August
> 1814. ½ past 5 o'clock PM

Not wishing to destroy the unoffending Inhabitants residing in the Town of Stonington, one hour is granted them from the receipt of this to remove out of the Town.

> T. M. Hardy Captain
> of H.M. Ship Ramillies

To the inhabitants of the Town
of Stonington.

This letter is the most interesting in the whole saga of the attack on Stonington (with the possible exception of the letter Hardy wrote the following day, which we will get to in due time). It is valuable as an indicator of Captain Hardy's state of mind only a few hours before the fighting began. At Eastport we saw him at his best—cool, efficient, and sure of every step, with each one of his written communications precise—if pedestrian—and clear. But his note to the "unoffending Inhabitants" of Stonington is uncharacteristically confused and ambiguous. Given Hardy's blunt directness, we would expect from him a simple, clear declaration, such as "The squadron under my command is about to bombard the village." But the threat of attack is never stated, and only clumsily implied. The lapse would be insignificant for some men, but not for the punctilious, by-the-book Hardy.

Most uncharacteristic of all, he has allowed a letter of this importance to go out with his signature both smeared and blotched. A psychiatrist might have some interesting things to say about this note.

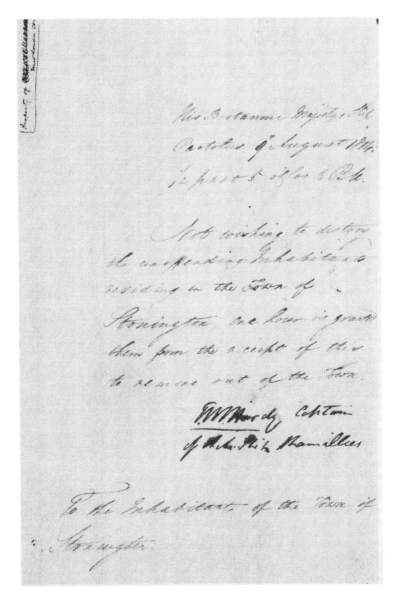

Captain Hardy sends his compliments. The 9 August letter warning the
"unoffending Inhabitants" to vacate the village was sent from the *Pactolus* and
bears evidence of hasty composition (see text). Note Hardy's blotted signature.
(Beinecke Rare Book and Manuscript Library, Yale University)

Ambiguous or not, the meaning was clear enough to the magistrates, who were stunned by the message. In spite of Hardy's apparent desire to avoid bloodshed by giving the unoffending inhabitants enough time to save their lives, the note conveyed an unexpectedly brutal finality. It was not even an ultimatum. There was no "either," no "or," no doorway lying open that might allow for discussion or compromise. It was not a threat but a sentence—a sentence of death for the village, as arbitrary and capricious as an act of God, and presented without the least attempt at justification.

As unsettling as the message itself was the signature at the bottom. How could the famous Captain Hardy put his name to such a letter? How could a man of such celebrated probity and decency, a man who had demonstrated time and again his evenhanded fairness be a party to such an unwarranted attack?

Captain Palmer, working hard to keep his anger and outrage under control, looked up from the note to the British lieutenant and asked if it were possible to discuss this matter with Hardy. He was told that no such arrangement could be made. The Americans, still shaken and incredulous, asked for confirmation that Captain Hardy had indeed determined to destroy the town. The officer, who had obviously been coached by Hardy, took pains to answer their question very precisely, so that there could be no misunderstanding. Commodore Hardy, he explained, was acting specifically on an order from the admiral and had determined to carry out the order most effectually.

The magistrates tried to be equally precise, so that there could be no misunderstanding on Hardy's part either. In carefully chosen words they told the lieutenant, "We shall defend this place to the last extremity; should it be destroyed, we shall perish in its ruins!" Such, in any case, are the words reported in the newspaper accounts of the scene. If the modern reader wonders how anyone, overwhelmed by the emotional intensity of the moment, would have been able to couch a response in such grandiloquence, we should remind ourselves that a heightened diction came easily to people in that day, and that it is entirely possible that what the newspapers reported is precisely what was said.

The magistrates rowed back to shore, where virtually the entire population of the village was standing at the dock waiting for them. Captain Palmer read Hardy's message aloud to them. The effect was instantaneous and universal—to a man, the village elected to fight.

The more bellicose gave intermittent cheers and whistles, but the general reaction was sober defiance. Everyone understood clearly that they were facing an impossible situation.

Just offshore, a stone's throw from the crowd, the British sailors rested on their oars so that their lieutenant could listen to the response of the villagers. When he was certain that he understood their reaction, he ordered the oarsmen to pull away and headed back to the *Pactolus*.

The spontaneous defiance of the villagers of Stonington is the key incident in the entire battle. Without it, there would not have been a battle, only a bombardment. Their intuitive protest against Hardy, even when viewed from almost two centuries' distance, expresses a degree of raw bravery that merits profound respect. Those people were neither fools nor romantics. They knew precisely how dangerous their situation was. (So did Hardy, which is why he gave them an hour to clear the village.)

The people of Stonington may have drastically revised their opinion of the once magnanimous Hardy upon reading his note, but they knew he was no liar. They understood clearly the power of the British navy, which had been leveling forts and cities for centuries. If Hardy said he was going to destroy Stonington, then that is what he was going to do. And without question, he had the means to do it. Standing up against such a tangible threat took enormous determination. Undoubtedly, some of the villagers could expect to die in the action.

It is difficult to imagine that a similar group of Americans today, faced with an equivalent danger, would show the same kind of spirit. What was it that motivated such universal courage? Undoubtedly, a major factor in stiffening the villagers' resolve was the memory of the attack by the *Rose*. Fighting off attacking British ships was something that one just did. To have failed to meet an almost identical challenge to the one their fathers faced up to would have been difficult. Another goad must have been their desperation. The entire worldly goods of almost every man and woman in the village were in their homes and furnishings. No one had insurance in those days. There was no fail-safe position. If your house went, you were left with nothing. Such a prospect, not only possible but likely, made it easier to risk death to protect your possessions.

Courage and fear are a powerful combination, but additionally Stonington's residents had almost certainly a third reason for their daring defiance. Simply put, they were Americans. Only thirty years had passed since the end of the Revolution, and only fifteen years since Washington took the oath as the first president. Their new nation was still in an undefined, ill-formed, almost adolescent stage. But for all that, it was their country, not the king's, and they were acutely aware that they were participating in a unique political experiment—the first democracy in more than two thousand years. They were their own people, not some despised and powerless colonists dependent upon the patronage of some faraway power. It must have been a heady experience to be an American in those days, a matter of great satisfaction and pride. What was seen as the disdainful arrogance of Hardy's letter undoubtedly kindled unkind memories of colonial times and touched at the roots of the people's patriotic pride. It was well worth the risk of death to regain the sense of independence.

It was just after six o'clock when the British barge left Stonington and returned to the *Pactolus*, so by the terms of Hardy's letter the village had only until seven o'clock to prepare for his attack. Stonington quickly turned into a confusion of running men shouting orders, women calling for their children, and small boys shrieking happily at the unexpected excitement and the promise of loud noises and fire. The best china was packed up in barrels and buried in the back garden, and the family silver hidden away or put down the well to protect it from fire and possibly the greedy hands of British looters. Everyone knew the stories of Cockburn's raping and thieving troops in the Chesapeake and Delaware Bays.

A messenger rushed off to General Cushing, the federal army commandant in New London, and to Colonel William Randall, of the 30th Regiment of militia, with pleas for help. Teams of men collected ammunition or helped to remove the sick and aged to safety. Mrs. Lucinda Palmer, whose late husband Jonathan had witnessed the raid of the *Rose* and had chronicled Stonington's feisty response in 1775, busily cut up carpets and flannel skirts to make wadding for the guns. Long before seven o'clock most of the population of the village had moved to the outskirts of town, leaving behind only those needed for defense.

Seafarers of the day were thoroughly familiar with the operation of guns, so Lieutenant Hough left the cannon to the civilians and stationed his small force of musket men around the edge of the village where they could watch for attack by barge and spread the alarm in time to fight off any incursion. Everyone was aware of the approaching hour, but as the appointed time drew near the villagers could see no activity on the ships indicating a preparation for attack. At seven o'clock, with the light fading fast (daylight saving time still lay many years in the future), Stonington had little left to do but wait.

Where was the bombardment? What had happened to Hardy?

It was not until eight o'clock that Hardy finally gave the order to attack. (The possible significance of this will be examined separately.) The lateness of the hour presented a problem to the British gunners, who preferred to begin a bombardment in daylight so that they could establish an idea of the direction and distance to their targets before the night closed in. It was also helpful to start some fires on shore with incendiary bombs before the sun went down, again as an aid to night aiming. The only advantage to night bombardment lay in its ability to terrorize an enemy, but since Hardy had deliberately warned the villagers to leave town before the shooting began, terror was clearly not his motive.

The British began their bombardment by lowering barges and launches, fitted with rocket launchers, from the larger vessels. Each boat carried a supply of rockets, and some were equipped with carronades, which were short guns that fired heavy charges but were effective only at close range.

Before moving to their assigned stations, the barges helped warp the *Terror* into position. Each boat took one of the *Terror*'s kedging anchors and rowed it forward, toward the shore. On a signal from the ship, each boat dropped the bomb ship's anchor and stood by as the sailors in the *Terror* winched in on the cables to pull the ship forward. The kedges were then raised and handed over once again to the barges, and the process repeated until the captain of the bomb ship, after consultation with his ordnance expert, determined the *Terror* had reached the optimum distance from the target, at which point the barges began the process of positioning the vessel. For greatest accuracy, and to best withstand the immense impact of the mortar recoil, bomb ships had to be anchored securely in all directions. By planting kedging anchors at all four points of the compass so as to keep the ship as stationary as possible, and then setting springs on the anchor cables, the sailors made the *Terror* ready for the attack. The barges were finally dismissed, and the oarsmen pulled away to their alloted positions.

All of this activity was carried out quite openly—there was no need for secrecy—and on the shore the tense American gun crews could see the signal lanterns hanging from the ships' spars and hear the British officers and petty officers calling out in the dark.

On the shore, not a light shone within the deserted village. At the breastworks, where men moved haltingly amid the ammunition and guns, the only light came from the tiny burning ends of the slow matches carried by each gun captain. These were needed to fire the guns. Any greater illumination would have given their position away and, more importantly, created a danger because of the gunpowder.

The *Terror* now stood a little over a mile from shore, the outer limits of the range of Stonington's 18-pounders. The barges with their carronades and rockets moved in considerably closer and surrounded the point on three sides. The Americans waited.

Abruptly, at eight o'clock, the bright glare of the huge 13-inch mortar in the *Terror* suddenly lit up the rigging on the bomb ship and dazzled eyes on shore with its unexpected brilliance. Seconds later the rumble of a deep, crisp "crump!" floated across the water as the sound chased after the explosion. Squinting to recover their sight, the Americans saw a faint streak of sparks hurtle high into the air and arch slowly down toward them. Carcasses! Those men not busy with the guns turned to the matter of fire patrol. There were shouts for assistance, and a covered lantern down on Water Street showed the fire fighters the way.

Before anyone had a chance to see where the carcass landed, the defenders were treated to a magical sight. Suddenly, incredibly, the entire seascape was thrown into relief as the first Congreve rocket rose eerily from one of the barges and arched toward the village. The rocket made almost no sound, which made the effect all the more mysterious. How could something so magical be so dangerous? For a moment the startled gun crews on shore and the hundreds of villagers watching from positions of safety beyond the northern limits of the village stood enchanted and beguiled, like children at a pantomime. The beauty, the abstract excitement of the moment drove all thoughts of fear or peril from their minds. As their eyes followed the arching path of the first rocket to its destination, a second rocket suddenly distracted them

. . . dazzling, mystical, unreal. Then, with a thunderclap, the almost simultaneous crash of their own two cannon, blasting away at the *Terror*, brought their attention back to reality.

When the men on the guns saw the flash from the *Terror*'s mortar they determined its position and sighted in on it as accurately as possible. The gun crews worked with a will, using crowbars to edge the enormous weight of gun and carriage into the right position, and when both captains fired their weapons at virtually the same time the men cheered and made brave jokes. The crews had, of course, no way to know if the shots had struck. The chances of a hit were very slim, as everyone knew. Still, it felt good to return fire.

Both of the crews on the 18s as well as the two men firing the 6-pounder soon realized that trying to hit the bomb ship was pointless, and determined that the barges made much better targets. They were smaller but closer. The men took to waiting for the glare of a rocket to show them the location of a boat, then methodically aiming and firing. They didn't manage to hit anything, but the relative accuracy of their fire forced the British oarsmen to keep well back from the shore.

On the British side the work was just as feverish, particularly in the barges, where the rocketeers struggled with the long, ungainly missiles and the even more ungainly twenty-foot-long launching apparatus. Working with rockets on a small, unstable boat was a little like juggling with lighted torches. The weapons were apt to be just as dangerous to those who fired them as to those fired upon. The flaming tail of the rocket on the launcher could ignite the other rockets in the boat, and of course the boat itself could always catch fire. To help ensure against such a mishap, wet leather tarpaulins covered all of the boat's surfaces. Even the sail was made of leather.

Rockets, of course, had been in use for hundreds of years, first as fireworks and eventually as weapons of war. The British military became interested in them as a result of the battle of Seringapatam in India in 1792, where General Cornwallis's army suffered heavy losses in a rocket attack launched by the troops of Tippoo Sahib. (This was the same Cornwallis who lost the Battle of Yorktown that ended the American Revolution. He seems to have had trouble with all sorts of colonials.)

William Congreve, who was employed at the Royal Laboratory in Woolwich, enthusiastically took up the challenge to produce an

English rocket. He eventually turned out an entire family of such weapons, some of which the British employed to great effect at Boulogne in 1806 and even more spectacularly at Copenhagen in 1807, where they triggered a fire storm that leveled one of Europe's great capitals.

Inevitably Congreve's rockets found their way into the war with America, and within the first six months of hostilities the British reportedly shipped over a million rockets across the Atlantic. Their greatest use in the War of 1812 still lay in the future. They would terrorize the militia in the attack on Washington two weeks after the attack on Stonington, and a month after that they provided "the rockets' red glare" that Francis Scott Key glorified in his poem about the unsuccessful assault on Baltimore. The British also used rockets, but without noticeable effect, in the Battle of New Orleans.

Congreve rockets fired from a ship's boat. Rocket attacks destroyed Copenhagen in 1807, and while they proved ineffective at Stonington, a fortnight later at Bladensburg they caused the American militia to panic and opened the way to the destruction of Washington. (William Reid's *Arms Through the Ages*)

Although Congreve developed several different kinds of rocket, including quite large ones armed with an explosive charge, the rockets used at Stonington were for the most part incendiary. They were made of rolled steel casings about two feet long and looked like ordinary fireworks, with a long, wooden guide pole. They were said to cost the Royal Navy about £5 apiece.

In theory, incendiary rockets were precisely the right weapons to use against Stonington. The village's neat rows of wooden houses made it a miniature Copenhagen, distinctly susceptible to any attack by fire. But as a practical matter, they proved ineffective. The members of the fire brigade were quick to find the rockets that managed to land in the town and extinguish any conflagration they might have started. The fact that they left a spectacular and highly visible trail made them easier to deal with than the carcasses, and there was no real danger to Stonington from fire until the bombshells started.

The *Terror* was equipped with two sea mortars—a small one with a ten-inch diameter and the larger, thirteen-inch version, which weighed five tons. At first only the bigger one was used, hurling two-hundred-pound carcasses. These were round iron shells, hollow and filled with fetid combustibles that the gunner's assistant set alight just before the mortar itself was fired. These incendiaries were designed to crash through the roof of a structure and to roll around inside, setting fires and causing confusion. While they were known officially as carcasses, they were commonly referred to by British and Americans alike as "stink pots."

Stink pots by themselves were not particularly effective because any fire brigade that could stand the smell of them could usually douse them before they did much harm. They were more dangerous when used in conjunction with rockets, and most effective of all when used in conjunction with the more sinister cousin of the carcass, the bombshell.

Bombshells were as dangerous and deadly as their name implied. Structurally they were virtually identical to stink pots; but instead of being stuffed with incendiary matter, bombshells carried some seven pounds of gunpowder—a fearsome amount of explosive that was powerful enough to destroy a manor house. In the words of one authority of the day, "The shell is a great hollow ball, filled with powder, which, falling into the works of a fortification, &c. destroys the most substantial buildings by its weight; and bursting asunder, creates the greatest disorder and mischief by its splinters."

Bombshells were as difficult and dangerous to fire as rockets. The gunner figured the distance to the target, worked out the trajectory he wanted the shell to follow, set the mortar to the correct angle, and measured out the requisite charge of powder calculated to throw the shell into its target in a given number of seconds. On his orders, his assistant would carefully cut a fuse, or quick match, to precisely the length calculated to burn that same number of seconds before it reached the bombshell's charge and detonated it. Just as the gunner prepared to fire the mortar, his assistant would thrust the fuse into the bombshell, light it, and step back quickly. If all went as calculated, the bombshell would be thrown high in the air and, because it weighed 216 pounds and was falling from a great height, would crash through whatever obstacle it encountered and explode moments later, scattering jagged, lethal fragments of shrapnel in all directions.

Experience with mortars had shown that getting all the calculations precisely right was not always necessary. If the fuse were a little too slow, that is, too long, the shell might roll around a bit before exploding, but it would still explode eventually, and the "disorder and mischief" be done. (On the other hand, Francis Scott Key's "bombs bursting in air" were examples of ineffectual bombs, whose fuses had been cut too short.)

One story of the Battle of Stonington, published in the Mystic *Pioneer* many years after the event, tells of one of the defenders who was in need of a light for his pipe. When a sputtering bombshell landed nearby he calmly reached over and plucked the fuse out of it to light his pipe, thereby disarming the bomb. Any reader desiring to believe such a story is of course free to do so.

An hour or so after the bombardment began, the gunners on the *Terror* shifted strategy and began alternating their barrage into Stonington between stink pots and bombshells. This shift made the fire brigade's job much more difficult. Since the spherical shells of the stink pot and the bombshell were identical, the men could not tell whether they might be dealing with a relatively harmless stink pot or a lethal explosive that might go off at any moment. The net effect was to cause the fire fighters to avoid all shells and allow the stink pots to start more serious fires than before. When a little later the ten-inch mortar joined its sister and began hurling a straight diet of bomb-shells, the fire brigade grew even more wary.

At about eleven o'clock the defenders learned that a considerable number of militia had assembled at the northern end of the village, including elements of the 30th Regiment of Foot and the Norwich Artillery. The presence of these troops was reassuring. With a large contingent of ground troops in place, Hardy would be forced to think twice before attempting any sort of landing.

By midnight the barges ran out of rockets, and when the boats returned to the mother ships to resupply, Hardy called an end to the barrage. The *Terror*'s guns grew quiet. The new silence settled slowly over the village, releasing the tension of the bombardment. It took a while for the villagers, huddled along a hillside just outside the bor-ough, to readjust to the ordinary sounds of life: a crying baby, a little boy asking questions, two adults discussing the possible reasons for the attack. Some of the people drifted cautiously back into the vil-lage—not to stay, but to find out what had happened to their homes. They soon learned that four hours of concentrated bombardment and rocket attack had damaged several houses in part but destroyed none. Most importantly, there had been no fire. Copenhagen had not hap-pened here.

The first day of the Battle of Stonington was over.

11

The Battle:
10 August 1814

Where was Jeremiah Holmes?—an 18-pounder at
the point stops a landing—Holmes arrives and
holes the Dispatch—*the high water mark of the*
*battle—search for gunpowder—*Dispatch *driven*
off—a letter to Hardy and his puzzling reply

WHERE was Jeremiah Holmes? Where was the one man everyone in Stonington would have selected to lead them at this crucial juncture? Holmes was a well-known figure in the town, an elected official and local celebrity, and everyone knew his story. They knew of his impressment, his skill with cannon, his hatred of the British navy. He was the most appropriate of all men to be standing at the breastworks that night, but he was not there. Where was he?

The fact that there is no record of Jeremiah Holmes's whereabouts that evening makes it likely he was involved in some other aspect of the defense of Stonington, possibly of a clandestine nature. Despite the loss of his first torpedo the previous March and the accidental explosion of the second near the *La Hogue*, Holmes still had in his possession a third torpedo, and it is probable that he and a few of his friends spent the night of 9 August out beyond the attacking squadron, seeking some means of getting close enough to one of the ships to sink it. If so, the bright lights of the rockets would have frustrated them, preventing them from stealing in on the attacking squadron undetected.

There is another, less dramatic explanation for Jeremiah Holmes's absence. In his official capacity as selectman of Stonington Township he may well have been the man chosen to carry the village's plea for help to Brigadier General Thomas Cushing, the commander of the U.S. Army in New London. If so, Holmes failed to convince the general of the urgency of his message. Cushing's reaction to the news was skeptical. He could conceive of no military value in attacking a harmless village like Stonington and, therefore, suspected Hardy's attack was a feint, designed to draw troops away from some real target. The only real target he could possibly imagine that was important enough for such a complicated maneuver was Decatur's squadron, dismantled and deserted up the Thames. The frigates were still worthwhile prizes, he reasoned, and if he were to take his troops out of Fort Trumbull and Fort Griswold and send them off to help beleaguered Stonington, a couple of British brigs could easily storm up to Allyn's Hill and burn the hapless ships.

General Cushing agonized for a moment and then decided emphatically to stay precisely where he was and leave it to the militia to help little Stonington.

Late that night Thomas Hardy, still in his temporary headquarters aboard the *Pactolus*—the *Ramillies* would not get to Stonington until the tide the next morning—sifted through the hurriedly scribbled reports of ammunition expended and estimates of damage, both received and inflicted. In four hours of bombardment his men had poured enough incendiaries into Stonington to burn it to the ground three times over. The expenditure of ammunition was enormous for such a paltry result.

Before dawn on 10 August the mortars on the *Terror* started up again, aiming their fire toward the western or harbor side of the village, to distract attention from the several barges and the single launch filled with red-coated marines making their way around to the east side, out of sight of the guns.

As the marine transport drew near enough to effect a landing, the barges began to lay down a barrage of rockets, and the sudden activity to the east immediately alerted the volunteers ashore. In a panic, half a dozen defenders began hauling the 6-pounder with its ammunition across the open ground leading to the southernmost point of the peninsula, where they could get a sighting on the boats.

Fortuitously, Colonel Randall of the 13th Regiment of militia had just brought up a detachment of troops to the breastworks, and the extra hands immediately went to work, manhandling one of the big guns—almost a ton and a half, including the field carriage—down to the point to join the 6-pounder. From this new vantage the gun crews had an excellent view of the landing party, but they were also totally exposed on all sides.

Almost unnoticed in the confusion, the brig *Dispatch*, which had the shallowest draft of all the attacking vessels, had moved close in to the shore—actually to less than half a mile of the men at the point—to cover the landing. At any moment she threatened to bring her cannon to bear on the exposed American gun crews.

Working feverishly, the volunteers managed to load the 18 with shot and about fifty pounds of grape, and aiming by the glare of the rockets, they torched the touch hole. Simultaneously with the explosion of the cannon, an enormous confusion of carnage erupted amid the boats. One of them was suddenly in splinters, with sailors and marines turning crazily through the air like catherine wheels, clutching at gaping wounds and spraying blood.

The Americans roared their delight and heard more cheers from the direction of the battery. The sky was reddening to the east, but no one thought to worry that they were as vulnerable as babes to every British gun in range, and no one gave a thought to the poor souls mangled and dead in the water, or clinging desperately to one of the remaining barges. The village was under attack—Stonington was under attack—and the volunteers were simply doing their damnedest to save it.

Almost at once the remaining barges, after picking up survivors, edged around and began rowing back toward the ships. Having lost the element of surprise, the British saw no point in trying for a landing. They quickly moved out of range. By now the brig *Dispatch* was almost within a pistol shot's distance of the point, and for the first time the cannoneers saw her rigging looming over them and recognized the danger of their position. Reluctantly, they spiked the 18-pounder where it stood and hurried back to the battery, dragging the 6-pounder with them.

As they made their way north over the rough dirt tracks from the point, the sun broke over the horizon behind Block Island, and the returning gun crew heard shouts from the breastworks. They climbed the four-foot wall protecting the battery in time to see Jeremiah Holmes and a group of his Hornet's Nest cronies bounding down Water Street on foot, followed by the cheers of the fire fighters. It was such a glorious, theatrical entrance that even Holmes himself, the tough, unsentimental, gritty torpedoist, must have sensed the drama of the moment. He would not disappoint them.

As soon as he arrived at the remaining gun he immediately assumed command. The *Dispatch* was so close he could clearly see her crew standing to the guns. Her imminent broadside would include devastating 32-pound carronades, deadly effective at such close range. But all Jeremiah Holmes could see was a once-in-a-lifetime opportunity. At such close range the *Dispatch* was a perfect target, so close that he could not miss. Carefully, with an eye trained in wars with the French, the Spanish, the Danes, and anyone else England picked a fight with, he sighted on the brig, then with the edge of his boot marked the ground where he wanted the gun carriage moved. Helping the men lever it around, he shouted for a double shot, no grape. The *Dispatch* had set her springs and would commence firing any moment, but no one in the Stonington gun crew—perhaps ten men in all—had the time to be worried. Their minds were totally engrossed with the idea of putting holes in the brig. Later they would be called heroes, but right now they were just being boys, and having a glorious time of it.

Finally snatching the slow match from Amos Palmer, Jeremiah Holmes thrust it to the touchhole and jumped back as the gun lurched with a great roar. Magically, two 18-pound rounds hulled the brig, one just below the waterline. The men went wild with excitement over their perfect hit and fought to grasp the hand of the legendary Holmes.

It all really happened, just like that. Within minutes, the crew at the point forestalled a British landing, and then the gun in the battery scored a direct hit on the *Dispatch*. It must have been an incredible moment of triumph for Jeremiah Holmes. After years of frustration and anger, endless dreams of retribution, and bitter disappointments—to actually send a cannon shot into the navy that had so miserably used him! What a moment to savor!

Did Holmes ever stop to think that some of those men he was shooting at might have included old shipmates from the *Saturn*? No, he did not. Enough that he had found his revenge, that at last the years of impotent fury were at an end, vengeance was here, now, at the end of a government-issued 18-pounder!

Suddenly the whole side of the *Dispatch* exploded with her first broadside, a combination of 32-, 24-, and 18-pound rounds ripping through the air above them. The same short range that made the brig an ideal target made the village a good target too, and even a ten-gun broadside at such close range was murderous.

Crouched behind the breastworks, Holmes noticed he was running short of gunpowder and sent back for fresh cartridges. The messenger returned with bad news—there was no powder left in the village, and the militia had already sent to New London for more. All that was left in the whole of the borough were the five cartridges in the breastworks. The crew turned to Holmes. Without hesitation he took a spike and hammered it into the touchhole, rendering the cannon useless to the British if they captured it. Then he and the others hurriedly gathered up the swab and the screw and the precious cartridges, which they might be able to use in the 6-pounder if Hardy sent in another landing party, and made ready for a dash back into the village.

One of the crew suggested they take with them the huge American flag displayed over the battery, an immense nine-by-sixteen-foot banner. Jeremiah Holmes, animated with triumph and patriotic fervor and sensing instantly that the British might interpret the removing of the flag as an overture to surrender, objected violently. "No!" he shouted. "That flag don't come down while I'm alive!" He grabbed the hammer and nails he'd used to spike the gun, and climbing onto a fence beside the flagpole, Holmes hoisted little Dean Gallup onto his shoulders and had him literally nail the flag to the pole. Finally, abandoning the 18 where it stood, the crew hurried off to search for gunpowder.

That same flag, its colors faded to a gentle pink, cream yellow, and robin's egg blue, shot full of holes and fragile as cheesecloth, is still reverently cherished by the village to this day. It is something of a patriotic nonesuch—the only American flag in existence with sixteen stars and sixteen stripes. Apparently the ladies of the Stonington Congregational Church sewing circle designed it some time after Tennessee entered the union, assuming that Congress would authorize an additional star and stripe for the new state; but Congress never did,

The Stonington battle flag, as it appeared in 1909, almost a hundred years after the bombardment. The sixteen-star canton (never authorized by Congress) suggests that the flag was designed sometime between 1796, when Tennessee was admitted as the sixteenth state, and 1808, when Ohio entered the Union. (Photograph by F. Stewart Greene)

and the official American flag in use throughout the War of 1812 was the fifteen-star-and-fifteen-stripe design authorized in 1794 and celebrated by Key as the *Star-Spangled Banner*. Thus it was that one more star spangled the banner at Stonington than at Fort McHenry.

The lack of gunpowder threw a pall of nervous anxiety over the group. They could see that the *Terror* had started firing again, and the only good news was that the *Pactolus* had run aground near Napatree Point and was having a desperate time trying to free herself. Unfortunately for the defenders, the *Pactolus* was out of cannon range, so even if they found some powder, they could not take advantage of her vulnerability. It was now a little after eight o'clock in the morning, and the *Dispatch* was firing at will into the village, with no one to stop her. It would be noon before further supplies could possibly arrive from New London. Meanwhile, the men cringed behind the breastworks as best they could while the *Dispatch* and *Terror* continued to pour shot and shell into Stonington.

The direct hit on the British landing barge, quickly followed by Jeremiah Holmes's holing the *Dispatch*, was probably the high-water mark for the Stonington volunteers. It in no way marked a victory, but it registered the moment when the citizens of Stonington stopped being victims and became instead a fighting force to be taken seriously. Their careless exposure to fire at the point represented heroism of a very superior order, and even when viewed from all these many years later, their gallantry demands respect. Not one man in that crew was standing on the point because he had been ordered to go there. Each man in that exposed position was there for his own reasons, which might include patriotism, a sense of community, and probably a yearning for a little excitement as well.

For the best part of an hour the villagers searched frantically for gunpowder. Finally a fourteen-year-old boy, Dickie Loper, uncovered a cache of six kegs of powder hidden under some seaweed near the States Pottery works on the east side of the village, not far from where the British marines had attempted a landing. The kegs were off the privateer *Halka* and were the property of a Mr. Thomas Swan, who was away on business at the time of the battle. One group of volunteers started packing the precious powder into cartridges and getting them over to the breastworks. Another group corralled an ox and had him haul the remaining 18 in the battery up to the blacksmith, a Mr. Cobb, to drill the spike out of the touchhole. The fire from the *Dispatch* was still so heavy that the men abandoned all thoughts of trying to retrieve the other cannon down at the point.

With one gun back in working order, Jeremiah Holmes ordered it immediately double shotted and, much to the surpirse of the British, started firing again at the *Dispatch* with such rapidity and accuracy that it made them believe that there might be two guns operating from the breastworks.

It was now about ten o'clock in the morning, and the noise and confusion in the battery reached new levels of frenzy and fever. The volunteers were hitting the brig with every shot now, but with only one gun the pace was maddeningly slow. It is an indication of the brute strength built into those old wooden warships that the *Dispatch* could continue her fire unabated in spite of the holes being punched into her side once every two minutes or so.

The men at the guns were now as black as the powder itself. One of Jeremiah Holmes's brothers-in-law, nineteen-year-old Frederick Denison, stepped clear of the breastworks to try to relight the slow match with a flint. While in this unprotected position he was struck in the knee by a chip of stone knocked off a rock by a shot from the *Dispatch*, and fell to the ground in pain. The wound put him out of the action, but no one—including himself—took it all that seriously. Everyone assumed his injury would heal quickly, but it never did; and the young man eventually died from complications three months later—the only American to die in the Battle of Stonington.

With the slow match gone, Jeremiah Holmes was forced to hold the flintlock of his musket over the cannon's touchhole and strike a spark to fire the gun. The cannon eventually grew so hot from rapid working that a cartridge of gunpowder exploded prematurely when the crew pushed it into an overheated chamber. The accidental explosion injured several of the men, and one of them, John Miner, never fully recovered his sight.

The volunteers continued firing until noon, by which time the *Dispatch*, now visibly in distress and beginning to take on more water than her pumps could handle, took advantage of a shift of wind to the north, cut her cables, and began moving out of range.

The men in the battery stopped to cheer, but Jeremiah Holmes insisted on another shot. After the crew hurriedly loaded the gun, he charged the touchhole and, using his musket one last time as a slow match, fired a shot that went into the brig's starboard quarter and, some say, killed or wounded eleven men.

Suddenly, after eight or nine hours of deafening noise and smoke and confusion, the village was almost quiet. For the first time in what must have seemed a week, the defenders were able to stand at ease and look at the world around them. The *Pactolus*, they noticed, had floated off the sandbar and now stood anchored near the newly arrived *Ramillies*, about two and a half miles out. Still another vessel had joined the squadron since dawn—the brig *Nimrod*. The heavy crump of a mortar reminded them that the *Terror* continued to lob shells into town occasionally, but for the men in the battery there was nothing more at which to shoot.

The magistrates picked their way through the rubble on Water Street—the *Dispatch* had done a great deal of mischief in the two hours of unopposed bombardment—to thank Jeremiah Holmes and the rest of the volunteers and to study the situation. With the enemy vessels all anchored out of range, there seemed very little that anyone could do in the way of defending the village.

After consideration the magistrates decided to send a letter to Hardy to ascertain his future plans for the village. As one newspaper reported, at least some of the village officials were of the opinion "that there must exist some latent cause of a peculiar nature to induce a commander who had heretofore distinguished himself for a scrupulous regard to the claims of honorable warfare,—to induce him to commit an act so repugnant to sound policy, so abhorent to his nature, so flagrant an outrage on humanity."

By this time, General Isham of the Connecticut Militia had arrived to take command of the disorganized collection of citizen soldiers on the scene, and the magistrates sought his permission to send a note out to the attacking squadron. The general was reluctant to sanction the act but pointedly did not forbid it; so the magistrates quickly composed a letter to Hardy, which they hoped combined the right mixture of determination, inquiry, and respect.

Stonington, August 10, 1814

To Sir Thomas M. Hardy
Sir—Agreeable to notice received from you yesterday, this town is now cleared of "unoffending inhabitants," and they feeling anxious about

the fate of their village, are desirous to know from you, your determination respecting it.

> Your most humble servants,
> Amos Denison, Burgess
> William Lord, Magistrate

With no idea of what might transpire, Dr. Lord and Colonel Isaac Williams climbed into a launch and set off for the *Ramillies*. They could hardly have expected that Hardy's answer to their note was to come in one of the oddest official papers ever dictated and signed by an officer of the king.

By one o'clock that afternoon Commodore Hardy was back in the *Ramillies*, surveying the situation. He watched his men patching up the *Dispatch* and hoped she would be fit to sail when the tide returned. She certainly was not in any condition to fight and would need permanent refitting in Halifax before she would be ready for action again. The *Pactolus*, he was cheered to see, had managed to free herself, but he wondered how much weight she had been forced to jettison to get clear.

A midshipman approached and, touching his hand smartly to his hat, announced that a launch with a white flag had left the village and was heading for the *Ramillies*. Hardy ordered the *Terror* to continue firing at the desultory pace the gun crews had maintained for several hours, but he cautioned the gun captains to be particularly careful to avoid the launch. Then he left the quarterdeck and retired to his cabin.

When the boat containing Dr. Lord and Colonel Williams came alongside, Hardy saw to it that the men were met with all due formalities. He himself was as affable as the circumstances would permit. This was the first time he had come face to face with any of the citizens of Stonington. The two Americans appeared serious and reserved and had the demeanor of educated men of affairs. They were clearly not rustics, and Hardy noted that they expressed themselves with the same casual self-confidence that he had come to associate with Americans since his tour of duty in the Chesapeake in 1807. They were deferential but not in the least servile.

Hardy invited them into his cabin and in a friendly manner pointed toward a couch standing against a side bulkhead. "It may interest you gentlemen to know that on that couch Lord Nelson lay in his death, after I had given him my parting embrace," he told them. They regarded the relic respectfully and mumbled something appropriate.

The three sat at a table, and Hardy opened the letter handed to him by Dr. Lord. Hardy read the note casually—he would already have guessed its purport—and put it on the table. One wonders whether he—or the Americans—noticed the letter's slightly mocking tone, the sarcasm implied by the use of quotation marks around "unoffending inhabitants." If Hardy sensed an unseemly truculence in the note, he chose to overlook it. From later evidence we can reconstruct the ensuing discussion.

"This is not another Eastport, Captain Hardy," Dr. Lord said quietly but with authority.

Hardy nodded and then began discussing the war in general, and the history of his experiences in Long Island Sound in particular. He invited an interchange; in time a conversation, at first halting, but with increasing ease, arose. Hardy, with the practiced eye of a man versed in leadership and negotiation, was careful to note the reactions of the two Americans as he began to bring the discussion around to the reasons for his attack.

Having guided the conversation to the point that was of primary interest to his visitors, he unveiled his surprising and totally unexpected reason for the attack in one word: Torpedoes.

The two men bristled, but Hardy continued, claiming that he had good reason to believe that Stonington had been for some time now a leading source both for the manufacture of torpedoes and, still worse, their distribution.

His accusations clearly angered the two Americans. They denied the charges vehemently, assuring him that the village had never been used as either a manufactory or a repository of torpedoes, and that the villagers, in fact, strongly disapproved of their use.

It then seems likely that Hardy changed the subject entirely, and switched from torpedoes to a completely different matter, namely, Elizabeth Stewart, the wife of the recent consul to New London. The commodore would have expressed his interest in having that lady and her children rejoin Mr. Stewart. What the Americans had to say on the subject—if indeed Hardy ever brought it up—is unknown.

The one statement that we do know Hardy made at this point, because the papers widely reported it afterward, is significant not only for its frankness but also because it helps us judge his state of mind less than twenty-four hours after the start of the bombardment. At one point he turned to the Americans and stated quite openly that the attack on Stonington, which he was careful to point out was not of his own doing, was the most unpleasant expedition he had ever undertaken.

Hardy then proposed to bring in his secretary and draft an answer to the letter the two Americans had delivered. He told them that since it might take some time, they could dismiss the boatmen waiting to return them to shore, and that he would be happy to provide transport. He also assured the Americans that he was ordering the *Terror* to stop firing and that his forces would commit no further hostilities against the village at this time.

Hardy turned the magistrates over to his second officer, Lieutenant Claxton, who showed them around the *Ramillies* and otherwise kept them occupied while the captain prepared what one journalist later characterized with considerable understatement as "a very singular and extraordinary communication."

The two magistrates probably thought they would soon return to the captain's cabin, where they would read through Hardy's letter in his presence so that they could question him on any points that might need clarification. But Lord and Williams were not to see the commodore again. After pleasantries with Lieutenant Claxton, they were ushered into a launch and handed Hardy's reply as the boat pulled away. We can imagine their confusion and distress upon opening and reading the following:

Ramillies, off Stonington,
10th August, 1814

Gentn

I have received your letter and representation of the State of your Town, and as you have declared that Torpedoes, never have been harbored by the Inhabitants or ever will be, as far as it lies in their power to prevent—and as you engaged that Mrs. Stewart the wife of the British vice consul late resident at New London, with her family, shall be permitted to embark on board this Ship tomorrow morning, I am induced to wave the attempt of the total destruction of your Town, which I feel confident can be effected by the Squadron under my Orders.

I am
Gentn
Your most obedient servant,
T. M. Hardy, Captain

To Doctor Law [Lord] and Colonel Williams, Stonington.

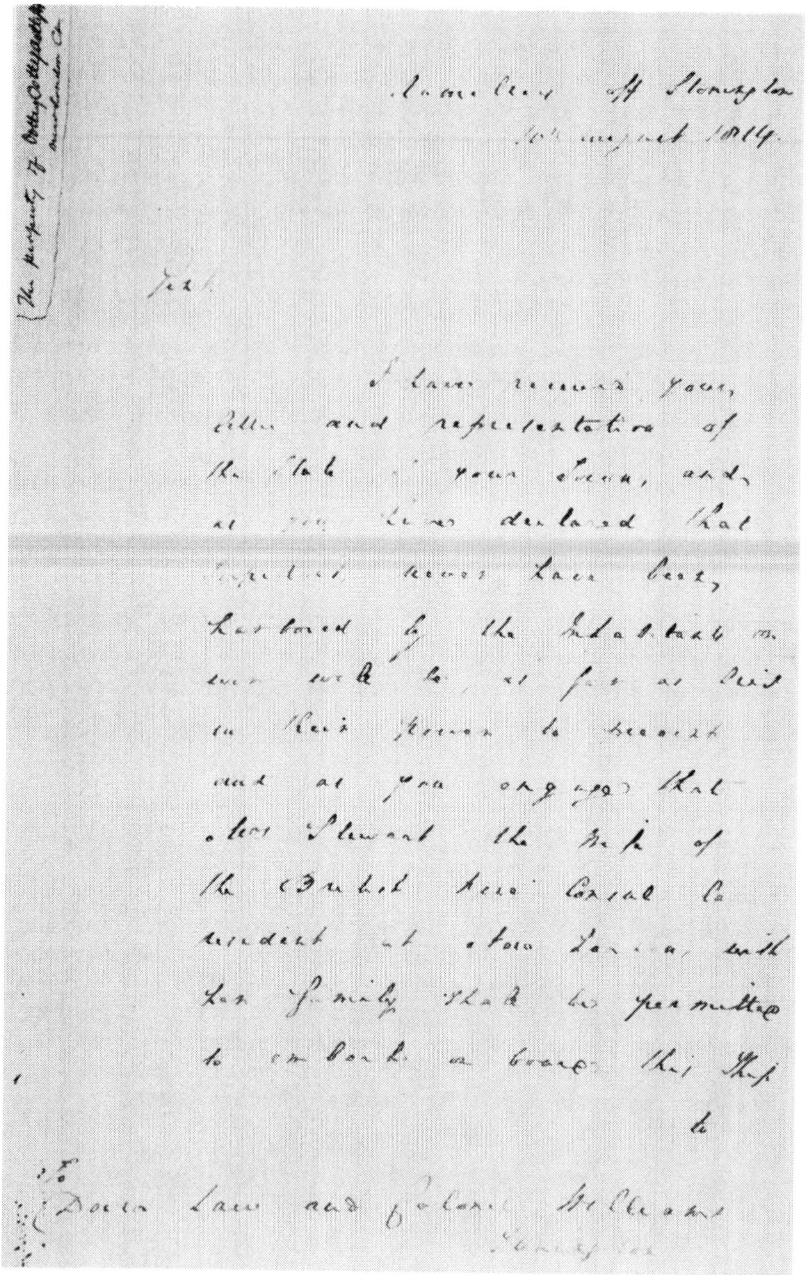

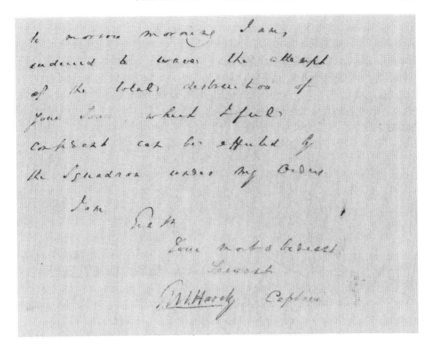

Hardy's 10 August letter to the village of Stonington, in which he refers to torpedoes and Mrs. Stewart. The letter, dictated in the *Ramillies*, differs in handwriting from that of the previous day because it has been written by Hardy's personal secretary, who presumably did not accompany him in the *Pactolus*. (Beinecke Rare Book and Manuscript Library, Yale University)

Such are the recorded facts concerning the strange confrontation between Hardy and the American emissaries on the second day of the Battle of Stonington, and the even stranger letter generated by that confrontation. Any reasonable interpretation of the facts shows conclusively that Hardy's story about torpedoes and his interest in Mrs. Stewart were nonsense, concocted out of thin air to serve his own purposes and having no bearing whatsoever on the attack.

If Hardy truly believed that Stonington was guilty of trafficking in torpedoes, he would have been morally justified in destroying the place. But his open admission to the Americans that the attack was the most unpleasant expedition of his career proves that he knew the torpedo story to be a fabrication.

Likewise, he knew that Stonington could not deliver Mrs. Stewart. Hardy was actually with Hotham the previous Sunday when the admiral learned that the American general in New London did not have the authority to release Mrs. Stewart but was sending to Washington to try to make arrangements. If an army general couldn't release Mrs. Stewart, how could Hardy expect some magistrates from Stonington to do so?

The best evidence indicates that Thomas Masterman Hardy was simply trying to find a way to bring this pointless battle to an end in a tidy and reasonable manner.

We know today what no one in Stonington could have known at the time—that the actual impetus for the attack was Cochrane's 18 July order to "destroy and lay waste such towns and districts upon the coast as you may find assailable." By raising the torpedo issue, which Hardy privately knew to be spurious, he was providing himself with some seemingly legitimate reason for the attack. But the next element—the introduction of Mrs. Stewart into the proceedings—was Hardy's happiest invention. He knew full well that Hotham had been unsuccessful in obtaining her release, and that in all likelihood he would not be able to do so either. But by using the threat of his continued bombardment as an inducement to force a speedier response from the Americans, Hardy might just possibly succeed where Hotham had failed.

With a very singular communication, Hardy had explained the battle either as a response to torpedo warfare or as a means of rescuing the vice consul's wife and family. Either way, he stood to justify his actions and cover his backside.

Not surprisingly, Hardy's letter was received indignantly by the village elders. They were outraged to learn that their town had just undergone two days of bombardment for what they were now informed was a spurious reason. But they were also indignant that Hardy could assume they would take action to ensure no torpedoes ever came through their village. How were they supposed to enforce such a guarantee? By posting guards on every road and dock to search incoming wagons and skiffs for contraband? Such was impossible, and Hardy must know it. Dr. Lord and Colonel Williams had to defend themselves against allegations that they had overstepped their commissions, and could only repeat that they had barely discussed the subjects broached in Hardy's letter and had made no agreements with him despite Hardy's implication to the contrary.

As to Mrs. Stewart, most of the village officials had no idea who she was. Even those who knew something about her could not understand how she had managed to find her way into the negotiations. A few rude suggestions were raised concerning Hardy's possible interest in the lady, at which everyone laughed. But the problem remained. If they wanted the British to go away, apparently Stonington had to give them Mrs. Stewart, or at least make an attempt. Those were Hardy's conditions. Protesting that they lacked the power to deliver the consul's wife was pointless. The only alternative was to send a request to the authorities in New London, even though the village officials knew they would be refused.

In the meantine, they could prepare for another day of bombardment.

12

The Battle: Aftermath

*Thursday, 11 August—a misunderstanding cleared
up—the bombardment resumed—Friday, 12
August—162 cannonballs—the British retire—the
creation of a myth—contrast of British and
American perceptions of the battle—Hardy's
probable motivations.*

THE truce called by Commodore Hardy on Wednesday afternoon gave some of the more adventurous villagers another opportunity to cautiously reenter the borough and take stock of their property. The *Dispatch*'s broadsides had done considerable damage, but as Captain Wallace had learned in his 1775 bombardment, wooden houses can absorb a lot of cannonballs without falling down. A number of unexploded bombshells lay scattered through the village, and groups of frugal men went about collecting the seven pounds of unburned gunpowder from each one they came across. Handling two-hundred-pound shells was cumbersome work and potentially dangerous, but no one was injured.

Amos Palmer, as head of the committee of public safety, organized a team to retrieve the 18-pounder that still stood abandoned at the point. The men brought an ox down with them and hitched him to the gun carriage, all the time keeping a cautious eye on the ships. From the point they could see British sailors standing idly by the shrouds and on the ratlines watching them as they struggled with the great weight of the gun. The men hauled it back to the smithy and once again called upon Mr. Cobb to drill out the iron spike in the

178

touchhole. When he was through, they returned the gun to the battery, and Stonington was once again in possession of both 18s in working order.

As the civic leaders had expected, the New London authorities turned down the petition for Mrs. Stewart's release. By eight o'clock Thursday morning, when the cease-fire was due to expire, the borough officials were putting the finishing touches on a letter to Hardy, explaining why they were not able to produce the lady as demanded.

While they deliberated, Hardy, who was anxious for any news concerning Mrs. Stewart, decided to send Lieutenant Claxton on shore with a message of inquiry. Claxton arrived off the point under a white flag, and what ensued was a scene out of a comedy of manners worthy of Richard Brinsley Sheridan.

A Mr. Faxon, who owned one of Stonington's two ropewalks, was standing on the shore and saw the British boat enter the harbor. He immediately recognized a potential problem and with all the good intentions in the world hurried off to stop Claxton. Under the rules of war as practiced at the time, an enemy bearing a flag of truce was not allowed to come within the opponents' lines without first obtaining permission. This stipulation ensured that no one used the flag of truce as a cover for spying.

Acting on his own, Faxon hailed the British boat and warned Claxton that he was in danger of creating an incident that neither side wanted. Faxon then offered to deliver whatever message the lieutenant might be carrying. On his guard, Claxton demanded to know Faxon's credentials. When Faxon explained that he was simply a private citizen with no official position in the village, the British officer questioned the American's authority to receive the dispatch from Commodore Hardy. Had Mrs. Stewart arrived in Stonington? Claxton wanted to know. Did she have her children with her? Faxon knew nothing of the matter and admitted as much. This reply apparently irritated Claxton so much that he broke off the discussion and announced he would come on shore. Faxon warned that if the officer attempted to do so, he would undoubtedly be fired upon.

Claxton, who apparently could not bring himself to believe that the villagers in an obscure backwater like Stonington could practice the rules of war with such punctilio, continued on his course. As he approached the docks, a militiaman attempted to fire a musket forward of the boat—a warning shot across the bow, as it were—but as luck would have it, the ball passed through the after sail. The lieutenant was incensed at what he saw as an insult to his flag of truce, and immediately put the boat about and steered for the *Ramillies*, swearing revenge.

A few minutes later, when the news of the incident reached General Jirah Isham, commanding the 3rd Brigade of the State Militia, he immediately saw the unhappy consequences that might arise. Eager not to give the British any excuse for renewing the attack, Isham hurriedly dictated a note of explanation to Hardy, begging his pardon for any misunderstanding. After Isham sent his note off under the obligatory flag of truce, he learned that the civil authorities had already sent off a boat with their own letter concerning Mrs. Stewart, carried by Gurdon Trumbull, Burgess of the borough, and the ubiquitous Dr. Lord, Magistrate. Three messages, in three different boats, each with its own flag of truce, were now scurrying about between Stonington Point and the *Ramillies*.

When the magistrates' boat reached the *Ramillies*, a lieutenant—not Claxton—met Trumbull at the head of the gang-ladder and informed him that the outraged commodore would not receive any communication from the shore until the Americans should explain the insult offered to his flag of truce.

Trumbull replied that he came as a messenger from the civil, not the military, authorities. He was not instructed to offer any explanation, but as an eyewitness to the event he was willing to describe the circumstances as they had occurred. He then did so, and the lieutenant left to report to Hardy. The officer returned a few minutes later all smiles, to say that Hardy was "perfectly satisfied" with the explanation, and that Lieutenant Claxton had been in the wrong. The officer then conducted the two Americans to Hardy's cabin, where they found the commodore in consultation with all the other commanders in his squadron. Trumbull bowed and presented his message to Hardy, who opened it and read quietly to himself:

Stonington Boro', Aug. 11, 1814

To Thomas M. Hardy, Commander of H.B.M. ship Ramillies Sir—Since the flag went into New London for Mrs. Stewart and family [that is, on the previous Sunday, when Admiral Hotham's boat bearing a letter requesting Mrs. Stewart and her children went into New London], General Cushing, who commands at New London, has written, we are informed, to the Secretary of War on the subject, and it is our opinion that the request will be complied with. But whatever may be the result of the communication from Gen. Cushing, you will be satisfied it is not in our power to enter into any arrangement with you respecting her.

Your most obedient servants,

Issac Williams,
William Lord, } Magistrates
Alexander G. Smith,
Joseph Smith, Warden
Geo. Hubbard
Amos Denison } Burgesses

Having finished reading, Hardy put the letter aside and said easily to Trumbull, "I learn from this, sir, that I am under the necessity of resuming hostilities, which I shall do at one o'clock." The magistrates returned to shore with the gloomy news that the bombardment was about to resume.

In fact it was not until three o'clock that the *Terror*, still far beyond range of Stonington's 18s, began throwing shells into the town again. The principal parts of three full regiments of militia were now encamped at the northern boundary of the borough, and the presence of such an overwhelming number of troops made the village secure against any possible British landing party. General Isham assigned fifty men to patrol the streets of the town on fire watch, ordering all remaining troops to stand by.

The shelling continued until sunset.

That night the villagers speculated on Hardy's intentions. The Americans were convinced that a British landing was now out of the question, given the strength of the militia. What then was he to do? Did he plan to spend the rest of the war sitting out there in Fishers Island Sound throwing ineffectual bombshells into the town? It seemed a great waste of time, given that Stonington held no military value. It was also reprehensible, since the village had done nothing to merit such treatment.

Perhaps they had it all wrong. Perhaps Hardy was not trying to do anything—that is, perhaps he was trying *not* to do something. Even in the earliest newspaper reports of the battle, written while the attack was still in progress, the idea had surfaced that there was something puzzling in Hardy's behavior. As the Connecticut *Gazette* speculated, "It was impossible to discover whether he [Hardy] was most doubtful of his ability to accomplish the destruction of the town, or desirous of a pretext to save it.''

At dawn on Friday, 12 August, the fourth day since the British anchored off the village, the people of Stonington crawled out of their makeshift beds, many of them in barns and stables at neighboring farms, to hear the now familiar boom of the *Terror*'s mortars pumping shells at a deliberate rate into the village. By standing near the edge of Lambert's Cove and craning their necks, the people could make out the two largest ships, the *Ramillies* and *Pactolus*, warping in to expose their broadsides.

By eight o'clock in the morning the two ships were in place, each lying in deep water far off the point, well beyond the range of Stonington's guns. With a great roar, the *Pactolus* let go a broadside that enveloped the whole ship in smoke. Most of the rounds whistled over the village and landed in the marsh beyond.

General Isham, as a precaution against the unlikely event of a British landing attempt, ordered the two cannon brought north from the breastworks to join the militia. A group of about twenty men under a Lieutenant Lathrop marched south to the battery to retrieve the guns. As the squad arrived at the battery, the *Ramillies* let go with a broadside that was as badly aimed as the first one and ended up in the same marsh.

Broadsides were designed for fighting at sea, where the massed power of a large number of rounds hitting the enemy simultaneously could actually shake loose the scantlings that held the ship together. When fired at land targets, the effectiveness of broadsides was limited, at best. The standard practice was to fire an initial broadside and then allow the gun crews to fire at will so that the faster crews could maximize the actual number of shots reaching the target. But the *Ramillies* and *Pactolus* did not follow this practice. Instead, each took enough time to make sure every gun was properly loaded and ready and then fired another broadside. And then each ship fired a third. It came to a total of 162 cannonballs, all aimed a little too high to do much damage.

It seemed almost a salute.

Then the two great ships made sail and returned to their former positions.

The *Terror* continued sending the occasional shell into town until about noon. Then she, too, pulled up anchor and moved off to join the two others. By four o'clock the ships—minus the *Dispatch*, which had limped away earlier under the protection of the *Nimrod*—were once again where they were on Monday afternoon: out of harm's way but still in a menacing position.

The Battle of Stonington was over, but the villagers did not know it. That night they remained away from their homes for fear that those huge, unpredictable, and murderous ships standing three miles or so off the coast might surprise them again and return.

Saturday morning the British settled the matter when the entire squadron weighed anchor and proceeded up Fishers Island Sound to the Hummucks.

The returning residents found their village altered but not significantly changed. About half the houses in the borough had been hit, but only eight or ten were seriously damaged, and only two or three so badly damaged as to be beyond repair.

As suspected, the principal damage resulted from the cannonading by the *Dispatch*. The uninterrupted point-blank firing during the two hours when Jeremiah Holmes and his men were out of gunpowder had been devastating. A considerable number of the mortar shells—both bombshells and stink pots—failed to explode or burn their combustibles. The Congreve rockets, which spread great fear the first night, lost their power to terrify when the villagers saw how little damage they in fact inflicted. In the end, the rockets appeared to be totally ineffective.

Total damage was estimated at $4,000, which, under the circumstances, was negligible.

The Americans reportedly recovered and duly buried the bodies of four British seamen that had been thrown overboard from the sinking barge. Some mystery surrounds the identity of these men since Hardy reported a total of only two British deaths for the whole action. The four appear in Amos Palmer's official published account of the battle, and while no one has found corroborative evidence to support his claim, he is not likely to have invented them, with so many witnesses. Palmer also claimed that after the war was over, officers from the *Dispatch* visited Stonington and admitted a total of twenty-one killed and fifty badly wounded in the action. No one has ever satisfactorily accounted for the discrepancy between Hardy's figures and Palmer's, and the number of killed is likely to remain an unresolved statistic forever.

The villagers collected about three or four tons of bombs, carcasses, and shot within a fortnight and estimated the total weight of metal expended in the battle by the British as between fifty and sixty tons, including more than five tons of shot deliberately thrown overboard from the *Pactolus* and later recovered by a team working with a diving machine. Amos Palmer, reporting on the action a year later to the secretary of war, wrote that the villagers eventually picked up more than fifteen tons of iron, and that "we have now more 18 pound shot than was sent us by the government."

The news of the attack on Stonington was first brought to the world by the *Gazette* of New London, which ran an excited account of it while the battle was still in progress. The New York *Columbian* quickly copied the *Gazette*'s story, and the Connecticut *Courant* in Hartford ran an extensive record of the events in its issue of 23 August. By then the battle was already a national story, with a long piece in *Niles' Weekly Register* in the issue of 20 August.

For obvious reasons, editors delighted in the story of Stonington's defiance, and it would undoubtedly have remained a staple item in the news for several more weeks had not Admiral Cockburn's devastating attack on Washington later in August immediately monopolized the public's attention. Cochrane's subsequent and somewhat less successful assault on Baltimore a few weeks later pushed the defense of Stonington even further into the background.

It was November by the time *Niles' Weekly Register* was able to return to the Stonington story, and the battle had started to take on the mythic qualities that were to characterize it thereafter. A detailed recapitulation of the battle in *Niles'* concluded with a mock epic, written by the best known American poet of the day, Philip Freneau. His many errors in the details of the attack indicate that the writer's understanding of the battle was more poetic than factual, although his estimate that "It cost their king ten thousand pounds/To have a dash at Stonington" is probably pretty close to the mark.

Three gallant ships from England came,
Freighted deep with fire and flame,

And other things we need not name,
 To have a dash at Stonington.

Now safe arrived—their work begun—
They thought to make the yankees run,
And have a mighty deal of fun,
 In stealing sheep at Stonington.

A yankee, then, popp'd up his head
And parson Jones' sermon read
In which the reverend doctor said,
 That they must fight for Stonington.

The ships advancing several ways,
The Britons soon began to blaze,
And put the old women in amaze,
 Who fear'd the loss of Stonington!

The yankees to their fort repaired,
And made as though they little cared,
For all their shot—though very hard
 They blazed away at Stonington.

The Ramilies began the attack,
And Nimrod made a mighty crack,
And none can tell what kept them back
 From setting fire to Stonington.

The old Razee, with red hot ball,
Soon made a farmer's barrack fall,
And did a cow house sadly maul,
 That stood a mile from Stonington.

The bombs were thrown, the rockets flew,
But not a man of all their crew,
(Though every man was full in view)
 Could kill a man at Stonington.

To have their turn they thought but fair—
The yankees brought two guns to bear,
And sir, it would have made you stare,
 To see the smoke at Stonington!

They bored the Nimrod through and through,
And kill'd and mangled half her crew,
When riddled, crippled, she withdrew
 And cursed the boys of Stonington.

The Ramilies gave up the fray,
And with her comrades sneak'd away—
Such was the valor on that day,
    Of British tars at Stonington.

But some assert, on certain grounds,
Beside the damage and the wounds,
It cost their king ten thousand pounds,
    To have a dash at Stonington.

The poem, with many of its inaccuracies corrected and a few satiric stanzas added, survived until the present century and was a standard item in the assortment of ballads and patriotic poems offered by street vendors in every city. It had an established place among the "declamations" offered at school festivals, and almost every Connecticut boy knew it by heart.

By 1817 the Hartford *Times* could report on a speech to the Congress by Erastus Root of New York, who extolled the Battle of Stonington as the exemplar of how patriotic Americans should behave. "A more brilliant affair had not taken place during the late war," he declared. "It was not rivaled by the defense of Sandusky, the glorious triumph on the Niagara, nor the naval victories on Erie and Champlain." Having sent havoc and death among the enemy and saved the town, the heroes of Stonington had "crowned themselves with never fading laurels."

In 1869, more than fifty years after the event, Benson Lossing, in his bestselling *Pictorial Field Book of the War of 1812*, called the battle "one of the most gallant affairs of the war."

The truth, in the end, had survived in the form of myth.

In reference to the Battle of Stonington, C. S. Forester, the English novelist and authority on naval history, wrote, "To the historian of the present day the main interest in that affair now lies in the profound difference between the official accounts on either side; the reader can hardly believe they are describing the same action." The reason for this profound difference lies in the quite separate ways each nation chose to interpret the same data. If the American version developed into a sort of heroic myth, the British version, as it passed through various shifts of emphasis and detail from Hardy's original report to its eventual appearance in the London press, developed into a righteous crusade for decency.

The process began with Hardy's report to Hotham, written on the last day of the attack:

To Admiral the Hon'ble Henry Hotham
      Ramillies, off Stonington
      August 12, 1814

Sir:—Agreeable to your orders of the 8th Instant, I proceeded with His Majesty's Ships named in the margin [*Ramillies; Pactolus; Dispatch*, brig; *Terror*, bomb] to make an attack on the town of Stonington, and on the Evening of the 9th many Shells and Rockets were thrown into it, without any apparent effect—The next morning I directed the Captains of the *Pactolus* and *Dispatch* to anchor as near as possible to the Town—in endeavouring to do so, the former ship took the ground for a short time, and was thereby prevented supporting the *Dispatch* most gallantly anchored within pistol shot of the battery, from which the Enemy kept up a fire so well directed from two 18 pounders I judged it right to recall her. I am sorry to add, not until she had suffered the loss of 2 men killed, and 12 wounded—and I beg most strongly to express my approbation of Captain Galloway's conduct, as well as that of his officers and crew (more particularly described in his letter to me enclosed herewith.)

On the evening of the 11th I directed Captain Sheridan to throw a few more shells and carcases into the Town which not setting the houses on fire as expected, I this morning anchored the *Ramillies* and the *Pactolus* as near as we could place them to the shore, from the shallowness of the water, and both ships fired several broadsides at the town, which was very much damaged, altho' from the houses being constructed of wood, none were seen to fall. The enemy, on commencing our fire, withdrew the guns from the Battery and retired outside the town, where were assembled 3000 militia under the command of General Isham. I therefore did not think it proper to continue any more operations against this place, but shall proceed in further execution of your orders. I feel particularly obliged to Captain the Hon'ble F. Aylmer, for his zeal and assistance on this Service, and also to Captain Sheridan and his officers for the steady manner in which the mortars were fired.

        I have the honor to be Sir,
           your most obedient humble servant,
               T. M. Hardy, Captain

There is no mention of torpedoes here, and nothing of Mrs. Stewart, nor is there any reference to any promises that might or might not have been made by the villagers concerning either.

On the following day Admiral Hotham sent an extract of Hardy's report to the commander in chief of the North American Station,

Admiral Cochrane. Hotham's report mentions torpedoes for the first time and closes with a rueful admission.

> Sir, His Majesty's Ship Ramillies and the Terror Bomb having joined me at this anchorage on the 7th instant, and being informed by the officers who had commanded here, that the town of Stonington has been conspicuous for preparing and harbouring torpedoes, and giving assistance to the insidious attempts of the Enemy at the destruction of His Majesty's Ships employed off New London, it appeared to be more deserving of the visitation prescribed in your Order of the 18th Ultimo, than any other place on this part of the Coast. . . . I therefore directed Sir Thomas Hardy on the 8th Instant, to take the direction of such an attack on the Town, with the ships and vessels named in the margin, with a view of destroying it by their fire, as he might find practicable, conformably to your order alluded to; and enclosed I have the honour to transmit to you an extract of the report of the execution of it, with a return of the casualties on board the Dispatch on the occasion. The destruction of the town has not been as complete as could have been wished. . . .
>
> Written on board Superb, off Gardiner's Island.

In due course Cochrane, busy with the burning of Washington and the subsequent attack on Baltimore, managed to forward the news to the Admiralty and to send a personal response to Hotham, again making a point of the torpedo aspect.

> Acknowledge receipt of your letter of 13 August—. . . Acquainting me of your having directed an attack be made upon the Town of Stonington. . . I very much approve of your having directed this measure, particularly as this Town has been the receptacle of Torpedoes and I request in all cases where you may find these insidious means reported to you do your utmost to distress and annoy the Town encouraging them.

By 3 October 1814 the news had appeared in the *Naval Gazette* in England, and the *Times* of London, after discussing various attacks on the American coast and claiming that "actual violence was never shown to the quiet and unresisting part of the population," made a significant exception in one case:

> The town of Stonington, however, having rendered itself notorious for preparing and harbouring torpedoes, and promoting other measures of a like kind, was deservedly cannonaded for two days.

The attack, which was originally prompted by Cochrane's order of 18 July "to destroy the coast towns and ravage the country," had undergone a radical sea change, and been transformed into a surgical incursion to eradicate the diabolical torpedo activity in Long Island Sound.

This investigation into the Battle of Stonington began as a search for answers to certain questions that continue to confound after all these years. Why did Hardy bother to attack such an inoffensive target? Why were the villagers so recklessly courageous in their response? Why did the British inflict so little damage? Most puzzling of all, why, with his overwhelming superiority in men and materiel, did Hardy lose?

We have now had a chance to examine all the facts bearing on the case, and they throw considerable light on some of the more straightforward issues. But the larger answer still eludes us, and as a result the Battle of Stonington continues to be a mystery and is likely to remain one so as long as we rely only on verifiable evidence. All the participants are long since dead, and no new clues are likely to emerge from attic trunks at this late stage. If we are to find some reasonable solution to the Stonington conundrum, one that conforms to the facts but manages to explain why certain things happened, we will have to move gingerly beyond historical objectivity into the realm of reasonable conjecture.

With that caveat firmly in mind, it becomes increasingly difficult to accept at face value all the details of the Battle of Stonington, and correspondingly easy to imagine that something quite out of the ordinary may have occurred in this little action, something perhaps unique.

The suspicion grows into a conviction that Thomas Masterman Hardy, who openly admitted his distate for the attack, deliberately sought to limit its effect and personally saw to it that the village survived his apparently lethal barrage. As we have seen in citations from contemporary published accounts, there were eyewitnesses at Stonington who suggested as much, and it is not at all difficult to construct a scenario from the known facts to support such a theory.

To recap the evidence, we start with Hardy's returning from Maine in early August. He has just distinguished himself by gaining still another significant victory without firing a shot. The capture of Eastport follows closely on his feat of neutralizing Decatur and his frigates in a bloodless action, and of maintaining the peace in Long Island Sound for a year and a half with virtually no loss of life.

Upon his arrival at Gardiner's Island Hardy learns that he has been replaced by Admiral Hotham. He also learns for the first time of Cochrane's order of 18 July calling for terror raids along the coast, a style of warfare totally at odds with Hardy's long-established policy of firm but gentle suasion.

When Hotham orders Hardy to implement the 18 July order by attacking some point in Long Island Sound, Hardy reluctantly picks Stonington as his target, not because it deserves attack but because it is geographically approachable and represents the fewest problems for his ships.

Because he does not wish to have noncombatant blood on his hands, he sends in a message before the bombardment, warning the innocent villagers—he characterizes them as "unoffending Inhabitants"—to save themselves by leaving the village. It is an uncharacteristically garbled and confused message, possibly reflecting the distress brought on by carrying out a distasteful order. When to his surprise the villagers defy him, Hardy finds himself on the horns of a moral dilemma.

Here he is, "Nelson's Hardy," face to face with a handful of defiant private citizens armed with two guns! Some officers might have found the circumstances comical, just another example of American hubris. Hardy knows better. How many martyred Yankees, he wonders, how many brave men killed in the act of protecting their homes will it take to permanently tarnish the honor of the Royal Navy in general, and one well-respected captain in particular?

He must obey orders, but to do so means he must not only deploy a vastly superior military force against a handful of villagers, which is beneath his dignity, but that he must also act in a dishonorable manner by ordering the killing of innocent civilians whose only crime is defending their homes. His personal code of conduct will not permit such a course, so he must find some means of obeying Hotham's orders while at the same time blunting the attack.

To make matters more difficult, Hardy must arrange this subterfuge on his own. It would be impossible to involve his officers in such a conspiracy. He cannot, for instance, tell Captain Sheridan of the *Terror* to misdirect his mortar fire, but he can see to it that the mortars do not get a chance to fire until after dark, thus ensuring inaccuracy.

Although Hardy wants to limit the action, he must make the battle look convincing. He manages this the following morning by sending the *Dispatch* in close to shore. For a while, when the Yankee guns are silenced, it looks as if Hardy is about to score his deliberately limited victory and will be able to depart that afternoon. But then the Yankees start firing again, and most distressful of all, they seriously damage the *Dispatch*. If he were to depart under these circumstances, he would appear to be running away. He withdraws the *Dispatch* and begins making new plans.

Shortly thereafter, the Stonington magistrates interrupt him, demanding to know why he is attacking their village. Hardy takes a shot in the dark and accuses the village of harboring torpedoes. If Stonington were in fact guilty of such activity, it would provide Hardy with the moral justification for the attack and allow him to leave as soon as the magistrates promise to discontinue their dishonorable traffic in infernal machines. But the surprised and indignant magistrates vehemently deny Hardy's allegations, so he must find another option.

He tries another shot in the dark: Mrs. Stewart. He is aware that the American authorities in New London have already shown themselves powerless to surrender her to Hotham without permission from Washington, but perhaps he might induce those same authorities to part with Mrs. Stewart if her release will save the village of Stonington. In other words, he will try to hold the village ransom for Mrs. Stewart. Delivering her to Hotham would indeed be a feather in Hardy's cap after the admiral had been so unsuccessful in obtaining her release the previous Sunday in New London. And, of course, her freedom would also justify the attack.

Unfortunately, the authorities in Stonington prove no more capable of delivering Mrs. Stewart than those in New London. The Yankees are not making it easy for Hardy to break off the action. While he tries to think up still another ruse, he orders the continuance of a sporadic and desultory bombardment.

On the fourth day of the attack, in an action that suggests showmanship rather than military ardor, he arranges for a grand finale of broadsides from his own ship and the *Pactolus*. Because of the deep drafts of the vessels, they must fire the broadsides from such a distance that accuracy is impossible. He then orders the squadron away and writes his report to Hotham.

If Hotham ever believed Stonington had torpedoes, Hardy would have certainly included mention of the "promise" not to traffic in torpedoes that he claimed he extracted from the village. But he makes no mention of the purported "concession"; obviously, neither Hardy nor Hotham even considered torpedoes as a reason to attack Stonington. What is equally obvious is that Hotham *wants* torpedoes in Stonington, either to enhance his own reputation or Hardy's, because he introduces torpedoes into the covering letter he sends on to Cochrane. The rest is "history."

Hardy did not "lose" the Battle of Stonington. It is probably more accurate to describe the outcome as a failure to gain the victory for want of zeal.

13

Postscripts

*The Stewarts reunited—Hardy's subsequent
career—Stephen Decatur's career—the* Hero
and Terror *in the Antarctic—how the war
ended—Jeremiah Holmes's long life—Stonington
today—an 1814 advertisement*

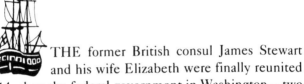

THE former British consul James Stewart
and his wife Elizabeth were finally reunited
on 25 August 1814 when the federal government in Washington—two
weeks after Hardy's demand for her release—approved her departure
from New London. She and her seven children and the family servants
embarked for the *Superb* anchored in Gardiner's Bay, and after an
affecting family reunion they soon set up housekeeping on a farm on
Plum Island, a few miles offshore. From there Mr. Stewart was able
to organize and then supervise his complicated scheme to smuggle
British goods into America so as to obtain American dollars with which
to buy food for the British blockading forces from the farmers they
were blockading.

But the couple, so long separated and so recently reunited, were
destined to be parted soon again. His smuggling operations were clearly
against the best interests of the U.S. government, and on 28 September
a long rowboat carrying a crew of thirty oarsmen emerged from the
Hornet's Nest in the late afternoon and at dusk came on shore on
Plum Island and spirited away Mr. Stewart to the mainland. By his
own account, he was then imprisoned aboard the *United States*, which

was still lying moribund far up the Thames. When Admiral Cochrane learned of the kidnapping, his response was characteristically simple and unequivocal.

> I have recently been informed that Mr James Stewart, a British subject late HM Consul at New London, has been carried away from the place in which he resides to New London. You will be pleased to intimate this to the Government of the United States that if he is not immediately returned and set at liberty I will not only retaliate by taking off every person I can lay hold of upon the Coast and sending them to England, but I will direct the retaliatory order hitherto suspended from the Northern States to be carried into immediate execution.

The government paroled Stewart on his promise not to make contact with the British fleet, and he spent the rest of the war living with his father-in-law in New London. Cochrane apparently accepted this arrangement as an appropriate response to his demand and left the coast in peace.

After the war James Stewart eventually received a new commission as consul in New London, and in the late 1820s retired to Great Britain, where, as mentioned earlier, a grateful crown provided him and his wife with a pension, chiefly in recognition of Mrs. Stewart's outstanding espionage work during the war.

Thomas Masterman Hardy was named a Knight Commander of the Bath in the New Year's List of 1815, but as if to temper that good news he found himself involved in an unsavory society scandal when he returned to England soon after.

Lady Hardy, who was closely related to the leading social figures of the day, was very much a part of the London scene. In 1814, while Hardy was busy in North America, a certain Lord Buckingham made improper advances to her, which the young matron stoutly rejected. Angered by the rebuff, Buckingham wrote a series of letters to friends, to newspapers, and to Hardy himself, accusing Lady Hardy of improprieties with a certain Lord Abercorn, a considerably older social leader who stood in a fatherly position to her. One of these letters accused Captain Hardy of accepting "complacency money" from Lord Abercorn.

When the matter could no longer be ignored, Hardy sued the *Morning Herald*, which had published one of the letters, and was awarded damages of £1000. Later that month he fought a duel with

Lord Buckingham. True to Hardy's style, the seconds were able to step between the principals before any damage was done. But the duel had served its purpose, for the letters stopped.

Hardy served for a time as captain of the royal yacht *Princess Augusta*, stationed at Deptford, and afterward returned to sea on the South American Station for a time. He was eventually appointed rear admiral and then vice admiral, stood twice for Parliament without success, and served as First Sea Lord and Governor of the Greenwich Naval Hospital. In 1837 he was awarded the Grand Cross of the Bath. He died in 1839 and is buried at Greenwich Hospital.

High over his native village of Portesham, on the brow of Blackdown Hill, rises a great, towering, homely monument that dominates the Dorset landscape for miles around and is visible far out to sea. Over the sealed door is inscribed the following:

ERECTED BY PUBLIC SUBSCRIPTION IN THE YEAR 1844
IN MEMORY OF VICE ADMIRAL THOMAS MASTERMAN
HARDY, BART, GCB,
FLAG CAPTAIN TO LORD NELSON ON HMS VICTORY
AT THE BATTLE OF TRAFALGAR

Nothing about the Battle of the Nile, or Copenhagen, and certainly not Stonington. As Hardy had always known, Trafalgar was the only one that really counted.

Stephen Decatur, after his ignominious return overland to New York to take command of the *President*, attempted in January 1815 to run the Sandy Hook blockade, unaware that the war had already ended. He outran three enemy ships but was forced to fight a fourth, the *Endymion*, 50 (ironically, this was the same frigate he had included in his four-ship challenge to Hardy the previous year). After a fierce confrontation he left *Endymion* dead in the water, but the battle delayed him and he was forced to surrender to his other pursuers.

Later that year he returned to North Africa, the scene of his first glory, the destruction of the *Philadelphia*, and used his squadron to force the dey of Algiers to sign a treaty ending American tribute to Algeria. He died in a duel in 1820.

Two vessels involved in this narrative, the American sloop *Hero* and the British bomb ship *Terror*, share a curious coincidence of nautical history, for each went on to play a significant role in the exploration of Antarctica.

In 1820 the *Hero*, now captained by a young Stonington mariner named Nathaniel Brown Palmer, penetrated deep into the South Atlantic in search of seal pelts for the China trade. In November Palmer came upon a landfall of such magnitude he concluded it must be the long-sought Antarctic continent, which is precisely what it turned out to be. The United States credits Palmer and his little forty-seven-foot *Hero* with the discovery of Antarctica, and even though the claim is disputed by the British who credit the Englishman Edward Bransfield, and the Russians who credit their man Count von Bellinghausen, the Stonington connection lives on in the Antarctic place names of Palmer Land and the Palmer Archipelago.

During the 1830s and '40s the British mounted elaborate exploration parties to survey both the Arctic and the Antarctic. They discovered that the navy's old bomb ships, with their massive oaken construction built to withstand the impact of recoiling mortars, were ideal for pushing through ice floes. In consequence the *Terror* and her sister ship, the *Erebus*, spent years in the Antarctic and left their names on volcanoes and on a gulf just a short distance from the Palmer Archipelago.

The *Terror* was last seen in 1845, thirty-one years after the Battle of Stonington, abandoned and locked into an iceberg, its massive bulkheads crushed and stove in by the relentless pressure of the ice.

The War of 1812 itself, that troublesome and unwanted headache, was finally settled on Christmas Eve 1814 when the ministers for each side signed a peace treaty in Ghent and sent duplicate copies off to be ratified in London and Washington. Incredibly, in spite of the Americans' well-informed pessimism of the previous August and the pressure on the British negotiators to teach the Yankees a lesson they would not soon forget, the treaty as it finally emerged called for a return to the *status quo ante bellum* (which meant, among other things, that the British had to give Moose Island back to the Americans). Every point of contention, from the question of British impressment to the future of the Great Lakes, was deliberately shelved and left for later negotiation. The overwhelming sentiment of the ministers at Ghent and their governments at home was simply to get the war over as swiftly as possible.

Why had the British, with a crushing victory within their grasp, given everything away? The answer in part was that they suspected America was more valuable as a free and unhobbled partner than as a sullen and reproachful enemy sitting on top of Britain's western hemisphere colonies. . . partly that General Prevost's forces came a cropper at Lake Champlain. . . partly that Britain suddenly discovered it was broke after decades of war with Napoleon. . . and not least that a sharper, more aggressive, and more intelligent bargaining team outnegotiated the British. As with the Treaty of Paris that ended the Revolution, the British continued to underestimate their ex-colonials and relegated negotiations to a team of second-string diplomats.

John Quincy Adams, son of a president and destined to be president himself, shook the hand of his British counterpart, saying, "I hope this is the last time that our two nations may ever be at war." Despite several close calls over the ensuing years, the relationship between the two countries has generally flourished as he had hoped. Given the number of times British and American national interests have been in conflict, the years of peace between these two aggressive and acquisitive powers merits more respect and attention than the relationship usually gets. Much of the credit for all those years of peace belongs to the Treaty of Ghent and the men who negotiated it, who had the wisdom to temper national interests with a sense of practicality and, therefore, set the style in which Anglo-American relations have ever since been conducted.

Jeremiah Holmes outlived all the other principals of the Battle of Stonington and died in 1872 at the age of ninety, a well-to-do merchant captain. Eventually, the area of Stonington Township in which he lived came to be known as Mystic Bridge and, in time, Mystic. His house beside the river no longer stands, but the road on which he lived still bears his name. His gravestone in Mystic is a white marble cenotaph that stands a proud twenty feet high, a worthy memorial to a warrior.

The village of Stonington prospered in the years following the war, particularly after the railroads established it as an important link between Providence and New York. Because the physical size of Stonington was limited to that of the peninsula it occupied, the village never grew much larger than it was in 1814, and today it probably

Jeremiah Holmes and his wife, Ann, from a drawing by
Benson Lossing made many years after the attack on
Stonington for his book, *The Pictorial Field-Book of the War of
1812*. Following the war, Holmes returned to the sea; after
devoting his life to maritime activities, he died a wealthy
man. (*The Pictorial Field-Book of the War of 1812*)

looks recognizably the way it did at the time of the battle. There are
about twice the number of houses in the borough as there were then;
though most of them were built after 1814, at least twenty or thirty
go back to the War of 1812, and each has a story to tell.

The two 18-pounders are still in the village, proudly displayed
in Cannon Square, and there are at least five permanent memorials
to the battle scattered throughout the borough. The anniversary of
the battle is celebrated every year with a fair on the village green. A
replica of Stonington's unique sixteen-star flag is proudly displayed at
every meeting of the Warden and Burgesses in Borough Hall, attesting
to the continued recognition that 10 August 1814 was the most important day in the history of the village.

The "Stonington jug," a patriotic design produced in Liverpool soon after the war for sale to the American market. The inscription circumscribing the scene of battle reads, "The Gallant Defence of Stonington, August 9th, 1814. Stonington is free whilst her Heroes have one gun left." An enlarged section of the battle scene is shown in the frontispiece. (Author)

The following advertisement appeared in a New York newspaper in November 1814.

English manufacture, and memento
of the "magnaminity" of Commodore Hardy!

Just received and offered for sale about THREE TONS of round SHOT, consisting of 6, 9, 12, 18, 24, and 32 lbs. very handsome, being a small proportion which were fired from his Britannic majesty's ships on the unoffending inhabitants of Stonington, in the recent brilliant attack on that place. Likewise a few carcasses, in good order, weighing about 200 lbs. each. Apply to S. TRUMBULL, 41, Peck-slip

N.B. The purchaser of the above can be supplied with about two tons more if required.

Swords into plowshares, New England style.

Appendix I

Names of Volunteers

(From the Connecticut *Gazette*, 24 August 1814)

The following is handed us as a list of volunteers (tho' presumed not entirely perfect,) of those who so bravely stood the brunt of the attack of Stonington point:—

Of Stonington:—

Capt. George Fellows,
Capt. Wm. Potter,
Dr. Wm. Lord,
Lieut. H. G. Lewis,
Ensign D. Frink,
John Miner.

Gurdon Trumbull,
Alex. G. Smith,
Amos Denison jun.,
Stanton Gallup,
Eb. Morgan,

Of Mystic:—

Jesse Deane,
Deane Gallup,
Fred. Haley,

Jeremiah Holmes,
N. Cleft,
Jedediah Reed.

Of Groton:—

Alfred White,
Ebenezer Morgan,

Frank Daniels,
Giles Moran.

201

Of New London:—

Major Simeon Smith,   Lambert Williams.
Capt. Noah Lester (formerly of the
Army),
Major N. Frink,

From Massachusetts:—

Capt. Leonard   Mr. Dunham

(From the Connecticut *Gazette*, 31 August 1814)

By an error of the compositor, the following names were omitted in the list published in our last paper, of volunteers who so greatly contributed to the glorious defence and preservation of Stonington, viz:—

Simeon Haley,   Thomas Wilcox,
Jeremiah Haley,   Luke Palmer,
Frederick Denison,   George Palmer,
John Miner,   Wm. G. Bush.
Asa Lee,

There were probably others, whom we have not learnt.

Appendix II

The Hornet's Nest

In the interest of narrative flow, the names of many of the mariners who were part of the "Hornet's Nest" along the Mystic River went unlisted. The names below include all those individuals cited in the series of stories entitled "Historic Leaves," which detailed the adventures of Mystic River men during the War of 1812, published in the Mystic *Pioneer* in the summer of 1859:

John Appleman
Henry Bailey
George Bennett
Ambrose Burrows
Guy E. Burrows
John Burrows
Paul Burrows
Silas Burrows
———— Coffin
Ebenezer Denison
Isaac Denison
Oliver Dewey
Elam Eldredge
Thomas Eldredge
Abel Fish

Anson Avery
Peter Baker
Avery Brown
Daniel Burrows
James Burrows
Lemuel Burrows
Nathan Burrows
Nathaniel Clift
Jesse Crary
Frederick Denison
Robert Deuce
Abel Eldredge
Nathan Eldredge
Benjamin Ellison
John Fish

John Fitch
Dean Gallup
Jeremiah Haley
Allen Holdredge
John Holdredge
———— Hyde
Alexander Latham
Isaacs Miner
Manassah Miner
Charles Packer
Elam Packer
George Packer
Roswell Packer
Henry Park
John Rathbun
Peter Rowland
James Sawyer
Edward Tinker
Peter Washington
Jonathan Wheeler
Thomas Wilcox
Eldredge Wolf
———— Wood
Zebulon Woolsey

Joseph Fitch
George Haley
Simeon Haley
Henry Holdredge
Jeremiah Holmes
Nicholas P. Isaacs
John McCan
Jonathan Miner
Nathaniel Niles
Dudley Packer
Elisha Packer
Hubbard Packer
Lt. Palmer
John Park
Nathaniel Rathbun
Havens Sawyer
Jeremiah Shaw
Ezekial Tufts
Amos Wheeler
William Wilbur
———— Williams
George Wolf
Perry Woodward

Sources

Because this book attempts to integrate a very small incident into a much larger historical mosaic, I relied heavily on Henry Adams's *The History of the United States of America During the Administrations of James Madison*, New York: Library of America, 1986. Almost as important to me as Adams was Benson J. Lossing's *The Pictorial Field-Book of the War of 1812*, New York: Harper & Brothers, 1868 (facsimile reprint, Somersworth: New Hampshire Publishing Company, 1976), a treasure trove of details and personal observations as well as solid reporting on virtually every incident in the entire war, with hundreds of illustrations and maps. To complement these two monumental histories, I relied for my sense of the war in its day-to-day aspects on the microfilm records of *Niles' Weekly Register* for the years 1812–15.

For information on the Battle of Stonington itself, I have relied primarily on four basic sources: an article in the Connecticut *Courant* of 23 August 1814, recapping the entire action; the letter of 21 August 1815, a year after the event, written by Amos Palmer of Stonington to the secretary of war; an article by Frederick Denison in the Mystic *Pioneer* of 2 July 1859; and finally, an article entitled "British Documents on the Stonington Raid, August, 1814" by

Richard K. Murdoch in the *Bulletin of the Connecticut Historical Society*, Hartford, July 1972. No one familiar with the reconstruction of past events will be surprised to learn that the four accounts have major discrepancies. In general, I have given most credence to the earliest documents, which are the British ships' logs quoted extensively in Murdoch's article, and the article in the *Courant*. I have relied on the later pieces only when I could reasonably assume that the earlier ones were in error. (The *Courant*, for example, lists the third cannon in the village as a 4-pounder, while the other two American reports—written by participants—indicate it was a 6-pounder. Here I've gone with later sources.) Both *Niles'* and Lossing cover the battle generally, but considerable additional material appears in *The Defence of Stonington* by James H. Trumbull, Hartford: Privately printed, 1864; *Stonington by the Sea* by Henry Robinson Palmer, Stonington: Palmer Press, 1913; *In the Village* by Anthony Bailey, New York: Knopf, 1971; and "The Battle of Stonington in Retrospect" by Captain Frank C. Lynch, Jr., USN (Ret.), *Historical Footnotes*, Bulletin of the Stonington Historical Society, August 1964, which is the first attempt to tell the story from both the British and American sides. For data on Stonington's 18-pounders I am indebted to "The Rejuvenated Cannon of 1814" by Henry R. Palmer, Jr., *Historical Footnotes*, Bulletin of the Stonington Historical Society, August 1982.

For information on the underwater and torpedo warfare in Long Island Sound, I relied heavily on *New York City and Vicinity During the War of 1812* by R. S. Guernsey, New York: Charles L. Woodward, 1889; "Blue Lights and Infernal Machines: The British Blockade of New London" by Joseph A. Goldenberg, *Mariner's Mirror*, Haywards Heath: Society for Nautical Research, November 1975; and "Robert Fulton's Turtle Boat" by W. B. Rowbotham, *U.S. Naval Institute Proceedings*, December 1936.

I have acknowledged elsewhere my indebtedness to Frank Lynch for his critically important research in the letter boxes of Admiral Sir Alexander Cochrane in the National Library of Scotland in Edinburgh and of Admiral Sir Henry Hotham at the University of Hull. Frank's research brought to light valuable information to flesh out the shadowy figures of James and Elizabeth Stewart as well as providing considerable extra information on other events connected with the Battle of Stonington.

Biographical material on Captain Hardy came largely from *Nelson's Hardy and his Wife* by John Gore, London: John Murray, 1935, with details on Hardy's 1807–8 duty in Chesapeake Bay from *The Commodores* by Leonard F. Guttridge and Jay D. Smith, New York: Harper & Row, 1969. Jeremiah Holmes's trip through the blockade was based almost entirely on his own account preserved in manuscript in the G. W. Blunt White Library, Mystic Seaport Museum. Details, such as those concerning prices of goods, are from *Niles'*. Information on the comparative value of money then and now—always a tricky measurement—came from "Spying's Dirty Little Secret" by Brock Brower, *Money* Magazine, July 1987, as well as a note on page 90 of *James Durand: An Able Bodied Seaman*, edited by George S. Brooks, New Haven: Yale University Press, 1926. My main source for Stephen Decatur's ill-fated attempt to escape the blockade via Montauk was *Decatur* by Irvin Anthony, New York: Charles Scribner's Sons, 1931. Additional details on the unfortunate lightning storm and the interlude where the two commodores were anchored on the opposite sides of Fishers Island are from *Niles'*. Hardy's discussion with the New London customs man is also from *Niles'*, and the information on the Torpedo Act is from Guernsey. The description of the *Eagle*'s explosion is primarily from contemporary sources as well as *The History of New London* by Frances Manwaring Caulkins, New London: Utley Press, 1895. The details of the attempted kidnapping of Hardy are from *Niles'*, augmented by Decatur's letter to Hardy of 1 August 1813 and Hardy's own letter to Major Case, quoted extensively in the text. Information on the "peace party" and spies is based on material in *Niles'* and Guernsey, with the significant addition of an entry in the Hotham files for 1824 confirming the "very important" espionage services performed by Mrs. Stewart. The account of John Carpenter's impressment and release is from *Niles'*. The various stories of the "Hornet's Nest," the group of mariners living along the Mystic River, are all from the Mystic *Pioneer* and ran as a series during the summer of 1859. Although published forty-five years after the events, the stories were written with the aid of participants and were authenticated by those who had taken part in the activities.

The complicated issue of grain shipments to feed Wellington's troops, as well as Britain's problems finding money to pay for the American goods, is covered at length in *The Age of Fighting Sail* by C. S. Forester, Garden City: Doubleday, 1956. James Stewart's involvement in a smuggling scheme designed to provide the British navy with U.S. funds is based largely upon letters in the Cochrane collection. Biographical material on Robert Fulton as well as much valuable information on the operation of underwater explosives is based primarily on *Robert Fulton: Pioneer of Undersea Warfare* by Wallace S. Hutcheon, Jr., Annapolis: Naval Institute Press, 1981, and secondarily on *Torpedo War and Submarine Explosions* by Robert Fulton, New York: William Elliot, 1810 (reprinted in facsimile by William Abbatt in *The Magazine of History*, 1914). For details on the burning of Newark, Ontario, I am indebted to *Flames Across the Border* by Pierre Berton, Toronto: McClelland and Stewart, 1981.

The story of Decatur and the "blue lights" of New London is well covered in a number of sources I consulted. The proposed duel between Hardy's and Decatur's ships is based on material in *Niles'*, Goldenberg's article in *Mariner's Mirror*, and *The Naval War of 1812* by Theodore Roosevelt, Annapolis: Naval Institute Press, 1987.

The significant change in Britain's war aims following the defeat of Napoleon is detailed in Adams and supported by contemporary pieces in *Niles'*. Jeremiah Holmes's unsuccessful torpedo attacks are from the Mystic *Pioneer* of 18 June 1859, and the subsequent story of "Torpedo Jack" and the raid on Pettipaug is based primarily on Goldenberg's article in *Mariner's Mirror*. Admiral Cochrane's arrival on the North American Station and the consequent stiffening of the blockade is based in part on Adams and in part on papers from the Cochrane collection. Hardy's letter concerning the USS *Washington* as well as all the details of the occupation of Moose Island are drawn from the Cochrane collection, except for the exhortation from the "Loyal American," which is from *Niles'*.

The description of the New England coastal reaction to Hardy's swing south is from Lossing, and the description of the British capture and destruction of the semisubmersible *Turtle* is largely from Rowbotham's article, with additional data from Guernsey.

The story of Midshipman Powers is found in Lynch's article and elsewhere, and the correspondence between Hotham and the New London authorities is in the Hotham collection, with additional details in Caulkins. The account of the first Battle of Stonington in 1775 is drawn primarily from *Colonel Jonathan Palmer's War Diary, Stonington, Connecticut*, Norman F. Boas, editor, Stonington: Seaport Autographs, 1985. The account of the peace negotiations at Ghent is largely from

Adams. The text of Mr. Trumbull's advertisement in New York is from *Niles'*.

In addition to the sources mentioned above, the following were useful to an understanding of the period and the incidents covered:

Baker, William A. *The Lore of Sail*. New York: Facts on File, 1983.

Beach, Edward L. *The United States Navy*. New York: Holt, 1986.

Crandall, Katharine B. *The Fine Old Town of Stonington*. Watch Hill: Book & Tackle Shop, 1975.

Dodds, James, and James Moore. *Building the Wooden Fighting Ship*. New York and Bicester: Facts on File, 1984.

Falconer, W. A. *A New Universal Dictionary of the Marine*. London: Cadell and Davis, 1815 (reprinted in facsimile, London: MacDonald and Jane's, 1974).

Forester, C. S., ed. *The Adventures of John Wetherell*. London: Michael Joseph, 1954.

Garitee, Jerome R. *The Republic's Private Navy*. Middletown: Wesleyan University Press, 1977.

Harland, John. *Seamanship in the Age of Sail*. Illustrated by Mark Myers. Annapolis: Naval Institute Press, 1984.

Hime, Henry W. L. *The Origin of Artillery*. London: Longmans, Green & Co., 1915.

Horsman, Reginald. *The War of 1812*. New York: Knopf, 1969.

Kennedy, Ludovic. *Nelson's Captains*. New York: W. W. Norton & Co., 1951.

Larkin, Jack. *The Reshaping of Everyday Life, 1790–1840*. New York: Harper and Row, 1988.

Lavery, Brian. *The Ship of the Line* (2 volumes). Annapolis: Naval Institute Press, 1983.

Lloyd, Alan. *The Scorching of Washington*. Washington: Robert B. Luce Co., 1974.

Lord, Walter. *The Dawn's Early Light*. New York: W. W. Norton, 1972.

Masterson, William H. *Tories and Democrats*. College Station: Texas A&M University Press, 1985.

Pack, James. *The Man Who Burned the White House*. Annapolis: Naval Institute Press, 1987.

Perkins, Bradford, ed. *The Causes of the War of 1812*. New York: Holt, Rinehart & Winston, 1962.

Richardson, Patrick. *Nelson's Navy*. Harlow: Longman, 1967.

Robinson, William. *Jack Nastyface*. Annapolis: Naval Institute Press, 1973.

Rodger, N. A. M. *The Wooden World*. Annapolis: Naval Institute Press, 1986.

Smith, Barbara Clark. *After the Revolution*. New York: Pantheon, 1985.

Tucker, Glenn. *Poltroons and Patriots*. Indianapolis: Bobbs-Merrill, 1954.

Wilbur, C. Keith. *Pirates and Patriots of the Revolution*. Chester: Globe Pequot Press, 1987.

Index

211

About the Author

James Tertius de Kay was born in New York in 1930 and attended Dalton and Trinity Schools in that city before graduating from Trinity College in Hartford. For many years he has written and produced wildlife television programs for Survival Anglia Limited. He is the author of biographies of Christopher Columbus and Martin Luther King, Jr., written for young readers, and has also written and illustrated a history of astronomy and several books on left-handedness. He is currently working on a history of the British-American frigate *Macedonian*, a ship that appears briefly in *The Battle of Stonington* and that at a later period was under the command of the author's great grandfather..

The Naval Institute Press is the book-publishing arm of the U.S. Naval Institute, a private, nonprofit professional society for members of the sea services and civilians who share an interest in naval and maritime affairs. Established in 1873 at the U.S. Naval Academy in Annapolis, Maryland, where its offices remain today, the Naval Institute has more than 100,000 members worldwide.

Members of the Naval Institute receive the influential monthly naval magazine *Proceedings* and substantial discounts on fine nautical prints, ship and aircraft photos, and subscriptions to the Institute's recently inaugurated quarterly, *Naval History*. They also have access to the transcripts of the Institute's Oral History Program and may attend any of the Institute-sponsored seminars regularly offered around the country.

The book-publishing program, begun in 1898 with basic guides to naval practices, has broadened its scope in recent years to include books of more general interest. Now the Naval Institute Press publishes more than forty new titles each year, ranging from how-to books on boating and navigation to battle histories, biographies, ship guides, and novels. Institute members receive discounts on the Press's more than 300 books.

For a free catalog describing books currently available and for further information about U.S. Naval Institute membership, please write to:

Membership Department
U.S. Naval Institute
Annapolis, Maryland 21402

or call, toll-free, 800-233-USNI.